Hitchhiking Through Europe
During the Summer of 1956

JOSEPH E. HAHN

Copyright © 2016 Joseph E. Hahn
All rights reserved
First Edition

PAGE PUBLISHING, INC.
New York, NY

First originally published by Page Publishing, Inc. 2016

ISBN 978-1-68348-344-1 (Paperback)
ISBN 978-1-68348-345-8 (Digital)

Printed in the United States of America

I would like to dedicate this book to my mother, Ruth Hahn, who encouraged me in the planning of my trip and did a great deal of bragging about her son upon his return. She saved all the letters I had sent to the Hahn family and typed them into a scrapbook as a gift to me on my fortieth birthday, nineteen years after my trip. All the twelve letters are made a part of this book and can be read at the conclusion of the book.

—Joseph E. Hahn

Disclaimer

The contents of this book were written in the 1950s and reflect the language and expressions during that period. Nothing that was said or implied was meant to offend any people or nationalities.

—Joseph E. Hahn

Hitchhiking through Europe
During the Summer of 1956

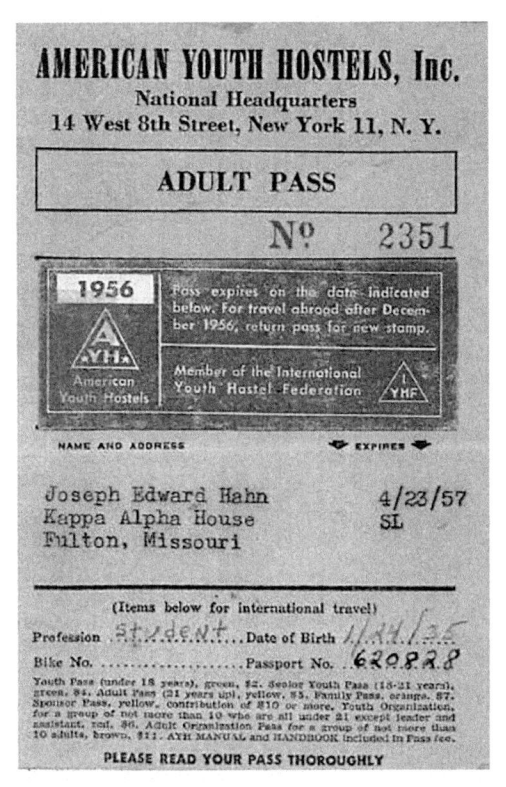

> **AMERICAN YOUTH HOSTELS, Inc.**
> National Headquarters
> 14 West 8th Street, New York 11, N. Y.
>
> **ADULT PASS**
>
> Nº 2351
>
> 1956 — Pass expires on the date indicated below. For travel abroad after December 1956, return pass for new stamp.
>
> American Youth Hostels — Member of the International Youth Hostel Federation
>
> NAME AND ADDRESS — EXPIRES
>
> Joseph Edward Hahn   4/23/57
> Kappa Alpha House   SL
> Fulton, Missouri
>
> (Items below for international travel)
> Profession ...student... Date of Birth 1/24/35
> Bike No. .... Passport No. 620828
>
> Youth Pass (under 18 years), green, $2. Senior Youth Pass (18-21 years), green, $4. Adult Pass (21 years up), yellow, $5. Family Pass, orange, $7. Sponsor Pass, yellow, contribution of $10 or more. Youth Organization, for a group of not more than 10 who are all under 21 except leader and assistant, red, $6. Adult Organization Pass for a group of not more than 10 adults, brown, $11. AYH MANUAL and HANDBOOK included in Pass fee.
>
> **PLEASE READ YOUR PASS THOROUGHLY**

Youth Hostel Pass
General Youth Hostel Customs

Hosteling is traveling simply—by foot, bike, canoe, horseback, or ski—and living simply, in a spirit of fun and friendship, using hostels as overnight accommodations. Hostelers follow the Golden Rule and observe local customs and laws.

Hitchhiking is not allowed!

Auto or public transportation may be used, so with these instructions, I have never hitchhiked directly from one hostel to another.

Introduction to My 1956 Trip to Europe

How It Came About

I guess you all want to know why I decided to hitchhike through Europe during the summer of 1956. A good question deserves a good answer, so here is the buildup to my summer travel in Europe during 1956.

I had graduated from Saint Louis Country Day School in June 1953 and enrolled at Westminster College, Fulton, Missouri, in the fall. I did very poorly in foreign languages in high school, not passing Latin, French, or German. Since there was a requirement of two years of foreign language in college, I enrolled in Spanish for the 1953 and 1954 years—and *passed*!

Since my ancestors came from Germany, I wanted to have a working knowledge of German, so I enrolled in the fall of 1955 in Dr. Felix Sharton's German class. He had participated in the Nuremberg Nazi trials and was an extremely interesting professor. Each year, he traveled to Europe in the summer and offered his students exposure to Europe as a tour guide. He gave his students a literature of European tour, and my parents became interested since they were about to celebrate their twenty-fifth wedding anniversary, so our family of five made plans to join his tour in the summer of 1955. This tour consisted of Mom, Dad, my two younger sisters, me, and six others.

Hahn family in Volendam, Holland, in 1955
for their Christmas card, dressed in native garb
(Dad, Mother, sister Janet, me, sister Carol)

No flying then; we took the ship for a seven-day cruise each way, and it was on the return trip that I met two University of Minnesota students, both girls, who were homeward bound and anxious to share their hitchhiking and hostel experiences through Europe with me. This sounded interesting, and with seven days of exposure to their travels, I had increased interest to do the same in 1956.

The drummer on the ship, Eric Hammond from Preston, England, invited me to visit him and his relatives, and a new girlfriend, Elfriede Butz from Rosswangen, Germany, had already invited me back to see her. I also had friends in Vienna, Austria, who wanted to see me, plus I had been told about L'Abri, a chalet in Switzerland run by Dr. Francis and Mrs. Edith Schaeffer where you could stay and "meet the Lord."

Thus, I had a nucleus of four stops with which I could intertwine my offbeat points of interest and plan a trip to and through Europe.

HITCHHIKING THROUGH EUROPE DURING THE SUMMER OF 1956

The two students shared their maps, places of interest, hostel life, and hitchhiking tips on safe travel with me. By the time we disembarked in Quebec, Canada, I was ready to go on my 1956 trip to Europe.

But *not* so fast! I had been given my parents' permission—using my own savings—but I was scheduled for ROTC summer camp at Fort Riley, Kansas, in order to receive my commission upon graduation from college in 1957. I wrote a letter through government channels to Washington, DC, requesting a postponement of my summer camp until after graduation in 1957 so I might have an *educational experience* in lieu of summer camp in 1956. My request was granted, and I was now able to proceed with planning the trip of my life as a twenty-one-year-old college student who would travel through ten countries on $160, with the entire trip costing $720, not including gifts and souvenirs.

To give a more colorful overview on the planning of the 1956 trip, I feel a detailed explanation is necessary to those of you who do not know me and may wonder why I went to certain places.

To be exact, as I planned my 1956 trip in the fall of 1955, I started with four planned destinations and just filled in the gaps with desire and curiosity. It began this way.

My first planned stop was Preston, England. Our voyage in 1955 allowed us to meet the ship's drummer, Eric Hammond, who resided in Preston. He was twenty years old and became keen on my teenage sisters, Janet and Carol. We socialized on his off time and, during the week, became good friends and exchanged addresses to become pen pals. During our exchange of letters, as it became evident I was going to Europe, I was invited to the Hammond home at 43 Elcho Street, thus my first stopping point.

My second planned visit was to Rosswangen, Germany. This town was the birthplace of my grandfather Joseph Hahn. I wanted to visit relatives and an attractive young sweetheart, Elfriede Butz.

This relationship needs to be explained, as to how I got a girlfriend in Germany. Here are the interesting details.

On June 1, 1932, my parents, Joseph Hahn and Ruth Due, were married in Saint Louis, Missouri. My paternal grandfather, also Joseph, had immigrated to Saint Louis at the age of fourteen. He started working in a bakery, stayed with the business, and years later, owned J. Hahn Bakery Co., which became the largest bakery in Saint Louis and the first to home-deliver bread via horse-drawn and electric wagons.

When my father became engaged, Grandpa Hahn offered to provide a honeymoon for four and half months to Europe, from June until October—on one condition, that they, Grandpa Joseph, Grandma Sophie, and the maid of honor, Dorothy Steffens, be allowed to accompany them.

The wedding party of five drove to New York in their Chrysler, boarded the ship with the car, and later arrived in Europe. They drove to Rosswangen, Germany, for an all-expense honeymoon. We now fast-forward to the July tour in 1955 to Rosswangen, Germany, a town of three hundred people that our family visited after the Dr. Sharton tour concluded.

As our week visit ended, Dad wanted to do something for the people of Rosswangen. He reserved the Adler Guest House, where Mother and Dad had spent their honeymoon in 1932. Beer and sausage, music, and dancing were to be provided for the townsfolk after 6:00 p.m. as a final going-away celebration.

The afternoon of the planned party, relatives realized that I, a lad of twenty, needed a companion, so quickly, a relative named Elfriede Butz was summoned to be my *date*. She was provided a German-to-English dictionary, and I was given an English-to-German likeness.

During the evening, we danced, drank beer, and chatted the best we could. After the social time, I escorted her home, receiving a good-night and good-bye kiss, promising to write. Thus, Rosswangen, Germany, and Elfriede Butz became my second planned destination for 1956.

My third planned visit was with Dr. Walter Hynek's family in Vienna, Austria. My best friend in high school, and later in college, was Roland Webb. We were always at each other's homes and chatted freely with the parents. This was how Roland's mother, Greta, learned of my planned trip. She was from Vienna, and her brother Walter still lived there. They had three teenage daughters, and Greta contacted her brother to inquire whether they would like a houseguest for a few days. Soon, an invitation arrived, and thus my third destination to visit Vienna was finalized.

My fourth destination was at a chalet in Switzerland near the French border. It was called L'Abri, meaning "shelter." It was established in 1955 by Dr. Francis and Edith Schaeffer as a place for people to visit in search of the Lord.

The two students I had met in 1955, who encouraged me to hitchhike and hostel, had recommended the chalet as a *must* place to visit. I had written Dr. Schaeffer and received a reply inviting me to visit them at their mountain chalet. The invitation letter from Dr. Schaeffer is made a part of this book and follows:

>Chalet les Melezes
>Huemoz sur Ollon
>Switzerland
>April 18, 1956

>Dear Mr. Hahn:

>We were so happy to receive your letter and do want to invite you to visit us.

It was a pleasure having Ruth Abrahamson with us last summer, and Dorothy Jamison of Los Angeles has been with us through the winter.

Yes, I was a pastor in Saint Louis, for four and a half years, of the First Bible Presbyterian Church of Saint Louis. We lived out on Waterman Boulevard. The church is now no longer in Saint Louis itself but has moved out to Town and Country, a nearby village.

Mrs. Schaeffer and I are in Europe, working especially with foreign students in Switzerland. Our chalet is usually running over with guests from many parts of the world, and I have a class for University of Lausanne students once a week and a class in Geneva for students also once a week, as well as Bible classes for students near where we live.

We live near Lausanne, up in the Alps. From Lausanne, take the Simplon line on the railway to Aigle (about an hour). When you get off the train at Aigle, you then take a little train marked Champéry. You get off this train at the mountain (about twenty minutes). Our address is at the top of this paper, and if you show it to the driver, he will let you off immediately in front of the chalet.

As you make your plans, please try to let us know when you will be arriving.

We all send our greetings.

Cordially yours,

Fr. Schaeff-
Francis A. Schaeffer

Thus, my fourth planned destination was determined.

It is now time for you to enjoy reading about my 1956 trip to Europe.

Enjoy.

This map of Europe shows the route I traveled after arriving in Southampton, England, where I then traveled through England, Scotland, Norway, Sweden, Denmark, Germany, Switzerland, Austria, Italy, and France, leaving from Le Havre to the USA. I walked, hitchhiked, and traveled by ship, train, and plane to complete this trip thru 10 countries, not 9, as stated in both of the local newspaper articles shown in this book. The distance Joe traveled in Europe was approximately 6,000 miles.

St. Louisan Visits Nine Countries In Seven Weeks, Spends Only $160

Little Jack Horner's thumb got him a plum. St. Louisan Joseph Hahn's got him a delightful low-cost trip through nine European countries.

Twenty-one-year-old Joe has just returned to his home at 5810 Kingwood dr. after reading newspapers by sunlight at midnight in Norway, picnicking in the Alps, burrowing through Medieval castles, and dozens of other Continental diversions—all for less money per day than an average tourist spends crossing Missouri.

"I'd like other students and young people to know how inexpensively they can enjoy Europe," said Joe, who is about to enter his senior year at Westminster College in Fulton. He was in Europe for seven weeks, and the expenses there, including tips, came to slightly more than $160.

All it takes is the ability to hold out your thumb in the time-honored tradition of the hitch-hiker, he continued. The transportation varied as much as the scenery—a hay wagon, a lorry full of fish, a German playboy's sports car careening along narrow mountain roads at 90 m.p.h.—but it got him where he wanted to go.

TROUBLE ON TRAINS

"As long as I stuck to hitch-hiking I did fine," he said. "The only trouble I had was when I got on trains. Twice I was taken in the wrong direction, with no one on board who spoke English."

"One of the best things about hitch-hiking is that you really get to know the people," Joe continued. If Americans are losing their popularity in Europe, as some sources of information insist, Joe found that Europeans do a fine job of concealing their animosity.

"They were friendly, hospitable to an extreme and anxious to help in any way." For example: A Scottish truck driver transported him many miles and then provided a room. A youth hostel in Norway offered dinner, lodging and breakfast for a grand total of 81 cents. The tourist bureau in Copenhagen got him a dinner invitation from a Danish family. A tour bus into Germany gave him a free ride and a passenger became his host for a day.

EAST BERLIN TOUR

In West Berlin, the United States Army's Columbia House sponsored a three-hour tour of the Russian sector for 25 cents. "Incidentally," Joe said, "there's a tremendous contrast between the Allied and Eastern sectors. The Russians have done little restoration of the destroyed streets and buildings and the people in their sector are shabbily dressed."

Students traveling in Europe routinely adopt methods of identification to speed their passage from place to place. Swiss wanderers carry small national flags and Danes wear distinctive student caps, for instance.

"I carried an old black suitcase with "U. S. A." painted in big letters on the side. It worked like magic all the way through," Joe said.

"Hitch - hiking is the major means of travel there, it seems. It's not viewed with suspicion, as it is here. Even in Norway, where so-called major roads are just sand paths and there are few cars, the going was good."

JOSEPH HAHN
Toured Europe 'By Thumb'

Newspaper article in *St. Louis Post-Dispatch* in August 1956 showing me posing in Norway with my *attractive* and *inviting* USA suitcase.

17

Tours 9 Countries...

Westminster Student Joe Hahn Gets Thumb-Level View Of Europe For $160

Joe Hahn will return to Westminster College this fall and one of his prized discoveries of the summer vacation will be his strong conversational piece. That is his educated thumb.

Joe, known to many Fultonians as a camera hobbyist and to sports fans as Blue Jay tennis player, has returned to his home in St. Louis after a seven-week, nine-country tour of Europe, carried out on a budget of $160.

To do this, Hahn brought his thumb's talent into full bloom. He discovered that clenched fingers and an extended thumb means the same in Europe as it does in America — "How about a lift, buddy?"

So by rule of thumb, Hahn was able to do such diverse things as read a newspaper by sunlight in Norway, picnic in the Alps, burrow through Medieval castles and enjoy dozens of other continental experiences. His costs were less per day than the average motorist spends crossing Missouri.

Joe was not particular about his mode of transportation. He rode in hay wagons, a lorry full of fish, a German playboy's sports car, or anything else on wheels that came along. He had no trouble hitchhiking, although the playboy took him on a 90-mile-per hour ride on narrow mountain roads, but he did learn to stay away from trains. "As long as I stuck to hitchhiking, I did fine," he told a St. Louis Globe-Democrat reporter, "The only trouble I had was when I got on trains. Twice I was taken in the wrong direction, with no one on board who spoke English."

Hahn said that one of the best things about hitchhiking is that "you really get to know people". He said he found no signs of growing European animosity toward Americans, as some sources have reported.

"They were friendly, hospitable to an extreme and anxious to help in any way." For example:

A Scottish truck driver transported him and then provided a room. A south hotel in Norway offered dinner, lodging and breakfast for a grand total of 21 cents. The tourist bureau in Copenhagen got him a dinner invitation from a Danish family. A tour bus into Germany gave him a free ride and a passenger became his host for a day.

In West Berlin, the United States Army's Columbia House sponsored a three-hour tour of the Russian sector for 25 cents. "Incidentally," Joe said, "there's a tremendous contrast between the Allied and Eastern sectors. The Russians have done little restoration of the destroyed streets and buildings and the people in their sector are shabbily dressed."

Students traveling in Europe routinely adopt methods of identification to speed their passage from place to place. Swiss wanderers carry small national flags and Danes wear distinctive student caps, for instance.

"I carried an old black suitcase with "U. S. A." painted in big letters on the side. It worked like magic all the way through," Joe said.

"Hitchhiking is the major means of travel there, it seems. It's not viewed with suspicion, as it is here. Even in Norway, where so-called major roads are just sand paths and there are few cars, the going was good."

Hahn will be a senior at Westminster this fall.

Newspaper article from the *Fulton Daily Sun-Gazette*, the local newspaper from where I attended college, printed upon my return to college in September 1956

My European Trip of 1956

After months of seemingly endless planning, my second trip to Europe suddenly became a reality when I found myself leaving 5810 Kingwood Drive for the airport. My plane was due to leave Lambert Airport at 12:15 a.m. on June 5th, but as Dad wanted to be sure I did not miss the plane, we left the confines of 5810 at 8:45 p.m. for the long drive to the airport.

Arriving at the airport, I checked in my baggage at forty and a half pounds and then watched other flights take off while waiting for the time to pass.

Boarding the Eastern Air Lines Silver Falcon at midnight after saying good-bye to the family for my 12:15 a.m. flight to New York, I occupied a seat at the rear of the plane and waved a last farewell to those on the ground as we taxied down the runway. It was my first commercial flight, and I was quite anxious to get off the ground.

We were aloft in a few minutes, and the view of lighted Saint Louis was beautiful. We crossed the Mississippi River, and then only inky blackness was visible. Bullion was served by the air stewardess, and I found myself sleeping until we arrived in Louisville, Kentucky, where we stepped down to solid earth briefly to refuel, as we were on our way to Washington, DC. We came in so low over the water of the Potomac River in the faint rays of the morning sun that for a moment, I thought the plane was going to land in the water, but we settled down gently on the runway and taxied over to the terminal. One could see the Capitol and the towering Washington Monument in the early-morning grayness, and as we took off, I found it most advantageous to take some pictures of the sunrise. The maze of highways below formed an interesting pattern, and before I knew it, we were over New York City and landing at LaGuardia Airport. It was now 6:45 a.m., and I called relatives of ours and our old neighbors, the Harry Stocks.

I boarded a bus to Manhattan and found myself one of two passengers. There was much traffic, and the going was slow, as we had to wait for many traffic lights. From the bus terminal I took a city bus to the port authority to catch the bus of the Holland American Line, which would take me directly to the pier. It was now eight thirty, and as soon as the bus was filled, we left for the pier.

I met two schoolteachers who were also going to Europe and found they were returning on the same ship as I was in late July. Their names were Joan Parrack from Oklahoma City and Grace Marston from Dallas.

Before boarding the SS *Maasdam*, I took a picture of it and then made table reservations for the second seating before heading to my cabin, 230, which was on the main deck.

We were to return on the SS *Ryndam*, the sister ship, of which a photo was available. Both ships were fairly new and very accommodating.

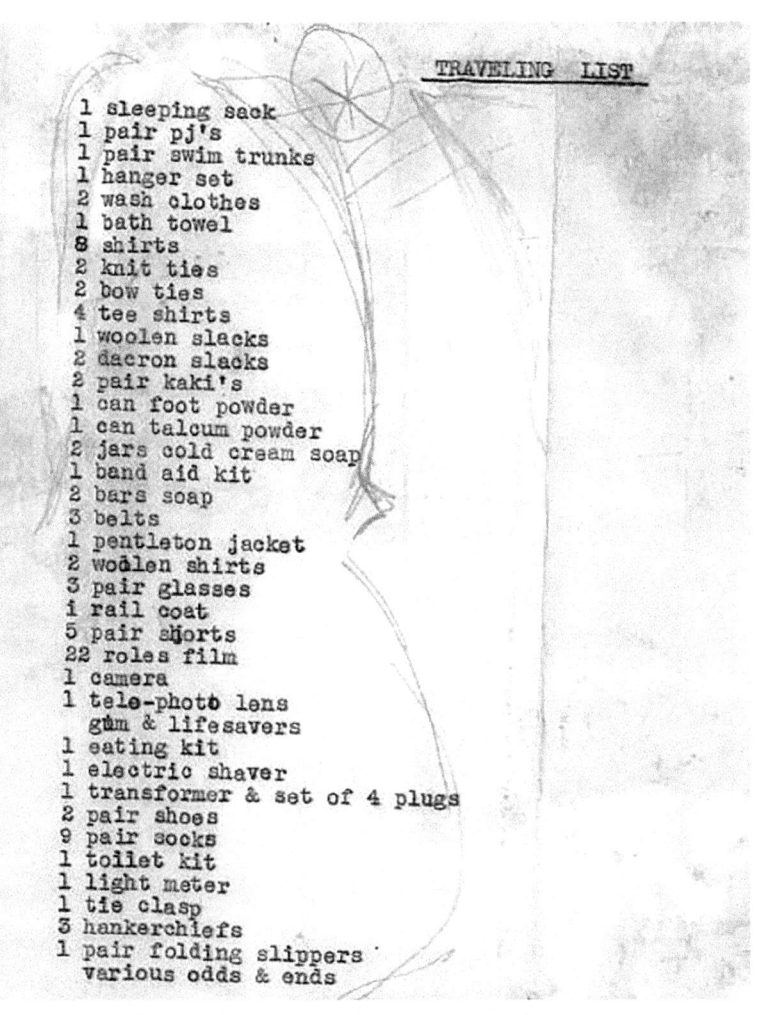

```
                                TRAVELING LIST
1 sleeping sack
1 pair pj's
1 pair swim trunks
1 hanger set
2 wash clothes
1 bath towel
8 shirts
2 knit ties
2 bow ties
4 tee shirts
1 woolen slacks
2 dacron slacks
2 pair kaki's
1 can foot powder
1 can talcum powder
2 jars cold cream soap
1 band aid kit
2 bars soap
3 belts
1 pentleton jacket
2 woolen shirts
3 pair glasses
1 rail coat
5 pair shorts
22 roles film
1 camera
1 tele-photo lens
  gum & lifesavers
1 eating kit
1 electric shaver
1 transformer & set of 4 plugs
2 pair shoes
9 pair socks
1 toilet kit
1 light meter
1 tie clasp
3 hankerchiefs
1 pair folding slippers
  various odds & ends
```

Traveling list prepared by my mother to keep track of my personal belongings (Note: The gum and lifesavers were to be given as gifts to German schoolchildren, as previously requested from our trip in 1955 to Rosswangen.)

After leaving my suitcase in my cabin, I took my camera and went out to take some pictures of the skyline and await our sailing. Joan and Grace were also on the top deck, watching the last-minute proceedings, and as the haze began to clear, I could see the tugs that were to take us from the harbor coming into view. It was twelve two when we pulled away from the pier and passed the New York skyline on our left. In a few minutes, the Statue of Liberty came into view, and passing her massive structure, one could appreciate our great land as a true land of freedom.

Feeling the pains of hunger, I went to the dining room for a filling lunch, and upon returning to my cabin, I found a bon voyage card from home. At this moment, I felt a little funny and again went out, and finding a deck chair empty, I availed myself to its usefulness and slept for two hours.

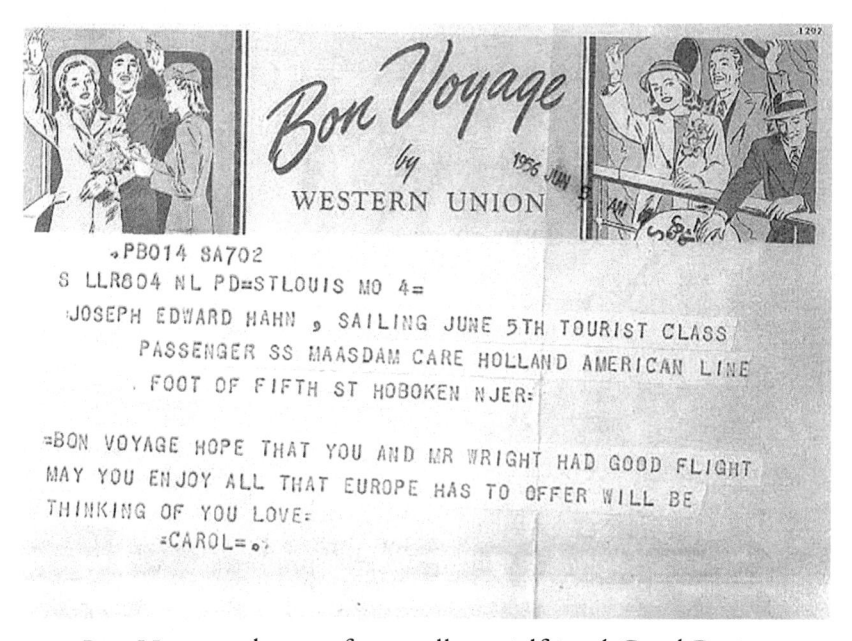

Bon Voyage telegram from college girlfriend Carol Ratjen

Waking up and feeling well rested, I found the sea shone calmly from the bright rays of the sun. The discomfort from the motion had long since passed, and I headed for the main lounge to listen to afternoon-tea music. Here I became involved in a three-handed bridge that shortly thereafter became four-handed, as my roommate Authur Naddell made the forth among Grace, Joan, and me.

Authur was a medical student from Brooklyn who was on his way to study for five years in Geneva. He had the typical accent of one from Brooklyn, and we found his company most enjoyable. We played bridge until it was time to dress for dinner, as the second seating did not have to arrive until 7:30 p.m.

Our dinner table party of six with our
waiter. I am at the far right.

We were now at our assigned tables, and our table was a large round one in the center of the dining room. Those sitting at the table included Roeli Boogerd, a Dutch girl of twenty-three from Winterswijk, Holland; Mary Hirschi from Guthrie, Oklahoma; Iva Hamilton, a dentist from Paisley, Scotland; Michel Craig, a young Frenchman who was the life of the table; Marie Morin, a Frenchwoman who was always laughing; Albert Valdman, a professor of modern languages at Cornell University; and Barbara, Pat, and Jim Blake from Bethlehem, Pennsylvania, who were traveling with their parents.

Dinner consisted of roast beef and many desserts, which were all quite filling. I had an interesting discussion with Prof. James G. Southworth, who advised me of traveling hints concerning Scotland and Norway.

Later, the three Blake children and I went to see the movie *The Leather Saint*, which was not up to expectations. Mr. Blake then bought a round of Dutch beer, which was very good.

At midnight, we were all quite tired and returned to our staterooms, where I was able to meet my other two roommates for the first time, which led to a general bull session. Besides Authur and me, the room was shared with Joe Lainer, a Jewish antique dealer from New York who was feeling the effects of the sea, and Mr. Michel Boudant, a professor at Princeton University.

I had been on my way for twenty-four hours at this point and had covered 1,400 miles. As our first day at sea drew to a close, our room steward, a reserved Dutchman, Theo Van de Hoek, came and inquired if there was anything we needed before we retired. This was quite a shock to me, for my observation of him tagged him as being quite lazy and successful in getting the job done only when asked the second time.

June 6—Partly Cloudy but Pleasant

I awoke at 9:00 a.m., dressed, and had a breakfast of prunes, tomato juice, and shredded wheat, eggs, bacon, toast, and honey. Barbara and I then engaged in some ping-pong as we snuck to the first-class side of the ship, where there were only thirty-six passengers, who never used the table.

Completing half a dozen strenuous games, we lounged in deck chairs until 2:00 p.m., which made us thirty minutes late for lunch. I asked Hank, our waiter, if I could have some ham and cheese, which I made into sandwiches, and some delicious Dutch pudding. Pat Blake and I played her parents in three rubbers of bridge and managed to win the last one as we held terrible cards most of the afternoon. While we played, we listened to a lecture by the social directress of the SS *Maasdam*, Mrs. H. Bijvoet. In the late afternoon, we played shuffleboard and deck tennis until 7:00 p.m.

I returned to our cabin to shave and dress for dinner of fried chicken, which was very delicious. Barbara and I took in the movie *Foreign Intrigue* and then went to the Palm Court to dance until 12:15 a.m.

I took this opportunity to dance with the Dutch girl who sat at our table. Roeli added much life to the ship by playing her guitar and singing when she was not engaged in her favorite sport of deck tennis. At the table, she was always telling jokes, as she brought her joke book to the table and read the more-involved ones. She had also been kind enough to help me learn some German that I needed to know.

Today she taught me how to make an orange sandwich, which was something new to me: After peeling the orange, you split the orange into two equal halves, and then after loosening the sections, they are inserted into each other and form a jointed entanglement that looks like a sandwich and can easily be held in the hand and eaten.

The tourist class literally had the run of the ship. They had access to the swimming pool, sports deck, and all other forms of recreation. Tomorrow, I would be entering the deck tennis tournament and the bridge tournament. It was now quite late, and I had just completed washing out my dirty clothes amid constant ribbing from my roommates, and being quite tired, I retired to a very soft bed.

June 7—Cloudy and Pleasant

I was able to sleep to nine fifty this morning and had to hurry to make breakfast by the closing hours of 10:00 a.m. After breakfast, I went to see the swimming pool, as it was now being filled. I was tempted to go for a swim, but the water appeared too cold for my blood.

Instead, I went to the sports deck and played some deck tennis and shuffleboard. While I rested from these tiring activities, I was able to take some slides of various people. Roeli began playing her guitar, and we all joined in the singing of popular songs until it was time for lunch.

Lunch consisted of the usual fine selection of foods, after which competition in the bridge tournament commenced. Again, the hands I held were nothing outstanding. Finding nothing else to do, I climbed the many steps to the sports deck and met Ms. Madeline Arnaudet, who suggested playing some more deck tennis.

As we left the playing area at 7:00 p.m., the sky was now clearing and small white caps were forming as the sun shone down on the sea, which glistened like a new-fallen snow. I hurriedly snapped some pictures of this spectacle and also some of the sunset. At this time, I had the pleasure of meeting a most interesting man from Australia who was interested in my camera, and seeing Professor Southworth again, I made the mistake of asking him if he was retired!

Tonight's dinner consisted of minute steaks, and the waiter, now knowing that I had a huge appetite, gave me two of them, not to mention the many servings of peach ice cream.

After seeing the movie entitled *The Brave and the Bold*, I had an interesting discussion with Barbara Blake concerning the general running of a ship and of boat life and its most unusual way of living.

The clocks were advanced forty-five minutes for the third successive evening, and after walking Barbara to her cabin, I returned to the Palm Court for a social gathering with two of my roommates and the two schoolteachers from the south whom we had previously met.

It was a gay celebration this evening with the telling of jokes between dances to keep us laughing. My roommate Joe Lainer, the Jewish antique dealer, had told everyone he was getting off the ship tomorrow at noon. Yes, we were 880 miles at sea, and old Joe kept insisting he was getting off the ship, as the *Queen Mary* was due to pass us the following day, and he was going to transfer to that ship in the middle of the Atlantic Ocean.

After this gathering broke up, several of us gathered in the main lounge, around the piano, where we sang until 3:00 a.m. I was not tired but returned to my room quite relaxed and looking forward to landing in England. I had met several American and Canadian students who were also going to hitchhike throughout Europe, which had helped build up my confidence in what I was attempting.

June 8—Warm and Sunny but Turning Cloudy

This morning, I slept until eleven thirty, which meant I received no breakfast, but I was able to eat from the bowl of fresh fruit that was placed in our room each day.

I dressed warmly only to find that the sun was beating down quite hard as we were now in the Gulf Stream. I watched the various deck games and strolled around the ship, taking in the sunshine.

I returned to our cabin and unpacked my suitcase, as I thought it was about time this task be done since I became quite tired of pulling the trunk from under the bed every time I wanted something. In the cabin was the funny antique dealer, and when I asked him when he was disembarking, he replied, "At the first stop."

Lunch was looked forward to by this hungry lad, and I again made ham-and-cheese sandwiches that hit the spot. After lunch,

Barbara suggested going to the sports deck, where we sat and watched some old Dutch people play various games and greatly admired them as we noticed they put their whole heart and soul into whatever they did. Mr. and Mrs. Blake asked us if we wanted to make a third and fourth for bridge, but Barbara chose to remain in the sunshine, so her sister Pat filled in, and in the next three hours, we played only two rubbers.

I returned to our cabin to freshen up for dinner, at which time I brought Roeli a piece of saltwater taffy. She was suspicious of me, so I had to take a bite of it first, as I had previously played a trick on her.

During the meal, we all tried to guess Roeli's age. Each of us was entitled to one guess to be written down on a piece of paper that was passed around. To our surprise, not one of us had guessed her age, and there were nine different guesses. She informed us that she was now twenty-three. She enjoyed this very much and now said to me, "Joe, now tell me, when is my birthday?"

Not knowing it, I fumbled around and said, "In February."

To my surprise, she said I was right, and then I went on and said, "Oh, you must be a Valentine baby. Your birthday is February 14."

She was most surprised and accused me of finding out from someone else but then came to realize that no one else on the ship would have cause to know her birthday. I could not explain how this happened, but it was a one chance out of 4,380 that I could give both the correct month and day of her birthday.

We excused ourselves from the table and went to see the movie entitled *The Angel Who Pawned Her Harp*. It was an English movie and was quite good for a change. We all went to the Palm Court for dancing, and at this time, they announced a game to be played that was similar to musical chairs but was played with couples instead.

Girls were placed back to back in the center of the floor, and the boys were to walk around them as long as the music played, but when it stopped, he was to latch onto a girl. The only trouble was that there was one less girl each time the music stopped. This continued until there were only two boys and one girl left. I was one of those boys who were then blindfolded and told to find the girl who was "somewhere on the dance floor."

I could hear people laughing, and as my hands touched someone's head, I thought I had found the lone girl. To my surprise, the "girl" was really a man with a wig on his head, who was sitting on a stool. I was given a cute small Dutch doll for finding the "girl."

I met a Dutch woman who was returning to Holland after a five-year visit to New York. With her were two students from Amherst who were planning to hitchhike in Europe also. They provided interesting conversation between dances, which allowed me to meet Ann, a girl from Cleveland, Ohio.

I returned to my cabin at 2:00 a.m. but found myself talking to my roommates until three fifteen, so little sleep was gotten.

June 9—Cloudy, Windy, and Cold

After my late retirement last evening, I was able to sleep until 12:45 p.m. and enjoyed a very restful night. For lunch, I again had ham-and-cheese sandwiches, but also at my place was the following poem and a baby's milk bottle:

> When you will go to sleep,
> We will sing this melody:
> Little Boy Blue, come blow your horn,
> The sheep's in the meadow, the cows in the corn.
> Where is the boy that looks after the sheep?
> He's under the haystack, fast asleep.

This type of proceeding was carried on by the people of my table for everyone who came late to a meal.

After lunch, I went on a tour of the engine room, which led from one stairway down to another. All the time it was becoming warmer and warmer. We were shown the turbines and the main shaft, which was over 150 feet long. There were five decks below the level of the passengers, where the complicated mechanism was situated. We were also shown the stabilizers, which jutted from the side of the ship when it started to toss in a heavy sea. There was a fin on the end of the stabilizer that helped ready the ship. The tour was certainly a most interesting experience even though it was very warm.

I joined the Blakes for some more bridge, which occupied the remainder of the afternoon, after which I took a short walk around the ship before returning to my room to wash out some clothes and squeeze an hour of sleep into my day's activities.

For dinner, we had lamb chops and then played bingo in the Palm Court. I lost two games and gave my card to Mrs. Blake, who promptly won $16 on it. Games on the dance floor occupied the rest of the evening as the men engaged in Pass the Hat, which saw Al, a man who sat at our table, and me hurriedly trying to place a hat on the others' head before the music stopped.

I danced with Barbara and Patty on a crowded floor until the music stopped for the evening, then I returned to our cabin and found myself in another bull session with my roommates, whom I only see before retiring.

June 10—Clear, Sunny, and Pleasant

I found myself getting up at nine thirty and making breakfast for the first time in three days, but to my surprise, I was only one of three out of ten who made breakfast.

I took a walk in refreshing sunlight and spoke to the Dutch woman and her two daughters, who were going to Munich to study music and art. I excused myself as I was scheduled for a tour of the bridge at 10:40 a.m., and I did not want to miss it. I found it most interesting. We were shown the radar set as well as the automatic pilot, which is just part of the wonderful modern equipment that makes navigation what it is today.

I then returned to speak with the daughters of the Dutch woman and asked Liz Hamers, her youngest daughter, to play ping-pong on the first-class side. We played until noon and then journeyed to the sports deck, where we played against Barbara and another partner until lunchtime.

I again asked for ham and cheese and was served bananas with cream for dessert. Hank, the waiter, had been very good to all of us as we'd always had excellent food.

I met Art, one of my roommates. We played ping-pong, which saw me suffer my first defeat on the ship. While I was playing with Art, an officer came along, and I thought he was going to tell us to stop playing since we were on the first-class side. However, he asked if he might play with us, and we switched partners throughout the course of the play. While not engaged in playing, I took the opportunity to ask the officer questions concerning the various assignments of the ships and various questions concerning life on the sea.

As I now looked down to see four gold stripes across his sleeves, I realized that I had been talking to the captain of the ship, none other than Captain Hogervorst, who had spent thirty-seven years on the sea and was quite an accomplished ping-pong player.

Finishing the games of ping-pong, I entered the main lounge only to be asked to play bridge with Art, Joan, and Grace. Four rubbers were completed in a very short time as good cards were held for the first time.

That evening, dinner consisted of Dutch steak, which was very good and put us all in the right mood for the talent show that was to follow in the Palm Court.

There were thirteen different performances put on by the passengers of the ship, and all were well received. The last consisted of ballroom dancing by Mr. and Mrs. Ed Cheney from Portland, Oregon, who were instructors known throughout the Far West.

Following this, there was dancing to the Maasdam Trio, and I took the opportunity to introduce myself to the Cheneys and asked Mrs. Cheney for a dance. It was so graceful dancing with her as we just glided along. They had been professionals for twenty years and taught dancing ever since they left the stage in New York.

The music ended shortly, but before I retired for the evening, I introduced myself to a Mr. Blattner from Saint Louis, who had sung in the talent show.

June 11—Clear, Warm, and Sunny

I did not awaken until 2:06 p.m. and had to hurry to make lunch of ham-and-cheese sandwiches. I then met one of the students from Amherst, who let me look at his maps of Norway and Scotland.

While walking along the deck for some exercise, I met Liz Hamers, who asked me to play ping-pong again. We played for two hours as a team and did not lose a game of doubles. As we went to the main lounge, we were surprised to hear the Maasdam Trio playing "Here Comes the Bride." We sat down to see what was happening and noticed that forty to fifty people were all standing in a circle in the center of the lounge as an elderly couple walked inside. As we later found out, it was this couple's forty-fifth wedding anniversary, and their Dutch friends were helping them celebrate. The singing was excellent and very lively as we were thrilled by the steady beat of the old Dutch songs and the various toasts. This singing carried on for nearly two hours and was most interesting to watch and listen to.

I left the lounge to sit in deck chair and met a girl who formally went to Stephens College in Columbia, Missouri, but left because she thought they were too strict.

Before dinner, I decided to head to the bar for a few beers at ten cents a glass and met a Father from Belleville, Illinois, who studied at Saint Louis University, and when I told him I lived near Kenrick Seminary, we found ourselves talking about home.

I dressed for the farewell dinner, and upon my entering the dining room, we were greeted with noisemakers, gay hats, balloons, and much fanfare to help us celebrate this festive occasion.

For our dinner, Hank saw that I had two lovely steaks and a plate of roast tom turkey topped off with two cherry sundaes. We had our picture taken and then made our way to the Palm Court for community singing to be followed by dancing. I danced with Barbara, Pat, and a girl from Vancouver, Canada, Ms. Laurel Noland, who was also going to hitchhike throughout Europe.

After I walked Barbara to her cabin, I returned to the Palm Court and had a round of beer with Joe, the antique dealer. I invited Laurel to join us as we sang songs, as we sat around the piano until 4:30 a.m. After I walked Laurel to her cabin, I took a stroll around the deck and viewed the faint rays of dawn appearing in the east, which was quite an impressive sight, before going to my cabin for some needed rest.

June 12—Clear, Warm, and Sunny

I again managed to sleep until 2:06 p.m. and had the same rush to have my ham and cheese for lunch. I then returned to my cabin to wash my clothes and take a refreshing bath, as I knew it would be some time before I would be so lucky to feel clean. Relaxing in warm sunshine, I saw the SS *United States* pass us like we were sitting still. It had left New York two days after we did and should reach Southampton shortly. We too were near the port but could not dock until tomorrow, so we had reduced our speed and would dock tomorrow morning.

I played Roeli in four games of deck tennis before having a refreshing glass of beer, as I was tired, and then headed for my cabin to rest up before dinner.

Our last dinner on the ship was roast beef in brown gravy, which we hurriedly ate as there was much to do on our last night aboard the ship. Laurel and I walked to the rear of ship and talked about the various adventures that lay before us, as we were both going to hitchhike through Europe.

It was now 10:00 p.m. and was very light out. We talked until 11:00, and then I walked her to her cabin and went to the Palm Court for dancing with Barbara until midnight. I took a stroll around the decks in refreshing air and returned to our cabin to pack and have our last bull session before retiring for the night.

June 13—Warm and Clear, Turning Cool with Light Rain

Our steward woke us at five thirty, but we remained in bed until 6:00 a.m., as Joe and I were the only two disembarking today. We dressed and took a quick glance outside to see land as we were nearing Southampton, the port where we would disembark.

I went to breakfast, where I had three glasses of orange juice, two bowls of cornflakes, hot toast, and honey. Hank had given me a plateful of ham and cheese so I could make some sandwiches to take with me for the long trip to Preston, England. Also at the table was a girl and her grandfather from the first setting who came from Jacksonville, Illinois. I thanked Hank, our waiter, for his lovely service and gave him his tip as I left the dining room, after saying goodbye to all my friends.

I returned to the cabin to tip the room steward, and with my suitcase in hand, I headed for the Palm Court, where the customs officials were located. There I met Laurel, and as we were talking, the Blakes came along and asked if they could take some pictures. I excused myself from Laurel and went with the Blake family to the main deck, where some last-minute pictures were taken.

I bade them farewell and returned to wait in line after I thanked them for all they had done for me. The line began moving quite rapidly, and in no time at all, I found myself through all the possible red tape that usually arouse at a time like this.

Disembarking, I watched the crew of the *Queen Mary* scrub and paint the huge vessel, and turning around, I could see the Blakes waving for the last time as I entered the huge green shed to have my suitcase checked for the last time. Laurel was still with me, and I wished her the best of luck in her journey as we parted ways.

Since I had carried my own baggage off the ship, I was checked through without any delay. I asked a bobby directions for getting out of the station since I was not taking the boat train to London.

I was given a green slip of paper that allowed me to leave the station. I hailed a taxi driver and explained to him that I wished to reach the edge of town so I could begin hitchhiking to Preston, which was some 380 miles to the north on the west coast of England.

The driver's name was Sidney Lewis Spencer, who informed me that the best way for me to reach northern England would be to get to the truck route going north from Winchester, which was eighteen miles to the north of Southampton. He was most interested in talking me into letting him drive me all the way to Preston for $60, but I informed him I was only interested in going to Winchester. However, he did help me map out the best route to take and instructed me to write down the names of the towns and cities I should go through to reach my destination.

The fare came to thirty-seven shillings, six pence, which was $5.25, but he was instructed to charge $10.50 since he would have to drive back to Southampton with an empty load. He had previously told me I would have to pay only $5.00, and though I did not realize it at that time, I now know he was speaking the truth; nevertheless, my trip did start out on the expensive side.

He dropped me on the northern outskirts of Winchester on the Old Banbury Road and said I would have no difficulty getting rides to the north.

I had been advised to display my nationality while trying to obtain a *lift*, so before I left on my trip, I had painted, in large letters, USA on my suitcase. Hitchhikers in Europe normally displayed the flag of their country as an armband, which allowed the oncoming motorists to know the country the hitchhiker was from. This was an excellent idea and provided knowledge about me before I was offered a ride. I was really a *curiosity* standing alongside the roadside, and with the USA showing an eager, youthful lad looking for a ride, getting offered a lift was normally an easy accomplishment throughout my trip.

I had to stand on the opposite side of the road since cars and trucks drove on the left-hand side of the roads. I was standing on the crest of a hill, and down the road I could see a truck coming. To my surprise, he stopped for me, but after seeing he was loaded down with bricks, I knew the going would be slow, but considering I had been waiting only thirty seconds for my first lift, I was not one to complain.

The driver was Peter Winter, who was most interesting to speak to even though he was a little hard to understand. He took me as far as Newbury and handed my suitcase down to me from the rear of the truck as I took a picture of him.

It was not over a minute when an Irish naval tailor named Mick stopped for me in his delivery truck and took me as far as his next business stop, which was in a small town thirty-three miles away. He took me to a petro station outside of town to make lifting easier for me, and no sooner than he pulled away, a United States Army truck driven by Chuck from Chicago and Tom from Brooklyn stopped for me. I tossed my suitcase into the rear of the truck with a generator they were transporting to another base and climbed into the cab. I rode with them for about an hour, and during this time, we finished the last of the box of candy Mother had given me the day I left home.

My fifth ride of the day was offered just a few seconds after I alighted from the army truck. It was in the form of a gravel truck driven by a fellow named Ron from Glester, England.

This ride was not a long one, but it helped me get the next one with a Mr. Morris, who was in the fruit and produce business and was coming from his farm when I was dropped from the gravel truck. Mr. Morris lived just outside of Stratford, the home of Shakespeare, and went out of his way to take me past the monument erected in his honor and the buildings that housed his great works. He stopped long enough to allow me to get some pictures and then took me to the edge of town, where I was picked up after all of a minute's wait by Mr. and Mrs. Upton and their daughter Sue, who were on their way to Birmingham to trade in their car after buying a new one that morning. They pulled into a service station to buy gas and, at the same time, bought me a map of England. They took me to Birmingham, but unfortunately, they dropped me in the center of the city.

Birmingham had one and a quarter million people, and here I was in the center of a busy city. After I took a few pictures, I approached a car that was parked along the curb and asked the people if they could direct me to the outskirts of North Birmingham. The couple inside the car was Mr. and Mrs. Nichols, and they told me to hop in and quickly took me to the highway leading north to Litchfield, where getting a lift would be an easier task.

I was left off in a poor factory section, where schoolchildren as well as the factory workers stared at me. Two small girls of around eight and ten asked me if I was looking for a bus and where I was headed to, but I smiled and replied that a bus would be too expensive.

Their clothing was ragged and dirty. All this was noticeable to me as they stood and stared at me. Just then, a young man approached me and inquired where I was headed. I told him I was on my way to Litchfield and Preston, and as I continued speaking with him and trying to get a ride at the same time, a truck used for carrying large steel beams driven by Harry Nuell from Hull, England, stopped for me. He was a nice gentleman, and after I told him my plans, he invited me to visit him in Hull if I ever came near his home. He told me his phone number was 16107 and said I should just call him when I came in town, as he would give me free lodging.

As we were driving along the road, and since he was about to let me off, he saw a moving van from Manchester, and stopping his truck, he asked the driver of the van if he would take me in the general direction I was headed.

I thanked Harry and climbed into the cab of the van driven by Sid and Bill. I thought we were on our way to Manchester, but somehow, we became lost, and in twenty minutes, we were again back in Litchfield.

This time we took the right highway and were soon on our way to Manchester. Feeling the pains of hunger, I opened my suitcase and ate the sandwiches I had taken with me from the ship, as it was now 3:00 p.m.

We arrived in Manchester at 5:00 p.m., and I was dropped off in the city at the main warehouse. Feeling a little lost in the rush hour traffic, I walked to try my luck alongside the road. I was not to be disappointed for long as a small pickup truck driven by two men in the real estate business stopped for me, but since there was no room in front of the truck, I had to make myself comfortable in the rear of the open truck.

It was a funny feeling to be surrounded by cars in the busy city, but I was quite comfortable as I was able to stretch my legs for the first time today. We rode through several small towns before the driver dropped me near his home, but he had made the mistake of not leaving me on the highway. His home was near Bury, and after walking a few blocks to again reach the highway, I was picked up by a man driving a confectionary truck, a person who was most difficult to understand.

As I indicated a preference to take a picture of the countryside, he was most willing to stop for me, which allowed me some excellent shots. He was soon to drop me along the highway again as we came to a fork in the road, and it was only a matter of minutes before my thirteenth ride of the day in the form of another fruit-and-produce truck driven by Bill Shaw and John O'Grady stopped for me and took me a few miles to their garage alongside the road.

The next car to offer me a lift was occupied by a young couple going out on a date. The lift was not long, but nevertheless, it helped. They left me on the road, where I was picked up by a businessman, William Bamber, on his way home from work, who went out of his way to take me to a junction where I might make better connections to Preston.

As this car pulled away, a fire department service truck that had been delivering hoses in Manchester came along and stopped for me. The driver was Fred Ryan, who had seen eleven years of service in the recent war and who happened to be on a United States ship on D-day, landing in Normandy. He was from Preston, and when I told him where I was headed, he suggested that it would be better if he would drop me off at my destination, lest I should never reach it.

My destination was the home of Eric Hammond at 43 Elcho Street, Preston, in Lanchester, England, and the driver of the fire department service truck left me off on Elcho Street, but not knowing where Eric lived, I went into a confectionary and inquired the whereabouts of the Hammond home. To my surprise, I was informed it was just three houses down the street, so after thanking the store owner, I made my way to the Hammond home.

Ringing the bell, I was greeted by Eric's aunt and then by Mrs. Hammond, who informed me that Eric was taking in a movie. His aunt went to fetch him while his mother told me of Eric's latest misfortune.

He had been run into while riding his bicycle on Sunday by a fourteen-year-old lad who couldn't control his bicycle. Both were taken to the hospital, and Eric was only released yesterday, which meant he would be out of work for the remainder of the week, which would allow him to spend some time with me.

I read my mail while a pot of tea was made for me, and in no time at all, Eric came rushing into the house, bustling with all the enthusiasm that I had known he possessed when I met him on my previous crossing of the Atlantic Ocean in 1955, when he was the drummer on the ship. It was now 7:30 p.m., and I related the long trip that had taken only ten and a half hours.

A fire was made in the hearth, and Eric fried me three sausages, some eggs, and sliced tomatoes, which all tasted very good to me after a tiring day along the highways. Also served with the meal was buttered currant bread and English barm cake, which was quite filling in itself. Barm cake is a soft round flattish bun made in Northern England that is leavened with barm. Barm is a product of scum from the top of a liquor and is also obtained from the scum of making wine.

Since there was no bathroom, we had to wash at the kitchen sink before we left for a walk around town. We took a double-decker bus, the only kind they had in England, to the center of town and then strolled through the old streets. We headed for the city park, which led down to the Ribble River, before we circled back to stop at a local pub, the Olympic, where we had a few drinks while meeting some friends and making plans for the weekend. The owner of the pub had an A-frame sign in front of his establishment that read "Chish and Fips," and when told of the misspelling on the sign, he replied, "It's done that way to get customers in the pub of course the pub was advertising "Fish and Chips," a popular English dish. Everyone wants to tell me of the error, but they always stay to eat and drink. It is a good idea to bring the customers into the pub." We then walked home in a light rain that had begun to fall, and Eric made some hot cocoa to warm us after the chilly walk.

We went upstairs, where he helped me unpack, which was followed by a "what have you been doing with yourself" topic of conversation.

It was good to have reached my first destination, which was only accomplished after sixteen different lifts in a most roundabout manner. The air was quite cool, but this situation was easily overshadowed by the warm hospitality of the Hammond family. The city of Preston was quite old and had a great deal of history. Tomorrow, Eric would be taking me on a general tour, at which time I'd have much explained to me, but for now, I was quite tired and should retire at 12:30 a.m.

June 14—Cool and Partly Cloudy, Becoming Sunny

I found it difficult to awaken from my feather bed as the morning sun came into the room. I wanted to remain in bed, but the aroma of food from the kitchen had drifted into the room. Eric was preparing breakfast, and after dressing, I went to the kitchen to wash as they had a small hot-water heater hanging from the wall, which was run by electricity.

Breakfast consisted of oatmeal, eggs, bacon, sausages, and barm cake, which was very delicious. Eric was quite the cook.

I received letter from parents and found all was well with them and then departed for town dressed in a bright-red woolen shirt with my camera along to record my trip. We walked to the downtown section of the city, and after inquiring at an electrical appliance store about the correct procedure for using an electric shaver, we walked to the market square to see the various sights.

The whole city was bubbling with activity; we walked through a Woolworths department store to note the contrast in prices and found them to be about one-third of the cost back home. This comparison was only made on the common articles and did not include the dear ones.

Thinking he had some dates lined up for the weekend, Eric took me to a record shop, and although the girls were nice, they were not interested in going out. After buying some air letters to write home, I was able to take some pictures of street scenes of the double-decker busses and of the bobbies directing traffic.

We then walked to Avenham Park to watch schoolchildren playing games on their lunch hour, as this was the gathering place for most of the children in this area. Each school had a different type of uniform to increase the rivalry in the various activities. Though most of the dress was similar, color represented the main difference, be it light green, blue, or maroon.

One schoolgirl saw me and asked me to take a picture of her, but I waited until she wasn't looking until I snapped the picture. Eric and I sat down in a shaded area to watch the children play various games and then walked to the Ribble River to see its muddy bottom as the tide was out. I took some pictures of Eric before heading for a café in the main section of town.

For two shillings and nine pence, about 38¢, we each had grapefruit juice, tomato soup, hamburger steak, buttered beans, mashed potatoes, and lemon pie. While we were eating, the presence of two girls sitting nearby caught our attention, and trying to learn more about them, we inquired from our waitress if she knew who they were, but this also drew a blank. Giving up hope of ever seeing them again as they had left before we finished eating, we paid the check and walked on down the main street of Preston.

We had not walked more than half a block when the two lovely girls we had just seen were spied coming toward us. We smiled as they walked past us and were now left pondering what to do when Eric grabbed my arm and turned me around as he headed after the girls, replying, "Come on, man, this is what we've been waiting for!"

Reluctantly, I followed Eric, and walking up behind one of them, he tapped her on the shoulder and said, "Pardon me, but my friend and I have a bet on whether or not you're American, and we figured the only way to find out was to ask you."

Eric, having tapped the better looking of the two, then looked at me, and I forced an "Oh, yes, I said you were American, and he says you're not."

She quietly replied that she was English, though of Italian decent, and introduced herself as Joan and her friend as Mary. They were from Grange, near the Lake District, and were working as secretaries in Preston and were now on their lunch hour.

Joan went on to say she was shocked to see me in such a bright-red shirt and wondered where I had purchased it. As we talked on, Eric nodded at me and then asked them to join us for lunch tomorrow at the same café. They accepted the invitation, but when asked out for the weekend, both replied that they were busy.

Saying good-bye to them, we walked over to the bus stop, and I noticed all the local shops were closed. Eric told me that most shops closed at noon on Thursday and remained open all day on Saturday, which gave them a five-and-a-half-day week.

We boarded a bus for Halfpenny Bridge, which crossed the Ribble River, and upon reaching the Ribble Valley, we strolled through the green fields that were sprinkled with yellow buttercups while herds of cows lazily basked in the sun. The fields were very fertile and quite a contrast to the city that lay just beyond the green hills.

We walked along the bank of the river as we headed back to town and arrived at 43 Elcho Street in time for afternoon tea. I also found time to write home while listening to a radio program from London and spent most of the remainder of the afternoon in a state of relaxation.

Eric prepared the evening meal, which was overly filling, and before long, we were both resting again. We were up at seven thirty and went to the city park to watch some tennis matches and see a good game of bowling on the green. This game was played on a green grass similar to that of a golf course green and was begun by rolling a *jack*, a small wooden ball, to any location on the green. Each person had two chances of rolling a larger wooden ball closest to the jack, with the closest person scoring a point and gaining the right to roll the jack where he wished for another round of play.

We returned to Eric's home to dress for a dance to be given by the Young Conservative Party of Preston at Worsley's Ballroom, noted to be the best in town.

On the way to the ballroom, we stopped to see Eric's aunt who lived in the slums of the city and who was shortly to lose her home to the city for a new construction project. She had four darling children, one by her first husband, an American from Alabama, and the other three, including a set of twins, by her second husband, a Canadian.

As we arrived at the ballroom, I was easily recognized as an American mostly due to my dress and height. Eric and I had decided to play it cool by first looking over the girls, but it wasn't long before we were going strong on the dancing. The music was outstanding; it consisted of a six-piece orchestra, dressed in formal attire, that would play a series of three similar dances then take a short break. While dancing, one moved in a counterclockwise direction around the dance floor, which added to the ease of dancing. The orchestra would play a series of three foxtrots, waltzes, fast fox, or what have you, but they would always play three dances of a similar nature.

Dancing with many girls from Preston and Blackpool, a nearby resort area, I made many friends, all seemingly interested in knowing how I contrasted them with American girls. I was told I danced differently than they were used to but was not hard to follow.

A girl by the name of Mary, a waitress in Blackpool, was interested in being with me and always found it convenient to be standing near me, but I displayed no interest in her as I elected to dance with them all.

Toward the end of the evening, Eric introduced me to the girl he had been dancing with, Margaret Butler, and as the music began to play, I asked her to dance. Eric had a surprised look on his face but couldn't say too much, for in a moment, we were dancing away. Margaret seemed to be a very lovely girl, and before too long, I had asked her out for the following evening. She was a model working in Liverpool and returned home only on the weekend, spending one night with her parents while going out the other.

Wishing to remain at home on the evening, I had asked her out and go out the following evening instead, I found myself doing a fast job of talking before she said, "All right, I'll come out with you."

After I asked her if she meant she would go out tomorrow evening, she replied "Yes, I guess I don't speak like an American" and went on to say "I'll meet you in front of the town clock at seven o'clock. Will that be all right with you?"

Not knowing what to say, I stammered around and asked her If I could pick her up instead, but she was quick to say that she lived outside of town and it would be difficult for me to find her home. I wasn't about to complain but felt much better when she went on to say that normally, the boy did meet his date in front of the town clock and assured me I would not be the only one waiting there.

The music had stopped, and we walked back to Eric, who was waiting for his turn to dance; he gave me a funny look and went on to say that it was a fine way for a guest to take one's date away from his host and added he wouldn't do the same to me when he came to America to visit me.

Margaret spent the rest of the evening with Eric, or should I say, Eric saw to it that she spent the rest of the evening with him. He accomplished this by asking her if she cared for anything to eat or drink. When she accepted and did not offer to pay, it was a sign that she would remain with him for the rest of the evening, as an English girl did not take advantage of her date by accepting anything from him without offering to pay for it when she did not care for him. If the girl allowed her date to pay for the food or drink, she was implying that she would remain with him for the rest of the evening. At dances of this type, everyone came alone and met up with dance partners until they found a date they would like to remain with for the evening. If the girl offered to pay for food or drink herself, it was a signal that she preferred to remain available to dance with others.

I spent the rest of the evening watching English couples dance various dances of European countries as they were competing in a contest, with a prize going to the couple that could do the most different dances.

Eric and I left the dance at about 1:00 a.m. and planned the following day's events as we walked home in the misty air. Now I had a date, but with Eric's girl, in a foreign country, not knowing where to go or what to do.

The day had been a most enjoyable one, for the weather was ideal and Eric and I had met many wonderful people, saw the historic city of Preston (Priest Town), and even saw a wedding in Eric's church as we passed there midmorning.

Most unusual to me was the fact that one could walk a few blocks from the downtown district and find himself in the beautiful countryside, with rolling hills and flowering meadow surrounding you. We were both very tired and eagerly jumped into our feather beds.

June 15—Partly Cloudy and Warm

I awoke at eleven twenty and hurried to the kitchen for breakfast of porridge, sausage, bacon, and some barm cake that Eric had prepared. Mrs. Hammond was washing in her outdoor pail, and after breakfast, I washed my dirty clothes and churned them in an old washtub with a wooden stick, as this was the only means of washing clothes.

Our plans called for a trip by train to Southport, some twenty miles to the south-southwest of Preston. We took a bus to the downtown area, stopping off at the market square. We noticed a great deal of buying and selling, but since it was Friday morning and people were buying for the weekend, we thought little of the crowded conditions.

It was twelve fifty, and we knew we were standing up Mary and Joan, the two girls we had asked out for lunch the previous day, but we walked onto the train station, passing the café quickly, and did not see our two friends.

Arriving at the station at 1:00 p.m. and buying our tickets for two shillings and six pence, we had but a short wait until our departure at one twenty. In the station, a notice caught my attention: Train Spotting Not Allowed. This, I found out to be, was a favorite pastime for the youth of England, which consisted of keeping a record of all the engine numbers on the locomotives of the trains throughout England, much the way an American youth had the desire to collect stamps. In the past, literally hundreds of boys would crowd into the stations and clog up the areaways, leaving little room for the passengers to stand or even move about, with the result the sport of "train spotting" had to be outlawed.

We rode third-class on nice, cushioned seats in a private compartment while stopping every mile or so for the many small towns. We arrived in Southport at around 2:00 p.m. and walked through the city until we came to the beach. There, a wide, open beach stared before us with many kiddy-land games and various recreational activities of boating, swimming, miniature golf on a large scale, and a high roller coaster. We took in all the sights and noticed two girls in blue uniforms who gave us the eye. We smiled and went on our way.

Southport was a resort area for British people. We saw very few foreign people, much less Americans. In fact, very few Americans came to the area around Preston.

Later, we walked back into town to check on our train departure and also found time to have something to eat at a Woolworths store that consisted of warm orange drink, ham sandwich, beef pie, and coconut muffin, all for eight pence.

We walked down Lord Street, the main street of Southport, and peered into one of the newer department stores, Timothy Whites, and to our surprise, we found ourselves looking at the two girls who had given us the eye before. Eric grabbed my arm, and we entered the store to find many more girls, all good-looking—no doubt to promote sales—but resisting any sales talk, we were quite content to merely walk through the store.

Walking up a side street to find the source of music coming to our ears, we found a daily concert in session. Featured was Jimmy Leach and His Organolians. We were not about to pay the six-pence admission price to sit down but stood near the entrance and listened to the music. As we started to walk away, the trio began playing "Yankee Doodle," which was quickly followed by "California Here I Come" and finished up with a few chords from "Chicago." The leader smiled at us and then played the first stanza of our national anthem. We nodded our approval and continued on our way.

Of particular note to me was that many women had huge baby carriages and wheeled them wherever they went, never leaving the baby at home. The carriages were quite large and were also used for packages since there was ample room for twins and then some.

At four twelve, we boarded the train for our return journey to Preston, and from the station, we took a bus back to Eric's home. Here I found some time to write a letter to the Holland American Shipping Line to confirm my return ticket while Eric was busy in the kitchen.

Dinner, and I use the term loosely, consisted of dry toasted buns since there was no other food in the house, and it was only listening to the music of June Christy that made me forget how hungry I was.

It wasn't long before I was dressed and on my way to the town clock for my date at 7:00 p.m. Eric had told me to be late for the date. "And if she is still waiting for you when you arrive, it's a sign she's keen for you."

However, I didn't heed his advice and arrived at six fifty-five to find my date stepping off a bus at the hour of seven. Asking her what she wished to do, she suggested a nearby theater, where we bought tickets for two shillings, nine pence apiece and sat down to see such *smash* hits entitled *Safari* and *Inside Detroit*. Tickets were sold by the seat in English theaters, similar to our reserved tickets for sporting events in America, with each section having a certain price.

My date's name was Margaret Butler, and quite a nice girl she was, as she was very eager to teach me the way things were done in England, though shocking at times. If your date lives in an inconvenient part of the town, for you to take her home, you merely put her on a bus or taxi and let her pay the fare when she arrives at her destination, as it is not always necessary to accompany your date home.

Margaret had made arrangements for her uncle to pick her up at the market square at 10:50 p.m., which was our destination after leaving the theater. She was very interested in American customs, and as we walked to the market square, I explained the difference in our dating procedure.

It was still twilight as we walked to the square, and she told me she had once been engaged to a doctor in Liverpool and had broken this engagement a fortnight ago and was now a model, making three guilders a showing. Margaret was nineteen years old, her birthday being August 28, and she stood a nice five feet, five and a half inches tall, with long blond hair slightly pulled to one side.

I thanked her for a most enjoyable evening and gave her some American bubble gum as I said good-night to her. Leaving the square, I had to struggle home on foot since the buses stopped running at ten thirty. Little trouble was encountered as far as directions were concerned as I only had to ask a bobby for directions once.

Eric was already home from his date, and I remained awake while I wrote for an hour the interesting things that had happened to me during the day, finally jumping into bed at 12:30 a.m.

June 16—Cloudy, Cold with Rain

I awoke at around eleven and had a light breakfast while we discussed our dates of the previous evening, after which we went into town so I might change some American currency into English pounds. Since this was Saturday and a big day for business in the market square, we walked through the crowded aisles before coming to the Midland Bank to receive three pounds, ten shillings, and five pence for my $10 American bill.

We continued taking in the sights of Preston and met some of Eric's friends before stopping by the tailor shop where Eric used to work. On the way home, we stopped at Rawlings for the best in fish and fries. We sat at a small table for four with two middle-aged women and enjoyed the friendly atmosphere. The lunch was quite tasty, and after I informed the English women that chips in America were crisp chips sliced thinly from the potato, Eric calmly replied that the English threw that part of the potato away, no doubt referring to the peelings.

The portion of lunch we received consisted of a nice piece of deep-fried fish, a liberal order of chips, four pieces of buttered bread, and a cup of tea for two shillings, six pence. For carryout orders, people were served on old pieces of newspaper, after which the paper was thoroughly read before being discarded.

Returning to Eric's home, I sorted out thirteen and a half pounds of clothing from my suitcase to send to Germany to lighten my load for travel, and after repacking my remaining clothes, we dressed for our trip to Blackpool, some eighteen miles to the west. Saying good-bye to Mrs. Hammond and taking the clothing to the post office on the way to the station, we had completed a busy day and now planned to see the sights of Blackpool. It was raining as we entered the station and watched the youthful boys in their favorite pastime of *engine spotting*, which occupied our attention until our train departed at 5:10 p.m.

The ride was enjoyable, but the rain continued to come down as we left the station in Blackpool and strolled about their Coney Island. Blackpool was the largest British attraction center, though few foreign people came to the area, as the gyp joints were all too familiar to the American people. Nearby was a small scale model of the Eiffel Tower, though quite large in itself.

Dinner consisted of meat pie and chips, buttered bread, and tea for 3 shillings and 9 pence. The café was dirty, and the linen was a disgrace to be on the table. Eric said he thought it hadn't been changed within the past week. Leaving the café, we headed for the Winter Garden, a large dance hall that had a charge of 3 shillings to enter and 3 pence for checking service. The hall was quite huge—massive would be more like it. I would say the dance floor was one hundred feet by two hundred feet, and that might be underestimating the actual size. It had two balconies and a twelve-piece orchestra in formal attire. The music played from 7–11 p.m., but the hall was so crowded all the enjoyment of dancing was lost. I had the pleasure of dancing with a Canadian and various girls from the area of Blackpool, and each one commented how differently I danced. One girl from Preston named Betty asked her English friend to tell me she wished to have another dance with me as she wanted to learn the American way of dancing. I spun her several times—quite gracefully—and she thought it was much fun.

The evening was enjoyable, but not to any great extent, as the crowdedness distracted my attention to the nicer girls, for one would see them once and then they were lost in the crowd. Toward the end of the evening, Eric introduced me to a Ms. Cynthia Rance; I was quite impressed with her, and as we unchecked our wraps, I told Eric that Cy was the type of company I would have enjoyed.

We left for the train station and got into a compartment all to ourselves and slept the entire way to Preston. We had asked friends of Cy if she would be riding the train but were informed she was meeting her friends at the station in Preston. As we showed our tickets (you must do so entering and leaving train stations), we again saw Cy with another girl and some boy. The other girl's name was Toni, but we didn't know the name of the boy with her. During the brief conversation that followed, Eric quite bluntly told Cy that it would have been nice if she had ridden home with us on the train, and when this got a twinkle in her eye, Eric suggested that we walk her home from the station.

Cy had left her date in the car, and after the suggestion by Eric, she turned and walked off with us arm in arm. I didn't get to see the expression on her date's face, but I was sure it was one of utter amazement. As we approached the center of town and the way to Eric's home no longer coincided with that of Cy's, Eric looked at me and said "See you later, Buster" and left me to walk Cy to her home.

It was only four short blocks to her home, and as I thanked her for allowing me to walk her home, she invited me to come inside to the parlor. Here we discussed the dating situation in both countries, and she was most interested to learn of our American customs. We talked until the hour reached 3:45 a.m.; hence, I bade her goodnight and started for home in misty rain. She called me back from the doorstep and said, "Oh, Joe, I'm so sorry my crinoline made so much noise when we walked home, but it was the first time I have ever worn one." And with that, she gently kissed me good-night.

The walk to Eric's home took thirty minutes, and I noticed the bobbies stationed at various locations in the city standing guard over the sleeping city as if waiting for something exciting to happen. I was quite tired when I crawled into bed beside Eric, knowing I wouldn't have too much sleep before I was to be on my way to Scotland.

June 17—Cloudy, Cool

It seemed like I had just crawled into bed when I was awakened by Eric and informed it was now nine thirty. I hurriedly packed while he prepared a breakfast of eggs, fried ham, bread, and jelly. I thanked the Hammonds for all they had done for me while living in their four-room house, which had been very uncomfortable; because of it only having outside toilet facilities—and this with no bath—I felt quite dirty but nonetheless pleased and happy that I had been with such wonderful people.

Eric helped carry my suitcase to the main highway north, A6, and as I again thanked him, he handed me a packed lunch that his mother had prepared for me.

I began the task of hitchhiking again and was told by a passerby that I would be more likely to obtain a ride if I would stand at the *zebra crossing*, a striped area across the pavement that was used by pedestrians to cross the road while cars must come to a stop.

Standing at this location, I was picked up by the very first car that happened to come by, although it appeared to be crowded, with three people in the front seat and the back filled with luggage and various other items. The trio was headed for Glasgow, Scotland, right on the way for me, and after putting my suitcase in the car trunk, I climbed into the rear seat of their four-door, six-passenger 1956 car.

Alex was driving, accompanied by his wife (Pam) and Ken, a business partner of his. They were both insurance brokers from London and were on a business holiday in Glasgow. I considered myself most fortunate in getting the ride on a Sunday morning; in a short while, we stopped at a café for tea and cookies. They insisted upon buying this for me, and in a few moments, our brief stop was a thing of the past.

Passing through the countryside, they stopped often so I could take slides of Lancaster and other shots of the nearby town of Kirkby in Kendal. At lunchtime, we stopped in the town of Penrith and dined in Musgrave Hall. I had scotch broth, stewed beef, green beans, three boiled potatoes, hot tea, and apple pie for sixty pence, but my friends from London again insisted on paying my bill, saying they would mark it off as traveling expense.

Before we entered the car, I took a picture of them, and we shortly found ourselves on our way to Carlisle, where the old Roman Wall cuts across England. Proceeding northward, they suggested I get off at a fork in the road that was only fifty-five miles to Edinburgh, my planned destination. I thanked them warmly for all they had done for me, and after exchanging addresses, I found myself again on the road, only this time I was now in Scotland. One passing note concerning my meeting the insurance brokers was that Pam was the cutest English woman I'd ever seen, though I doubted If I'd ever see her again.

As I waited at the fork in the road, a sign informed me I was fifty-three miles from Glasgow, seemingly on a good highway, the way my friends had gone. I was also fifty-five miles from Edinburgh, on a not too heavily traveled road, but within five minutes, a Volkswagen van stopped for me. The driver was Dick Fielding from Saint Boswells, fifty miles due east from where I was now and some thirty miles south of Edinburgh. It was his suggestion I ride with him through the "border country" and see the beautiful countryside, after which he would drop me on the main highway to Edinburgh.

We stopped at various places of interest, where I was able to take pictures of the hills and sheep often found grazing on the hillside. One shepherd was having his dog bring in the sheep, and the faithful dog quickly obeyed his master.

During our conversation, I informed Dick I had to be in Edinburgh by 10:00 p.m. if I wanted to stay in a hostel, to which he offered me the invitation of his home for the night. I was most surprised but willingly accepted his invitation. We continued slowly, stopping often along Saint Mary's Loch and the scenic valleys of Scotland.

As we passed through the town of Selkirk, I took a picture of Sir Walter Scott as a huge festival was in progress, as flags and banners hung quite gaily from the roofs in honor of this old Scot.

We arrived at his home in Saint Boswells, a nice, quiet town, and after meeting his wife and son, Derrick, I was given the opportunity to wash and freshen myself up for the first time since I landed in England.

After a most refreshing bath, I was shown to my room by Mr. Fielding as he placed my suitcase on the large double bed so I might hang my clothes to air out after being in the musty suitcase. Dick was a building contractor, and as I dressed and returned to the living room, his wife had prepared some snacks for us while we became better acquainted. It was during this get-together that Dick offered to drive me to Edinburgh the following day, as he had thought of going there on business since he had to see a firm concerning an order of plaster for some homes he was building.

His home was beautiful, and the full use of bathroom privileges was quite a thing for me, as I had not bathed in five days; to this day, I remember crawling into the tub and letting the cool water make me feel clean again.

Mrs. Fielding had also prepared some sandwiches for her hungry men along with a pot of tea, and as we sat there together, I couldn't understand why luck was with me all the way since I landed in England. Here I was, a stranger to these people, having been in their country only a few hours, and I was treated like an old friend. We continued our conversation, during which time Dick thought it would be interesting if we would visit Dryburgh Abbey, a series of old ruins dating back to the year of 1140. The entrance to the grounds closed at 7:00 p.m., but since Dick knew the caretaker, we were allowed to enter the grounds. The sight before me was one of utter beauty, as the green trees, grass, moss, and pines seemed to form a painting in itself. It was nearly 10:00 p.m. when we left the grounds and headed for the home of his mother-in-law, from a quite well-to-do family of Scotland, where Dick was supposed to pick up some bread. We sat around the hearth for thirty minutes and then left to buy some chips at a nearby café.

Arriving at the Fielding home, we continued our conversation while his wife prepared the evening meal. It was still far from being dark, which provided an opportunity to speak with some of the neighbors who were sitting in the yard. It wasn't long before we were called in for dinner of eggs, pancakes, bread and jelly, chips, and hot tea. Being in no hurry to leave the table, I was asked questions as to my plans after leaving Scotland, after which questions centered on the modern way of living in America. We remained at the table until 12:30 a.m., and after helping Mrs. Fielding with the dishes, I began to wash my shirts. She began laughing at me and finished the job, saying I was doing the job in a most awkward manner. By the time we were ready for bed, it was one thirty, and as I went upstairs and climbed into bed, I thought myself indeed lucky and most thankful for the way I was being treated in these foreign lands.

June 18—Light Rain, Gradually Clearing

Before I begin on this day's events, it may be well to say something about Saint Boswells, a small village to the southeast of Melrose named after Saint Boisel, a preceptor of Saint Cuthbert. It is famous for its annual sheep fair held in July, which attracts large numbers of flock masters from the surrounding country. A monument of Sir William Wallace is located near the town. The above is all interesting, but I have achieved my greatest expression of people in the way Mrs. Fielding insisted she would never put on a "bathing costume" for fear people would laugh at her when she and her husband went south for a few days on the beach. Instead, she was going to wear a new, stylish dress "for fear of drawing comment" if she displayed her white legs in public.

I was allowed to sleep until ten thirty before a knock on my door by Mr. Fielding informed me it was time to go down for breakfast. I quickly washed and dressed and found breakfast ready in the dinette, consisting of shredded wheat, two fried eggs, fried potatoes, Canadian bacon, buttered bread, jam, and cold milk. It was truly an American breakfast served in the finest style.

After reading the morning paper, I shaved and packed, but it was while I was shaving that their twenty-month-old son received a kick from watching me, as he couldn't understand why I made so much noise. I made my bed and, before leaving, took a photo of the Fielding family, a family that had treated me as their own son during my brief stay.

Dick, his wife, and his son were all to accompany me to Edinburgh, but Dick thought it would be a good idea to see Dryburgh Abbey once more so I might have some information on the old buildings.

The buildings were begun in 1140 by the Canons Regular of the Premonstratensian Order for the first home in Scotland. Today, what was left depicted beauty in some small way of the beauty that was once the pride of Scotland. Although it was raining, I took some pictures after Dick paid my way into the grounds and purchased an official guide to the grounds for me.

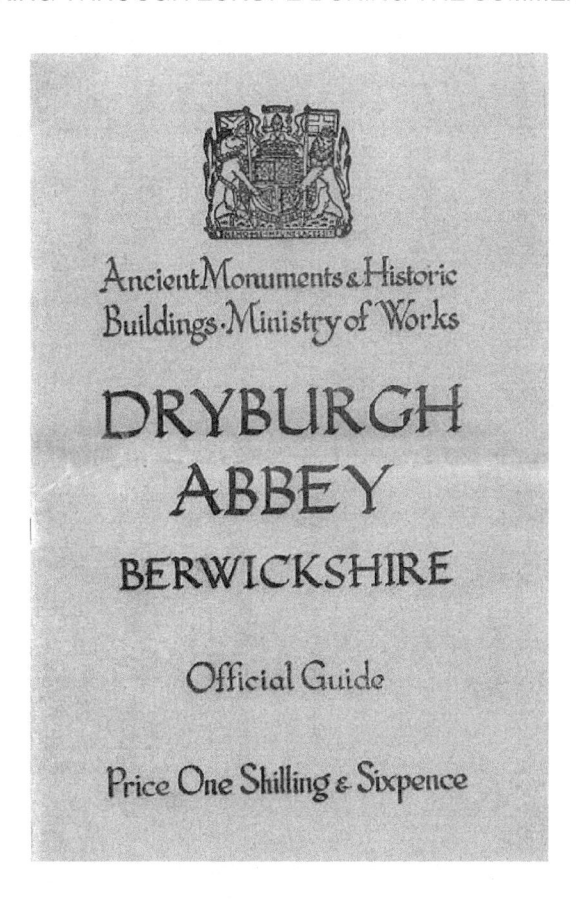

HITCHHIKING THROUGH EUROPE DURING THE SUMMER OF 1956

> Ancient Monuments & Historic Buildings · Ministry of Works
>
> # DRYBURGH ABBEY
>
> ## BERWICKSHIRE
>
> Official Guide
>
> Price One Shilling & Sixpence

Leaving here, we journeyed to Scott's Summit, a beautiful view over the Tweed River, where it was said Sir Walter Scott drove daily.

We were now on our way to Edinburgh, family dog included, and headed for the Waverly railroad station, where I checked my suitcase for 6¢, and then we drove to Princes Street, which went directly below the Edinburgh Castle, which was situated upon a high hill in the heart of the city. We were pleasantly surprised to see ladies dressed for a festival, and after watching them pass in their gay colors, we were directed to Lillywhites, a department store, where I purchased cashmere sweaters for my sisters.

Bidding farewell to the Fieldings and thanking them for all they had done for me, I boarded a number 10 double-decker bus for

Leith, paying the fare for 4¢, which would take me to the office of the Norwegian Shipping Line, where I had hopes of hitching a ride to Norway across the North Sea. Arriving at the main office, I was directed to another office, but this netted me nothing as they were uncooperative, but they did say I might try my luck on the first floor. This so-called place on the first floor was really on the second floor, and entering the seemingly deserted office, as I could only see closed doors, I knocked on one of the huge wooden frames and, surprisingly enough, was told to go in.

Inside, I had my second surprise—two good-looking women taking an office break as I had come into the ladies room by mistake! I informed them what I was looking for, some way to reach Norway, and they directed me to the office of the president of the firm.

Reaching his office, I explained to him my problem, and he informed me that the taking of passengers on freight lines was no longer allowed but added a word of encouragement by telling me the names of the ships leaving Edinburgh during the week and replied, "Son, best of luck to you, and if you can talk one of our captains into letting you travel with his ship, I'm all for you."

Shaking hands and thanking him all in one breath, I boarded a trolley for the Midway docks at Leith. Before me stretched long piers, and after inquiring where I would go to find out where the ships the president of the line had told me about would be located, I went to the pier office on the extreme end of the longest pier. Here I inquired information concerning the freighter *Royal*, which was due to sail this week.

Informed my best bet would be to talk directly with the captain, I returned to the docks and set out on foot to the distant freighter. When I reached the *Royal*, a coal freighter, the foreman directed me to the captain's room while the chief steward went in search of the captain.

HITCHHIKING THROUGH EUROPE DURING THE SUMMER OF 1956

In a few minutes, the captain entered his quarters; he was a gray-haired gentleman of casual dress and undoubtedly had seen much activity on the sea. I introduced myself and told him of my plans, to which he checked my passport and, finally, after being convinced I was not trying to flee the country for some crime I had committed, said he would have to "hire" me as an assistant deck mate to keep his records in order, as he was not allowed to take on passengers. It was Monday, and the *Royal* was not to sail until Friday or Saturday; another drawback was the fact that the destination of the *Royal* was Copenhagen, Denmark, not Norway, as I had desired to reach.

It was the captain's suggestion that I try to obtain another means to the Scandinavian countries, and if I were unable to obtain some other means, he would hire me, and I would sail with him at the end of the week. I shook hands with my new friend and jumped ashore, and as I turned around, his smiling face greeted mine. Motioning with my hand and displaying my camera, I took a picture of him as he stood outside his quarters.

The freighter was still unloading coal from its hold; it appeared to be a very hard and dirty operation, and I didn't know what kind of a ship's hand I would make, but if worse came to worst, I was game to try any means to get to Norway.

As I stood on the pier, the foreman came up to me and said in a sincere way that it would be nice to have an American aboard but suggested I might obtain a faster ship in Newcastle, England, some one hundred miles to the south.

It was now 5:00 p.m., and my hopes of getting a ride to Newcastle didn't seem too good, but I checked at the Midway pier to see if any trucks were headed south in the direction of Newcastle (the British name for a truck is a *lorry*). On the main pier, a ship had just brought in 1,180 crates of fish, each crate weighing fourteen pounds without the crate, and I hopelessly asked if by chance the trucks were going my way. To my surprise, two of the three trucks being loaded with fish were going to Newcastle within thirty minutes, but this hardly left time for me to return to the railroad station to pick up my suitcase, which was stored in a locker. One of the truck drivers said he would wait for my return to the pier as I went to fetch my suitcase, and he walked with me to a nearby trolley stop. On the way, he spotted another truck he knew was on its way to Newcastle, and hailing the driver, he explained the situation to his friend, also explaining that my luggage was checked in the heart of Edinburgh at the railroad station.

Nonetheless, I was told to climb into the cab of the truck, and at the next corner, we turned around and were on our way to the railroads station to pick up my suitcase. My new friend was Bob Archie, who had ten tons of fish on board his lorry due in Southern England by the time the markets opened in the morning.

After I picked up the suitcase, it wasn't long before we were on the highway to Newcastle. I opened my bag and removed one of the sandwiches Eric had given me several days previously as I left Preston. I had almost forgotten I still carried some food, as all my meals had been provided during the past two days. To my surprise, the sandwich I had taken a bite of turned out to be nothing more than a butter sandwich, and although tasteless as old as it was, I ate it to quench my hunger.

The drive along the eastern coastline was very scenic, and before we realized the time, we were pulling into Newcastle. It was now nine forty-five, and finding the former hostel within the city was closed, I was directed to the YMCA only three blocks away.

I walked into the lounge, and a Mr. Stevenson offered to help me since all the rooms at the Y were taken. It was his suggestion that I try to obtain lodging in a *dig*, a home that catered to traveling people. Normally, there would have been room in the Y for me, but a truck drivers' convention was going on within the city and all available rooms were taken.

The prices in a dig were most reasonable, as a sleeping room and breakfast was provided anywhere from $1.00 to $1.50. We inquired at four digs, but the Full Up sign was displayed in the window. We were fortunate in being directed from one dig to another and felt the situation was not entirely hopeless. We finally arrived at the home of Mrs. B. B. Taylor, and there Mr. Stevenson, who had carried my suitcase the entire way, inquired of the possibility for lodging. Being convinced I wasn't a cheap runabout, she let me have her own room for the night and informed me breakfast would be served at nine in the morning.

An English *dig* is similar to what we know as a bed-and-breakfast. The dig is normally in a home that provides sleeping rooms by the night and breakfast in the morning. They are used quite often by truck drivers and businesspeople. When putting this book together for publication, I referenced the Saint Louis County Public Library as to the word *dig*—a place I used to eat and sleep in Newcastle, England. I was told the correct word was *digs*, being singular and plural, so in reality, I did not stay at a *dig* but went to a *digs*. Just want to get this matter correct for those of you with English culture as to what is correct. Nonetheless, those common people of England do refer to the place of lodging and breakfast as a dig.

Being served breakfast at 9:30 a.m. was most ideal for me, for most of her boarders got up at six thirty in order to be at work on time, and since she could not serve breakfast to all her boarders at one time, those wishing to could eat at the second shift. The cost per day for lodging and breakfast was $1.75, to be paid on my departure.

It was now 11:00 p.m. and not completely dark as yet. I had spent only 40¢ for the entire day and considered myself quite lucky for the breaks that had gone my way. Bidding Mr. Stevenson goodbye and saying good-night to Mrs. Taylor, I was in need of a good night's sleep for I was to check with the shipping agencies in the morning. It was now two weeks since I had left home, and what had happened to me in that time seemed like it would require many more weeks, but I was happy and fulfilling an ambition I had thought of for the entire year.

June 19—Cool and Sunny

Awaking when Mrs. Taylor knocked on my door at about nine thirty, as she had allowed me to get some extra sleep, I had had a restful night, despite the fact that the bed was too short for me. The room itself was large, with two soft chairs and a sofa. Next to the bed was a phone similar to our own, but there was a charge made for each call made. The room was chilly, but under three or four blankets, one obtained all the warmth needed.

Breakfast consisted of cornflakes, milk, fried eggs on toast, three strips of bacon, stewed tomatoes, and a pot of tea. I was urged to try adding milk to my tea similar to our own way of adding cream to our coffee. It didn't taste bad at all.

Going to my room, I phoned the Thomas Cook Travel Agency and was informed it would be best to come to the office. Quickly I read the morning paper and asked Mrs. Taylor for directions to the Cook office. Finding out it was only a ten-minute walk increased my desire to reach the office, and crossing my fingers, I waited patiently for my turn, as they were fairly busy.

Telling them I wished passage to Bergen, Norway, as soon as possible, I was told the next ship would leave at 4:00 p.m. tomorrow, but they didn't know if there were accommodations available. While a phone call was being made directly to the travel line for this information, the man next to me was being turned down on booking passage to Sidney, Australia, with the usual "Sorry, we're all booked up. This is the peak of the travel season." In this case, passage could not be obtained until January!

The man waiting on me returned and said all cheap tourist was sold out but I would be able to obtain passage in the higher bracket. The ticket cost $26.60 as travel time to Norway on this ship was only twenty-three hours. I purchased the ticket and paid for the ticket to a boat train that would bring me alongside the boat for 22¢, and I was also asked to pay the phone bill, 6¢, for the call the man had to make in order to confirm my reservations.

Finding it convenient to cash my travel checks for Norwegian kroner as well as the excess English pounds, I felt quite relieved knowing I would soon be in beautiful Norway.

Walking through Newcastle, I took pictures of interest and purchased air letters and postcards, intending to send some news home; I wrote Carol Ratjen in Chicago; Eric from Preston; the Fieldings; the Butzes, a family I would see in Germany; Dr. Hynek, whom I would visit in Vienna; and the Effinger family, another family from Germany where I would no doubt stay with.

While I had been in the travel agency, a gentleman told me that a visit to Jesmond Dene would be worth my while. Leaving the post office, I stopped a man and asked him directions to the Dene; he told me to hop in as he was going right by the Dene. My befriender was Mr. William Lamb, a well-to-do man of the community. He told me Jesmond Dene was quite large, but no matter what part I was able to see, it would be worthwhile. I was dropped at the upper entrance, whence I embarked on a scenic tour that took me to shady lanes and ponds flowing into waterfalls. Since there were only footpaths provided, no cars were to be found within the enclosure. Making a circular tour of one end of the area brought me to bubbling streams. I left the park by the lower entrance and walked back into town.

I caught a bus that took me to the area of the YMCA, and buying a bag of candy, I sat down for a noon snack. I was in no hurry as I was content to take in the nearby surroundings.

Returning to the dig, I changed into lighter clothes, as Mrs. Taylor suggested I take the electric train to Monkseaton, a nearby village, and spend some time along the coast. The walk to the railroad station was a little more than a block, located in an area called Jesmond, though not near the park area I had been earlier in the day. As I purchased my ticket, the train was pulling into the station, and in a few moments, I was on my way to Monkseaton.

Reaching my destination, I found myself alongside a city park where the old English sport of "bowling on the green" was in progress. I took some pictures of the interesting sport and continued on to the coast several blocks away.

Here a beautiful sight of green grass, sandy beaches, and blue sea met my eyes. People were taking in the warm weather and swarmed over the open stretches as I walked along the boardwalk and then went to the beach, as the tide was out.

After walking for some time, I took a rest on the sand and enjoyed watching the people relax, but my position was none too desirable as the wind was blowing the sand in gusts and pelting me quite hard.

I continued on my way along the beach to the promenade and found myself in the borough of Whitney Bay. Here I came upon a general store, where I bought a loaf of bread for 6¢, sliced cheese for 19¢, potato chips for 4¢, and a quart bottle of soda for12¢. I took these items to a nearby park area overlooking the bay and had my evening meal, returning to the store for my refund on the pop bottle.

It was at this time that I became acquainted with the owner, Nichol Rumney. He informed me of the village a short distance away, Cullercoats, where Marconi set up his first wireless station. Thinking the trip would be worthwhile, I went to see the tall poles with connecting wires, where a great event in history took place years ago.

I returned to the little store to take his picture before proceeding on to Tynemouth, where at the mouth of the Tyne River on the sea coast stood an old castle built in the tenth and eleventh centuries.

Admission was 7¢, and I met the keeper of the grounds, Bill Turnbull, who wasn't too busy at the time and offered to personally escort me on a tour of the grounds.

We came upon tombs enclosed in concrete, still very much intact, and many old ruins of the fortress. Massive walls, dungeons, ruins—behind it all lay centuries of history, as the fortress had been a defensive outpost against Scottish invaders.

The chapel, Percy Chantry, had been built by the Earl of Northumberland in 1450 and still had its original stained glass windows, the Rose Window. Also of particular interest was a monk stone that if touched by wrongdoers would give them thirty-seven days sanctuary.

I thanked Bill for his vivid explanation and walked to the railroad station, where again I was able to catch the train as it was pulling out of the station, saving me a thirty-minute wait.

The ride to Jesmond station took only a few minutes, then I walked to the dig, where I took a needed bath and removed the sand from my shoes and clothing. I also found time to do some washing after Mrs. Taylor did some ironing for me while we listened to the British light-heavyweight championship fight.

Her other six boarders came in shortly, and tea was served while we sat around and became better acquainted. I finished eating the loaf of bread I had bought earlier in the evening with some of Mrs. Taylor's jam. Conversation was easy to strike up with these strangers, and before long, we were talking like old friends. Most interesting to talk to were Charles Westwood and Philip Wolfsan, both from London, who were in Newcastle for an agriculture show. We talked until 1:00 a.m. before retiring, as we had not noticed the time was late, and needing a good night's sleep, I hurried off to bed to rest my tired legs.

June 20—Warm and Sunny

I slept until nine thirty and then slowly washed and dressed for a lovely breakfast of a heaping bowl of cornflakes, eggs, fried ham, fried tomatoes, tea, and toast. Mrs. Taylor sat down at the table with me while I read the morning paper, as I was the last person to eat.

I slowly went about the task of packing and then lay down to rest until 12:15 p.m. Awaking, I paid my lodging for two nights, twenty-five shillings, and took a picture of Mrs. Taylor, thanking her for all she had done.

Again I walked to the Jesmond station and took an electric train to Central Station, the cost just 3¢. Reaching Central Station at 12:41 p.m., I had to wait for the 1:10 boat train. It was during this waiting time I happened to see two girls hosteling via bicycle but said nothing to them at the time.

I occupied a compartment with a couple from South Bend, Indiana, who were traveling on a lush tour, having left the States the day before. I told them of my expenses and my mode of travel, to which they seemed surprised. The train pulled alongside the ship, and after checking my baggage through customs, I climbed aboard the *Venus*. It wasn't long before I met an eighteen-year-old lad who had been to sea on a tanker for over a year and was now on his way home in Kåfjord. His name was Reidar Daniloff, whose home was located in the most northern part of Norway. He seemed quite interested in talking to me, and as the time passed, we found ourselves in the first-class area of the ship. From this section one could easily watch the crew loading the many cars into the hold of the ship. It was while watching this operation that I met a Mr. and Mrs. John

Vogwill from Fort Lauderdale, Florida. I related my experiences of England and of my plans for Norway to them; Mrs. Vogwill went to her cabin and returned with an extra map of Norway and also one of Sweden and replied that if she saw me along the road, they would pick me up. She also gave me a list of chalets and hostels and suggested I visit certain sections of Norway, as they were returning to their native land for a visit.

I remained on the first-class side of the ship while talking to several other people before going to my cabin to clean up. My cabin was located on B deck, probably the only one left, as it was on the outside, port side. My roommate was a Mr. Bert Chambers, a supervisor of the bus lines in London. He was taking his first vacation since his wife died many years before.

Lunch was served cafeteria style, and looking for a place to sit down, I found it convenient to sit near the two girls I had seen in the train station, but there was still no conversation among us.

After a light lunch, I went to the sundry room to look at the various items, where I was approached by three girls from Texas, Linda, Honey, and Jane. They were looking for a fourth for bridge, and before long, we were involved in a good, fast game.

We played until it was time for dinner, and as we were leaving the lounge, I noticed a man who looked vaguely familiar. I walked around him from a distance, staring at him from all angles, but could not place the face.

I was about to leave the lounge when I noticed a woman coming toward the man who looked so familiar. Now I knew the man was no stranger, for both the man and woman were familiar to me. Going over to the couple, I asked if they were from Saint Louis, and they replied that they were. I asked them if they didn't belong to Sunset Country Club, and they replied that they had belonged several years previously but were no longer members. I introduced myself to them and told them of my planned trip. What a small world ours was, but how wonderful it was in all its beauty.

Returning to my cabin, I rounded a corner on the stairs and bumped into the two girls who were hosteling, and taking advantage of the situation, I brought up the topic of hosteling into conversation, hoping to become better acquainted.

Through the course of the conversation, I learned their names to be Carol Spaulding and Barbara Berry, but what really surprised me was that Barbara was from Ladue, a suburb of Saint Louis not far from my home, and her brother was a good friend of the boy who had pushed a log from an overpass onto a highway patrol car last spring, causing an accident.

The girls had studied the past year in Edinburgh and were now on vacation before returning to the States. We exchanged information and went to dinner together, eating roast beef, potatoes, salad, rolls, and vegetables, all for 70¢.

After dinner, I decided to buy the handwoven ski sweater I had previously seen in the sundry room. It cost $17.34. It was a beautiful large blue-and-white long-sleeve sweater ornamented with Viking-ship buttons.

We resumed our bridge game with the girls from Texas and followed this with several hands of Hollywood Gin Rummy between Honey and me. It was 11:00 p.m. when the game broke up, but it was very light out as the western sky was a golden orange and the full moon shone brightly in the east. I said good-night to Honey and went to my cabin to check my maps while speaking briefly with Bert. I retired at twelve twenty on one of the best ships on the Bergen Line, the *Venus*, built in 1948 to provide a faster means of transportation across the North Sea.

June 21—Sunny, Clear, Warm

I awoke at nine thirty, dressed, and went to look for Carol and Barbara, who were going to hostel in Norway by bicycle. I was unable to locate them, and not feeling too well, I thought some breakfast might liven up my spirits. I had half a grapefruit, rolls, jelly, butter, and hot tea for 56¢.

A gentleman who had ridden in my compartment on the boat train but who had spoken very little now sat down for breakfast. He was on his way to visit his 102-year-old mother, whom he had not seen for forty-five years. He also offered to help me map out my trip through Norway as I tried to finish eating.

Still not feeling too well, I finished the grapefruit and quickly excused myself from the table as I was soon to experience my first case of seasickness.

The North Sea was a rough sea, and although the *Venus* had stabilizers, they didn't help my case. After a thirty-minute rest, I felt well enough to be up and around, but as I was leaving the cabin, my roommate came in, complaining of being sick. I wished him the best of luck in his battle with the sea and again went to look for Barbara, the girl from Ladue. I waited in the main hall, where she was most likely to appear, but did not have to wait very long. She brought her hostel information with her to the lounge, but it wasn't long before the motion of the ship drove us elsewhere.

I copied down the location and regulations of the hostels I might visit, and then we went to the cafeteria for a lunch consisting of lamb chops, fruit salad, rolls, butter, and a glass of water. We then made the daring move to the first-class lounge for deluxe comfort in the soft chairs. I again happened to see the couple from Saint Louis I had seen the previous day, but as yet, they had not given me their names. They motioned for me to come over to their chairs and informed me not to tell my parents I had seen them on the ship.

"My real name is Mr. Boushet, but I'm traveling under the name of Ray Bardgett," he replied. "And I would appreciate you keeping this information to yourself."

I could not understand all the hush-hush but assumed it was because he was traveling with Mary Bouer, a woman who had been living with him for many years in Saint Louis though the couple was not married.

Land was now in sight as the mountains of Norway stood out against the gray sky. I quickly finished jotting down the list of hostels along with my mapped route of Norway and Sweden, and thanking Barbara, I went to my cabin to pack my suitcase.

Since I was in a hurry to leave the ship, I carried my suitcase with me rather than have it taken off the ship with the crane. Barbara and Carol were on the top deck with their bags as they had the same idea, but since their belongings were tied onto their bicycles, it could easily be seen why they traveled lightly.

The small huts seen dotting the shoreline seemed to be balanced on top of the rocky coast. Norway looked so inviting I could hardly wait to get inland to meet the people and see the country.

As I stood alongside of the ship's rail, a man came up behind me and began talking of my travels. I introduced myself, and he told me he was Herbert Bell, a retired superintendent of a girls' school and was now associated with a railroad line in England. He went on to say that I should visit him the next time I came to England and promptly gave me his address and added that he would have no trouble getting me a date.

We proceeded through the immigration line slowly at first and then moved at a moderate rate. I soon found myself going down the gangplank, passing customs, and meeting Barbara and Carol, who decided to remain in Bergen for a day to see the city. Before we departed, each on our own way, I took a picture of the girls and promised to see Barbara in Saint Louis when she returned from her trip.

I asked a truck driver directions but quickly discovered he didn't speak English as he seemed to grunt and mumble weird expressions. Pulling out my map, I pointed to the town of Voss as my destination. He motioned for me to remain on the road I was on and drove off down the road by himself.

It was 3:45 p.m., and within minutes, a man stopped to inform me it would be better to take a train since the only way to reach Voss by road was a round-the-way route going south and east before going north. He offered to take me to the town of Nesttun, which was nine kilometers south of Bergen. He had gone out of his way for me but directed me to a road that would take me to Voss, as he was a lumberjack and knew the country well.

There was little traffic as I waited for a lift, but I was amused by the conversation of a town bum who came along on foot and told me about his brother and sister from Texas. I realized my chances of getting a ride would be slim if I was standing with a bum, so I tried to ignore him. This didn't work, so I walked into a confectionary to buy some bread and cheese, hoping he would leave me alone.

He was not in sight when I again set up my vigil along the roadway, but now children were on their way home from school, and they peered with interest at my suitcase as they rode by. The large USA letters had attracted their attention.

I made a sandwich from the Italian cheese and fresh bread I had bought at the confectionary. Looking up, I saw a man coming toward me. He could speak English and offered to help. I told him I wanted to reach Voss, but he said I would be unable to go that far before darkness and suggested I remain in the town of Norheimsund, a town along the way.

As I talked to this man, another man came from his house across the street and offered me a lift in his car. His name was Gurstav

Liland, and though the lift was not a long one, I was on my way. He too advised me I would be unable to reach Voss in time to obtain lodging at the hostel by 10:00 p.m., the time the hostel closed.

My next ride was offered by Aksel Lien and Olav Hakvaag, two highway workmen who were taking wooden planks to a roadside storage shed near Norheimsund.

The scenery was beautiful. Words could not describe the beauty I saw as we traveled along the mountain passes. We came upon one accident that forced us to wait while the road was cleared in order for us to proceed. Only one car could use most of the road on the narrow passes, which caused one to wonder why there weren't more mishaps. If a car met another car, it was more than likely that one car would have to back up in order to let the other pass.

I took a picture of the highway workmen as I was left by the side of the road again. They were returning home after they unloaded their truck. It was a funny feeling to be alone without a town, house, or another person in sight as I stood along the bleak, rocky road somewhere in Western Norway.

I waited for over an hour by the shed while only a bus and one car came along the road. Finally, a Buick Roadmaster came shooting down the road, but by the time it stopped for me, it was a block away. Not knowing if the car had stopped for me or not, I waited where I stood. I was greeted by two men, Mr. E. Espeland and Hakon Rygh, who made room for me in the backseat of the big car.

This lift was the kind I had hoped for since their destination was ninety kilometers away at a ferry junction that would take them across the fjord. They were going on a fishing trip and were in a hurry to make the 9:00 p.m. ferry, which was the last one for the day.

We passed through many long tunnels and saw the old fortresses of the Germans after they invaded Norway. Machine gun nests were also evident along the road as they were located in convenient terrain locations that would afford adequate fields of fire.

I was dropped off at eight thirty a few yards from the ferry dock but had to wait until the ferry unloaded the passengers before obtaining my next ride from John Rasmussen, a Hansa Beer representative from Bergen. He thought highly of his product and carried an open case on the rear seat of his car.

He was drinking warm beer as he drove along and graciously offered me a bottle. I hadn't had a thing to drink since I left the ship and eagerly jumped at the chance to quench my thirst, even if it was warm beer. I was taken to the town of Granvin and was now only twenty-three kilometers from Voss, my destination for the evening.

Shortly before we reached the town of Granvin, we had passed a car whose trunk had popped open while driving along the road. It was this same car that was to stop for me and offer to take me to Voss. The car was driven by Dr. and Mrs. Hjerkinn from Hamar. The doctor told me that upon seeing my suitcase displaying the letters USA, he felt that he, as a citizen of Norway, owed the United States a great deal for all our country had done to help his country during and after the war.

He thought that in some small way, he could help me since I was an American. They were a lovely couple who were on their way to Voss. It seemed my luck would never run out, for as we drove along the road, they invited me to visit them if and when I reached their city of Hamar.

When we arrived in Voss, they inquired where the hostel was and willingly drove to it, which was located three kilometers outside of town. The closing hour in hostels was normally 10:00 p.m., but because of the additional daylight, it was now 10:15 p.m., but the hostel appeared dark and unoccupied as we approached.

The houseparent answered my knock on the door and said he wasn't expecting anyone for the night but welcomed me to lodge there for the night. The hostel was constructed of knotty pine, and each room was equipped with four bunks, a pillow, and mattresses.

The bathroom had hot and cold running water and was a relief from the strain of being on the road the latter part of the day without restroom facilities.

I returned to the car and thanked the doctor and his wife and went into the hostel, where I opened my sheet sack for the first time. I had a feeling of happiness as I spoke with the houseparents before getting ready for bed. I turned out my light at midnight and was surprised to see that the light coming through the window was still bright enough to read by, for it was now midsummer, and Norway had from twenty to twenty-two hours of daylight. My sheet sack consisted of two sheets sewn together with a gusset of about ten inches attached to the sides and one end and a pillowcase attached to the other end. This was like a sleeping blanket but made of sheets. The hostel provided blankets and a pillow that would be placed inside the pillowcase. Mother had made two of these sleeping-sheet sacks for my use in the hostels.

Norway was a wonderful country but had only three and a quarter million people. However, I believed it had some of the finest beauty in the world within its lengthy borders, and I would urge everyone to visit Norway if possible.

June 22—Clear, Warm, and Sunny

The houseparent woke me at about 8:00 a.m., but I was able to grab a few winks of extra sleep before rolling out of bed. I packed my sleeping sack and folded my blankets, and since there were no house chores to do, I paid my lodging, which amounted to 28¢. I asked to take a picture of the houseparent so I might remember my first night in a hostel and then walked to the main road to continue on my way.

Reaching the main highway, I found myself waiting for a bus back to Voss. Across the street was a bakery that was being remodeled, and smelling the aroma of the freshly baked cakes, I hurried across the street to buy something for breakfast. The name of the bakery was the Iverson Bakeri. I bought five sweet rolls for 14¢ and waited for the bus that was due at 9:00 a.m. It finally arrived at nine twenty, and I paid the fare of 60 øre, or 60 percent of 14¢, about 8¢ in our money. The bus was crowded, and I had to stand for the three-kilometer trip back to Voss.

In Voss I inquired the best way to reach Olden but was told I could not reach the town in one day as transportation to that town was rerouted, as the road was under construction. I was told to take a bus to Gudvangen and, from there, to take a ferry to Balestrand, from which I could take a bus to Olden.

I had gone into a small shop that had a sign saying English Spoken hanging in the window. The shopkeeper was very friendly and overly helpful. I asked him for a drink of water, and he showed me the back of his shop and also the adjoining grocery store, where I had my drink, as the bakery goods had left me dry; they were not sweet rolls as we knew them but were good nonetheless. The owner's son spoke a few words of English but was going to school to learn the language well.

We retraced our steps to the father's store; he hung a Shop Closed sign on the door as he locked the door and walked me to the bus stop located at the edge of town and waited to see that I caught the right bus. Unbelievable? But true! A man closed his business to see that a stranger from the United States caught the right bus!

Eight other people were on the bus as I paid nine kroners ($1.26) for the long bus ride ahead of me. We had only gone about five kilometers when the eight passengers got off the bus, and I found myself the only passenger for the hour-and-a-half trip to Gudvangen.

The driver could not speak English but noticed I had a camera and stopped the bus numerous times so I could take pictures. Pictures were taken of Twindar Falls and Opheim's Vann before it was time to have a rest stop at Stalheim, where a magnificent view of snow-covered mountains with falls dropping hundreds of feet to the green valley below was available for my viewing.

12-8-25. Kjelfoss (also called "The Bridal Veil") Gudvangen, Norway

We started down the steep grade in second gear and then shifted to first as we made many hairpin turns. The view was outstanding, one of the best I had ever seen. When we reached the bottom of the steep mountain and were about to enter the fertile valley, I had to open a cattle gate to let the bus pass into the valley, as I was the only passenger on board.

Farther ahead, we were stopped by a flock of sheep blocking the road. If a vehicle hit an animal, the driver must pay the owner, which accounted for careful driving to a large degree. The milling flock did afford a delightful picture as it passed through the farm gate with the dog standing guard.

I arrived in Gudvangen at 11:30 a.m. and discovered the next ferry wasn't due to leave until two thirty that afternoon. Placing my suitcase in a safe place, I walked into town a few hundred feet from where I stood as the road I had come on came to an abrupt end at the water's edge.

I bought a large can of plums for 28¢, three rolls for 5¢, soda for 10¢, and a package of cheese for 14¢. I asked the store owner to open the can of plums for me while I sent a postcard to my parents, telling of the latest events. Going outside to finish my lunch, I walked into the countryside and saw a woman using a crude hoe to till her field while her husband was cutting grass to be hung on wire to dry.

I lay down on the grass and noticed the town was completely surrounded by mountains, with waterfalls dropping from ledge to ledge. The heavenward view contrasted the mountain ridges against the deep blue sky as the warm sun caused me to shed my coat.

Walking back into town, I met a small boy who offered me an orange. We sat down together on a grassy bank; it wasn't long before a dark German car came alongside us, and to my surprise, the doctor and his wife, who had stopped for me the previous day, stepped from the car.

We chatted until our ferry came, and boarding it, we sat in the warm sun on the top deck. The deck chairs were comfortable, and in no time at all, we were pulling away from the dock, beginning our beautiful journey through the fjords of Norway. It was very warm, so I only had my T-shirt on, not having a care in the world.

After an hour-and-a-half ride on the fjord, we met another ferry that I changed over to, as the original ferry went up one fjord while the one I was now on went in another direction. Looking down, one could tell the water was very deep, and with the images and reflections from the mountains, beauty was shown all around us in the clear water.

We stopped at several villages bordering the fjord along the way, but the most distracting chatter of the many American tourists who were no doubt away from home for the first time annoyed many people on the ferry. They were very loud and noisy, always trying to look after the other person, fearing their friend might miss seeing a passing ship or rugged mountain peak, whence they would have had enough to do to look after themselves. I was quite disgusted with the American passengers, especially the women, who thought they knew it all and were fast to let everyone know about it.

I finally got into a conversation with one of the nicer and older women and thought I would speak loud enough so all the anxious tongues and know-it-all people would hear what I had accomplished in my travels to date. They were most surprised to learn I had traveled through England and Scotland during the past week and only spent $10.

Though I am not one to brag to the public, I could not pass up the opportunity to make them feel that their $1,000 tour was really nothing compared to all the experiences I was accomplishing. Their mouths dropped still farther when I told them my lodging for the previous night had been only 28¢.

We landed in Balestrand at 6:20 p.m., and hearing a man say he was from the town, I asked him directions to the Youth Hostel. It turned out he was on his way home and would pass the hostel, as he was a schoolteacher and had been proctoring exams in a nearby town. His name was Eirik Holen, and seeing my arm was getting tired as I carried my suitcase, he offered to help me by carrying the heavy suitcase.

The hostel was one kilometer outside of town, a few hundred meters from where the schoolteacher lived. Walking up to the hostel, I was met by Kjell Konstad, the sixteen-year-old son of the couple who ran the hostel. I was instructed to sign the register and was shown to my quarters, a nice room well equipped with a bed, dresser, and stove.

I was told to wash quickly since they would serve me supper at seven thirty, since everyone else had previously eaten and they would be going through extra trouble for me.

I was ready by seven twenty-five and found a place set just for me. A young girl served me some hot tea, fresh bread, butter, and a large bowl of rhubarb, which really hit the spot as I had been very hungry. There was also a large pitcher of fresh milk on the table, and before I finished eating, I consumed five glasses of milk, three cups of tea, four pieces of bread, and two slices of cheese.

The Norwegians covered their bread with rhubarb similar to the way we put jelly on our bread. In fact, this was the only way they eat rhubarb and were most amazed to find that I ate rhubarb from a plate or dish.

Kjell introduced me to his father, also a schoolteacher, and after speaking briefly, Kjell and I rode bicycles into town. Here I saw the largest wooden hotel in Northern Europe. We traveled along a country road to a spot where an avalanche frequently covered the road. Along the side of the road was piled much snow and rock, as a slide had come tumbling down the mountainside only a few weeks ago.

We parked the bicycles and began climbing over the rock and snow to the green mountainside, which displayed scars of the wrath that had come down from above. Trees were snapped off, and bushes were bent toward the ground. On we went to the higher patches of snow sheltered from the sun between two steep cliffs.

It was very cool in the mountain shade as we walked among the grazing sheep. Several black bodies lay on the packed snow, revealing the death of the younger lambs that were killed during the harsh winter. We were now surrounded by snow and ice, which presented a beautiful sight to see in the sunny month of June.

We could hear water rushing below us, but the ice we stood on was very thick, and there was no danger of a cave-in. Such beauty and thrills I had never experienced, and sitting down on a green patch to rest, I was surprised to realize that it was ten o'clock and not the slightest sign of darkness prevailed. The sun was still shining on the mountain peaks as we descended the mountain and returned to the hostel.

The full moon was coming over the mountaintops as we returned, and a beautiful reflection was shown across the water as both the sun and moon were visible at the same time. After we walked along the water's edge, Kjell came to my room to chat while I washed my socks, and bidding farewell for the night, I climbed into my bed at 1:00 a.m. As late as it was, the sky was very light, and enough light was coming through the window that I could write in my diary as easily as if it had been midafternoon. Having been in Norway only a few days, I was greatly enjoying myself in the land of the north and of the midnight sun.

June 23—Cloudy with a Light Mist Falling

Although the light sky kept fooling me on the time as I tossed and turned in bed, I did manage to remain there until 8:15 a.m. The room was cold to dress in, and the socks were still wet. On the way to breakfast, I hung the socks to dry and took a short walk along the water's edge.

Breakfast consisted of coffee, bread, butter, and rhubarb, and though it was just what I had eaten the night before, it did serve to fill me. Again, I was the only one eating. I paid my bill of $1.02 for lodging and food to the girl who had cleared the table. I had learned how to say "Thank you" in Norwegian, "Tusen takk," to which the girl giggled and then went about her duties.

Kjell helped me pack and helped me take the suitcase into town by holding it across the bicycle as we walked alongside, pushing the bike from the hostel to the large hotel, where I took some pictures. In the hotel gift shop I bought Mother a nut dish and Dad a pewter ashtray. Also in the shop were several of the women I had seen the previous day on the ferry; they were unable to make decisions on what to buy and created much confusion among the employees.

We checked on bus schedules and found one to my liking at noon, then rode to the landslide area again to take some pictures as we again climbed the mountain but didn't go quite as far into the snow-covered areas. From a good vantage point we could take excellent pictures of the valley and the town from where we had come.

I returned to the hostel, where the giggly kitchen girl made me five cheese sandwiches for 28¢, all buttered with good mountain butter. I thanked the houseparents for their warm hospitality and exchanged addresses with Kjell.

Going to the bus station, I passed an old English church of unusual construction, which afforded a good picture. It wasn't long before I was on my way to Olden, for the bus was on time, but the fact that an eight-hour trip lay before me afforded an easy means of transportation, costing only $4.45.

Who should be on the bus with me but the noisy Americans who had been on the ferry and in the gift shop. I was fortunate to sit next to a fairly reserved woman, Ann Rowland from New York, but the noise and chatter from the people who would shout when they saw a goat or some sheep was enough to give one a headache. I was quite certain most of these people had never left the city they lived in, and many had never seen farm animals before.

One consolation in being with the group was that all fifteen members of the tour had been given box lunches by the hotel, and the old women couldn't manage to eat the entire lunch, so I was given the leftovers. I don't think the fact that they weren't hungry entered into the picture but the fact that the food the hotel gave them seemed unappealing to them.

I had a tomato-and-pork sandwich and several ham-and-tongue sandwiches, but my favorite was a yellow cheese spread that was topped off with a shot of whiskey, which I found very powerful.

The road was very narrow, and often we crawled along and just managed to squeeze between boulders. Leaving the valley behind, we climbed into the hills and made our way through a mountain pass, where the snow was fairly deep. Along the side of the road was evidence of a heavy winter, and as we reached the top of the pass, snow was fifteen feet high on both sides of the bus. As both sides of the road were covered with fifteen feet of snow, the bus went between walls of snow until we saw a large craterlike lake covered with ice and snow before us.

The bus had a stopover for a few minutes at a mountain lodge, at which time I bought a Hansa Beer for only 14¢, the same kind that the sales representative had given me when he picked me up several days ago.

We soon left the sunny weather behind and entered clouds of dense fog that continued for the rest of the day. Our next stop was at a mountain hotel, where I bought another ski sweater that Dad might use for golf. We enjoyed an hour-and-a-half wait, resting in the lounge or walking through the tiny village, which brought me to a bakery, where I bought a bag of cookies for 14¢ and a bottle of Solo Water for 10¢. This was their name for our soda, and as I drank the refreshing drink, I wrote a letter home to my parents.

I returned to the lodge to warm myself before the crackling fire. We left at 6:00 p.m. for the remaining two-hour ride to Olden. We were still in a fog, which was disappointing, for we had hoped to see the scenery.

The guide for the American tourists, Mr. Keller from Switzerland but now living in Stockholm, was familiar with the city of Lausanne, where I would be in a month. He was very interesting to talk with and enjoyed being a tour guide.

The bus arrived in Olden at 8:00 p.m., and I said farewell to the noisy American passengers. Before me was a sign, Three Kilometers to Hostel, and walking there in a few minutes, I entered into a sitting room with four English-speaking people. Two of them were married, making their home in London, while the other two were still in the courting stage, the woman coming from Edinburgh and the man coming from Newcastle.

A young girl working in the hostel showed me to my room, and though she could speak no English, she informed me dinner would be served at 9:00 p.m. through the motions of her hands. My roommate was the boyfriend of the girl from Scotland, though they were to be married at Christmastime. The married couple was hiking, while the engaged couple was motorcycling, one having just come from Balestrand and the other in the process of going there.

I was called to dinner at nine o'clock and found before me a plate of ham, one of white cheese, another of Norwegian "gum cheese," a pitcher of milk, rolls, white and brown bread, butter, unsweetened strawberry jelly, a pot of tea, boiled potatoes, and a large plate of fresh fish. Truly, there was enough food to feed an entire family, and although there was a good bit of food before me, I only had one piece of the tasteless fish, three glasses of milk, three cups of tea, three ham-with-white-cheese sandwiches, a helping of potatoes, and two pieces of jelly bread.

The young girl asked my name, and introducing myself as Joseph, I cleared the table for her. She said, "Takk," and I replied, "Tusen takk," nothing more than exchanging thank-yous in her language.

As I went into the sitting room, the English people helped me plan my trip so I could get out of Norway within two days as I was running behind schedule. They had a list of bus and train schedules with them, and checking these over, I discovered I could arrive in Sweden in two days.

Before going to bed, my roommate and I went to the outside toilets, and upon leaving my privy, I latched what I thought to be the door from which I had come and returned to the hostel, but it wasn't long before I knew something to be wrong, for my roommate did not return. I returned to the outside toilets and found him pounding on the door, as he was securely locked in for the night.

We had a good laugh over the incident with the comment "It would have been a cold resting spot for the night." The wind continued to howl and blow very hard, and as we went to bed at 12:15 a.m., the usually light sky at night was now a pale gray due to the fog that had settled in the valley. Finding how cold it was as we undressed, we had to ask for extra blankets. We were not too far from the Jostedalsbreen Glacier, the largest ice mass in Norway. All along the roads we had traveled, there were orange sticks five meters high, marking the edge of the road, which was an indication of the severe winters, but now it was the middle of June and we were really cold.

June 24—Partly Cloudy, Nice

I awoke in a cold room at eight thirty and dressed while Bryan and I discussed the near-*fatal* incident of the night before. He said he would always remember me as the American who tried to lock him up for good.

Going downstairs, we found a breakfast of omelet, gooseberry jelly, bread, ham, cheese, milk, and coffee—again all you could eat for 39¢. I ate heartily, packed, and said good-bye to my friends and paid the houseparents for lodging and two meals, the striking sum of $1.06.

I walked into the town of Olden after taking a picture of the hostel with the engaged couple, Bryan and Crystine. It wasn't long before the nine-forty-five bus to Grotei came along and took me through a mountain pass 1,139 meters above sea level. The sky was now clear to partly cloudy, and the sight was magnificent. The snow was very deep, up to five meters high, along the side of the road, which gave me a feeling of being iced in as the snow had become compressed and turned into ice. The road we were traveling on was only open from the first of June until early fall as it would become blocked with snow by the end of September.

The glare of the sun on the snow was enough to blind you, but the sun shining on the many waterfalls created rainbow patterns on the rock surrounding the white spray. A beautiful view of the valley below from which we had just come created a scenic picture of beauty. It was fairly cool on the mountain pass; it was easily seen why the snow didn't melt, for the snow was packed ice many feet thick. We were now on the edge of the Jostedalsbreen Glacier, the largest in Europe. At the bus stopover, I changed buses, taking a bus that would take me to Lom. As we descended the far side of the mountain slope and once more viewed the green hillside, I was now one of three passengers on the bus.

Reaching Lom, I had to catch another bus that would take me to Otta. During this stopover, I did not buy Solo Water but thought I would try their cola, or what I thought to be a cola drink. Instead, it turned out to be the worst-tasting drink I had ever experienced, tasting more like a bitter medicine.

I boarded the bus to Otta and sat down to eat two more of the sandwiches that had been made for me at the hostel two days ago and finished a chocolate bar I had been carrying with me. I soon fell asleep, as it had been a long day. Many herds of goats were blocking the road when I awoke from my brief nap, but the road was wider at this point, and the bus could pass without too much difficulty.

I arrived in Otta at 5:25 p.m. and waited for the express train due at five forty-five. I was told there would be no seats available since this train was a direct run to Oslo, and since it was Sunday, everyone would be on their way home.

I was content to sit in the aisle as I ate the last two of my cheese sandwiches and spread the paper on the floor. I noticed a gentleman offer his seat to a woman and come toward me to stand at the open window. He spoke to me in good English and mentioned he was from Oslo.

I opened my billfold and showed him the calling card of Stein Bugge, playwright, who visited Westminster College and had given me his card when I said I was coming to Norway during the summer.

Well, the poor fellow nearly fainted for he was a student of his in the sense that he had studied under Stein in his desire to become an actor. He had just completed a tour of Northern Norway with his fellow actors and was now taking the summer months off. We talked for an hour, during which time he gave me his address in case I ran into trouble.

My destination was Hamar, the hometown of Dr. and Mrs. Hjerkinn, the couple who had invited me to visit them several days ago after picking me up along the road. We had only made one stop, going one hundred miles, and arrived in Hamar at 8:15 p.m.

Going into a phone booth, I called the doctor's home, but there was no answer. I tried again in a few minutes only to hear a squeaky voice in broken English. The voice was of the doctor's fourteen-year-old son, Olav, who informed me his parents had not returned from their vacation. This was most surprising to me since I had seen his parents several days ago, and to the best of my knowledge, they were homeward bound.

It was difficult to make myself understood on the phone, so Olav came to the station on his mother's bicycle shortly thereafter. He invited me to spend the night at his home, but since his parents were not at home, I thought it best not to accept the invitation.

I suggested staying at the hostel, if there was one, and he directed me to it, or what he thought was a hostel, which turned out to be the Grand Hotel. The girl at the desk was able to speak English, but she could not understand what I meant. I took a pencil and paper and drew her a picture of the hostel sign, usually found along the highways, directing travelers to the hostel. Once I printed the letters *YHF* inside a triangle drawing on the paper, she knew to what I was referring to and easily directed me to the location. YHF stands for Youth Hostel Federation and is a universal guide for hostellers.

Olav was shown the location on the city map by the girl, and together, we walked to the hostel with the suitcase resting on the bicycle. The hostel was only four years old and could house one hundred people; it was also open year-round to accommodate the skaters in the winter, since it was located across the street from an artificial skating rink.

I was shown to my room, which I was sharing with Steffen Klinfborg, a nineteen-year-old boy from Gotland Island living in the city of Visby.

Supper had already been served at the hostel, so I was forced to go to a café in town and purchased a piece of chocolate cake for 60 øre, about 8 1/2¢. I returned to the hostel and spoke with a youth from Amsterdam and others before retiring for the night.

June 25—Cloudy, Rainy All Day

Steffen awoke at 8:00 a.m. and shook me, but I was in no hurry to climb out of bed from under three warm blankets into a cold room; I was content to remain warm as long as I could. Knowing that I had to get up for breakfast, I finally set foot on the cold floor at eight twenty.

We occupied two rooms, and after washing and dressing, we packed and hurried downstairs for breakfast, which was one I did not enjoy; the milk was slightly sour, the bread was stale, the cheese was not moist, and there wasn't enough to eat. The only item that met my approval was the jelly.

As I paid the hostel owner for my lodging, I inquired for the best directions to Arvika, Sweden, and was directed to a well-traveled route by tourists. I walked to the highway and waited fifteen minutes for a ride but to no avail. It was raining hard, and no one wanted to pick someone up in the rain and get their car wet.

Thinking I would have a better chance for a ride if I went in the other direction, toward Oslo, I crossed the road, but after waiting for a ride that didn't come, I returned to the original position, hoping for a ride to Sweden.

This was just the beginning of a terrible day; it wasn't long before I was picked up by a man going north to the town of Elverum. By ten ten, I had only gone twenty-three kilometers, and I was most disgusted and very wet.

I waited at a busy intersection until an old man in an ancient Ford picked me up and took me four blocks before he came to a stop, saying this was as far as he was going. He was a big help! It was now misting as I walked to another intersection, hoping for a ride south. Many cars passed me by, but nearly all of them were taxies that I first thought to be passenger cars. It was most discouraging to see very few cars leave town.

Finally, a young boy, perhaps nineteen or so, strolled up to me and said, "Do you speak American?" Informing him that I did speak English and that I was an American, he informed me that his boss, the editor of the daily paper of the town, *Ostlendingen*, wanted to interview me for a story in his office.

I carried the suitcase to the newspaper office, where I was shown to the office of the editor, who inquired of my hitchhiking experiences to date in Norway and further asked why I had come and of any unusual experiences. I showed them my maps and talked quite freely, ending with an invitation to remain for the day and have a date in the evening with a friend of the boy who had asked me to come to the newspaper office.

I was told the newspaper article about me and the pictures taken would appear in their weekly edition. I requested they mail me a paper to my home in Saint Louis, Missouri, and gave them my address. (A copy of the article is enclosed, together with an English translation, exactly as written.)

Så utrolig vilt og skjønt,

sier amerikansk student og hitch-hiker om vestlandsnaturen - Joseph E. Hahn vil aldri glemme Norges-turen

Med tommelen elegant hevet og et smil av beste amerikanske merke fristet Joseph E. Hahn fra St. Louis bilkjørerne med hyggelig reisefølge fra Bankhjørnet i Elverum og nedover Solør i går formiddag. Om noen tok imot innbydelsen vet vi ikke sikkert, men det skal mye til om noen kunne motstå et så livsfriskt og ungdommelig muntert ansikt, så vi tipper han allerede befinner seg langt nede i Sverige eller Danmark.

— Vanskelig å komme fram for en hitch-hiker?

— Well, — det er så opp og ned. Enkelte dager kommer man praktisk talt så langt man behager, mens det andre dager er nesten umulig å komme lenger enn bena kan frakte en. Det skulle vel forresten ikke bli så rent kort det heller, da man er utstyrt med så velsignet lange underäxtter som student «Joe», som vanligvis ikke trasker rundt fra land til land, men studerer handelsadministrasjon ved Westminster College i Fulton, Missouri.

ENGLAND FINT HIKE-LAND»

Joseph forlot hjembyen 5. juni og liket seg fram til New York, hvor han gikk ombord i en båt og kom seg over til England. Her reiste han på tommelen fra sørenden av landet og omtrent opp til Scotland, og dette var et «nice country» for en hitch-hiker, bedyrer han. Man kunne knapt komme raskere fram med egen bil. Fra England bar det så med båt til Bergen, og der kom han i land onsdag.

HAR HØRT SÅ MYE OM NATUREN I NORGE

— Fra Bergen reiste jeg via Voss til Sogn, og maken til villskap og skjønnhet i naturen har jeg aldri opplevd. Det var denne naturen jeg har hørt så mye om og som fikk meg til å reise hit. Jeg vil aldri angre på det, og heller aldri glemme det. Så snart jeg kommer hjem skal jeg fortelle venner og kjente om alt det vakre jeg har sett her, og så sant jeg kan skal jeg få dem til å reise hit i stedet for til Mellom- og Syd-Europa.

SKAL BESØKE SLEKTNINGER I TYSKLAND

Joseph E. Hahn ser drømmende ut når han forteller om skjønnhetsinntrykkene fra Vestlandet, men kommer etter hvert tilbake til den harde virkelighet. Han skal til Tyskland å besøke slektninger, og skal også en snartur nedom Nord-Italia før han går ombord i Le Havre for å seile tilbake til Amerika i slutten av måneden, så han har ikke for mye tid å kaste bort. Han leverer sitt flotteste forretningsbukk til adjø, vender ansiktet smilende til første og beste bil, og slenger tommelen rutinert i været med et inderlig ønske om et riktig langt «lift».

kyrre.

Joseph E. Hahn hever tommelen rutinert med håp om å få «lift» nedover Solør.

SO INCREDIBLE WILD AND BEAUTIFUL,

says the American Student and Hitchhiker about the west coast of Norway, Joseph E. Hahn will never forget his trip in Norway.

With his thumb eloquently raised and with a smile of the best American brand, Joseph E. Hahn from St. Louis tempted drivers with nice company from Bankhjornet in Elverum and down toward Solør yesterday noon. Whether anyone accepted the invitation, we don't know, but it takes a lot to say no to such a lively and cheerful face, so we bet he is already way down in Sweden or Denmark.

IS IT DIFFICULT TO GET LIFTS?

"Well, it has its ups and downs. Some days you can practically get as far as you want, while on other days, it is impossible to get farther than your legs can carry you." However, that should not be too short a distance either, when you have such heavenly long underpinnings as student "Joe," who usually does not trod around from country to country, but is studying business administration at Westminster College in Fulton, Missouri.

ENGLAND IS A FINE COUNTRY FOR HITCHHIKING

Joe left his hometown on June 5th and hitchhiked to New York, where he embarked on a ship and went to England. From here he hitchhiked from the south end of the country and up to Scotland. "This was really nice country for the hitchhiker," he says, "for one can hardly get there faster with your own car." From England the trip went with ship to Bergen, where he came Wednesday.

HEARD SO MUCH ABOUT THE NATURE OF NORWAY

"From Bergen I went by Voss to Sogn, and I have never in my life seen a more beautiful and wild nature. It was this nature I had heard so much about and which made me decide to come here. I don't regret that decision, and I will never forget this trip. As soon as I get home I shall tell my friends about the beauty I have seen here, and I shall do my best to get them to go here instead of the Central and South Europe.

SHALL VISIT RELATIVES IN GERMANY

Joseph E. Hahn has a dreamy look in his eyes when he tells about the impressions of the nature on the West Coast of Norway. But after a while, he comes back to reality; he has to leave soon for

Germany, where he shall visit relatives. He shall also take a short trip through North Italy before he embarks in Le Havre to sail back to America in the end of the month. So he doesn't have too much time to waste. He says goodbye with his most polite bow, turns his smiling face to the first car, and thumbs a ride with a sincere wish of a real, real long lift.

(Editor's note: Joe did not hitchhike from Saint Louis to New York as the newspaper article states but rather flew this distance, as detailed at the beginning of the book.)

Joe in the newspaper office, showing his map to newspaper editor

*Joe posed for hitchhiking with the
newspaper building in the distance*

Pictures were taken of me looking at my map in the newspaper office, after which others were taken of me outside posed along the road in the usual hitchhiking manner with the large USA suitcase displayed at my feet.

I thanked the boy for the invitation, explaining I was behind schedule as I was having a hard time getting a ride to Sweden. Little did I know at that time how much I could have told them at the end of the day concerning my efforts to get a ride.

Again, I was told it would not be hard to get a ride, and so with my hopes built high, I set out again, raising my thumb in the time-honored way of getting a ride.

Two hours later, I was about to take the newspaper boy up on his invitation as I had not moved from where I stood, and to make matters worse, the gentle mist had now turned into a hard rain.

Finally, a man in an old car picked me up and took me a few miles and left me off on a country intersection, where I bought two oranges, a large can of plums, and a bottle of Solo Water for lunch. I ate the plums under a tree, which sheltered me from the rain until I was picked up by a young boy and his father, who was driving a taxi. This ride netted me three kilometers before I was again on the side of the road, looking for a lift.

I stood on the porch of a general store for forty-five minutes before a man driving a small van picked me up and took me to a small town where he had to carry on some business, and leaving me to go about his affairs, he was surprised to again find me standing where he left me the previous hour; he headed for the next town with me as his passenger, letting me off at his business stop. Two boys were standing nearby. They came over and spoke English, quite proud to show me what they had learned in school.

As we talked, a truck stopped for me, but finding he was only going three kilometers and being used to that type of ride during the day, I refused the ride. The driver seemed hurt that I did not accept his offer, so I then crawled into the truck and knelt on the seat as my suitcase and I occupied what space there was beside the milk pail on the floor.

I was taken to his farm, where I again found myself standing along the road in the nasty drizzle. A thirty-minute wait brought two cars along the road, but it was a large lumber truck that next stopped for me. Their load was a shipment of logs to a railroad siding that was only a fifteen-minute ride.

It seemed as though I was getting nowhere fast. Very few of the people that stopped for me could speak good English, and they only muttered sounds, but the people that made me mad were the ones who would speed past me, making sure I was a target of the puddles they would splash through.

I was now standing alongside a home in the countryside. A small boy was "car-spotting" nearby, but as it continued to rain, his mother came home and invited me to have shelter until I could get a ride. I would remain in the house until I heard the sound of a motor coming down the road before I made any attempt to get a ride. At least I was now out of the rain. Within thirty minutes, a double-trailer truck carrying more logs stopped for me. I hovered between two men in the front seat as we went to another lumber yard before we continued on to the town of Kongsvinger, where I was picked up within two minutes by a father and his son in a Volkswagen truck, to be taken a good distance, for my best ride of the day.

My next ride came from a road-repair service truck, my tenth lift of the day. Looking at the driver, I said "Sweden," and he nodded his head, yet to my surprise, his home was three kilometers from the border in the town of Magnor.

The rain was coming down harder than it had been during the entire day. I stood in the entranceway of a store until it became dark enough for the lights to be turned on—still no cars on the road. I walked to the front door of a private home to inquire of lodging for the night. I was directed to a home a block away, where I found a friendly home and lodging for seven kroners, or 98¢. I was the only boarder for the night. They had eaten earlier but were anxious to serve me a hot supper.

None of the people could speak English, but they tried to make me as comfortable as possible. Supper consisted of five boiled potatoes, three slices of pork, green peas, lettuce, and tomato. I cleaned my plate, even eating the dry crackers they put on the table.

The sixteen-year-old daughter of the homeowner entered the room and spoke good English, having only one year of instruction in school. We talked of school life before the hour became late, with her asking if they could serve me breakfast in the morning.

To sum up my day's activities, I was quite put out toward the people of Norway, at least the ones I had come in contact with during the day. Many were inconsiderate, selfish, and for the most part, utterly stupid, but one must have bad days in life. I retired looking for a better morrow.

June 26—Cloudy, Cool

I enjoyed a delicious breakfast of boiled eggs, cheese, sliced meats, orange marmalade, coffee, and milk. I then paid my bill, fifteen kroners, for lodging, breakfast, and supper. The walk to the main street in the cool, crisp air heightened my spirits for a lift that would take me to Sweden. It was nine thirty when I began hitchhiking, and by ten forty-five, I was still on the street corner, downhearted and out of sorts.

It was at this point I chose to make a drastic decision—to travel by train until I made up the time lost waiting for a ride in the unfriendly border country between Norway and Sweden.

This decision was prompted by the fact that the train station was in sight from where I stood along the road. A train that would take me to Halsingborg, Sweden, some 574 kilometers to the south, was due at eleven fifteen. The fare was 67.70 kroners. I took the eleven-fifteen train to Kil, where I was to transfer to another train that would take me to Gothenburg, Sweden.

Upon alighting from the train in Kil, I showed the conductor my ticket, asking him where to catch my next train, knowing it was due to leave at one two. At twelve fifty-five, a train came into the station on the track indicated to me by the conductor. I boarded the train, found myself a seat, and the train pulled out of the station at 1:05 p.m.

When the conductor came through to collect the tickets some fifteen minutes later, he uttered something I could not understand, but evidently, something was wrong, for everyone else suddenly looked at me. It turned out that I had gotten on the wrong train, going north instead of south; I was directed to get off the train in the next town, Deje, and wait until I could catch one going south to my destination of Gothenburg.

There was a terrible smell in the air as I waited in the station. It was now one thirty, and the next train due was at three fifteen. I had gone from bad to worse. I was farther north now than I had been when I started out this morning.

I set my case down in the station and asked directions to a grocery store and bank. Going first to the bank, I was able to obtain some Swedish krona. At the store, I purchased half a loaf of bread, three large slices of Edam cheese, a box of cookies, and a bag of gingersnaps.

I returned to the station to eat my lunch and wait patiently on a bench as I watched the laborers shovel sand from a flatcar into a wheelbarrow. Oh, what fun!

This was indeed a most unusual sight, one I came thousands of miles to see! I had come this far with all the luck in the world with me that it seemed right that things were finally evening themselves out.

As I watched trains come and go, I noticed all engines on the Swedish lines had a snowplow attached to the front. There were also cars built for the gauge of the track with iron wheels driven by electricity; the driver sat in the backseat and operated the controls. The railroad also had a three-wheel bicycle that fit the rails like a motorcycle with a sidecar.

When my train came, it wasn't long before I fell asleep and remained that way for some time. Waking up, I was offered a cigarette by a couple sitting across from me in our compartment. I declined this friendly gesture, which led to a conversation that lasted until eight thirty that evening. During that time, I was offered a drink of Swedish brandy, which tasted more like rubbing or denatured alcohol. We talked and joked around until we pulled into Gothenburg. I thanked my friends and set about to obtain some tourist information.

Just then, I heard someone say "Hi, USA," and turning around, I saw the smiling face of a United States naval officer. We introduced ourselves, finding it nice to meet someone from our own country. His home was in Minnesota, and his ship was sailing for Hamburg tonight.

I was interested in obtaining information of train schedules and on hostels as soon as possible. Trains left at 11:15 p.m. and at 7:37 a.m. for Helsingborg. I decided to locate a hostel, get a good night's rest, and catch the early train. Going to the tourist bureau, I was directed to a nearby hostel. It was now raining, but the hostel was only four blocks away.

The hostel was massive. One could hear the shouting of many children running through the halls. As I entered the building, the cold walls of the school served to echo the sounds from everywhere. A carpenter working on a doorjamb directed me to the reception room, a classroom with a harsh-speaking man to greet you, perched behind a desk.

Asking if I should sign the register, I was told there was no room in the hostel. I was told, however, that I might be able to stay in a private hostel on the other side of town for five krona, located about a twenty-five minute walk from the railroad station. I was given the address of the other hostel, and as I left, I inquired as to how many people could be housed in the hostel I was just refused admission. In a cold tone, I was informed there were three hundred beds.

What to do? Others had been turned away also, and together, we talked things over, trying to decide on a solution as we congregated in the halls. I decided to return to the train station and take the train and use a compartment for my place of resting, knowing if the other hostel was as noisy as the one I had just come from, I would get very little sleep.

I sat on a hardwood bench and ate the remainder of the bread and cheese before I bought my train ticket. Still being hungry, I purchased three oranges to eat with the cookies that were left from my noon snack.

At about ten thirty, a line of freight cars pulled into the station on track 11, the track my train was to be on. Could this be my means of transportation? Two middle-aged women also looked around for an explanation to the situation. They could only speak German, but I spoke with them the best I could. They were going to take the same general route through Germany and Austria as I had mapped out for my travels. The woman I spoke with was Christel Bothke from Regensburg, Germany.

As it turned out, the freight cars were part of the train I was to take, as the coaches were added to the train, forcing us to walk to the extreme end of the platform in order to board. I found an empty compartment and took the seat by the window, going backward, slipped off my shoes, and thought I'd catch some sleep but was soon awakened as a boy came in the compartment, wanting to read, while others who joined him thought talking at 11:30 p.m. was the thing to do.

The conductor came through for the tickets, and ignoring the distractions, I went to sleep with my head propped against my raincoat. And so ended the worst day of my trip.

June 27—Cold, Cloudy to Partly Cloudy

I awoke at 3:00 a.m. partly because of the daylight and partly because of the discomfort. I tried various positions for better rest but all to no avail. I was scheduled to change trains at 4:00 a.m. in order to make my connection for Hälsingborg, so I remained awake. We were fifteen minutes late, but that made little difference to me since the train wasn't due to leave until 5:35 a.m.

The Swedes were a very cold, hardened people extremely set in their ways, thinking only of themselves and caring little for anyone else, but a family who shared the same fate as me, waiting for an hour and a half in a cold coach, the Gustaf Strom family from Örebro, Sweden, became quite friendly with me and proved to be interesting people. Their two children, Leonard and Archie, slept while their parents talked with me. The father worked for the Swedish Railroad as head supervisor, and since he received free transportation, he must take the undesirable schedule since the more desirable ones were all filled with paying passengers. The family was on its way to Copenhagen so his sons could have their first visit there.

After the engine was hooked onto the train, the coach heated up, and I was soon asleep, to remain that way until we pulled into the station at 6:08 a.m. I accompanied the Strom family to the waiting room, bought my ferry ticket, and was invited to have breakfast in the railroad restaurant. Little was I to realize at that time, but the good fortune I was to have in the morning was to continue throughout the day.

Breakfast consisted of a pot of tea and cheese sandwiches. We then went through customs. I knew trouble would arise from the fact that no one had checked my entry into Sweden; no custom official or any of the immigration authorities had come into my compartment as I rode the train from Norway to Sweden the day before. Evidently,

I was to have filled out a white card, but no one on the train the previous day so much as looked like an official.

In a few minutes, the red tape was straightened out, and as I passed through the gate, I slyly remarked that previous to this, I thought I was still in Norway. The official stared at me with the typical cold expression that prevailed most everywhere on the face of the Swedes, or at least the ones I came into contact with.

The Strom family was waving to me as I boarded the ferry and set off for Denmark and the city of Helsingør. The ferry was also taking railroad coaches across the Danish Straits, the body of water that divides Sweden from Denmark. Within twenty minutes, I was in Denmark, and going through customs, I inquired where I might find the Danish Tourist Information Bureau and was informed it was only a block away.

Finding the door locked as it was only seven forty-five and the office opened at nine, I was told by a nearby Esso dealer I could wait at his filling station. I was given a map of Denmark and decided to try my luck hitchhiking to Copenhagen.

Within five minutes, a 1956 Ford driven by a Neon salesman on his way to Copenhagen stopped for me. We were on a four-lane highway with no speed limit, which accounted for the fact we were at our destination by eight twenty-five. He took me directly to the Tourist Information Bureau, where I had a ten-minute wait for the office to open.

I was warmly greeted by the personal service director of the office. I expressed a desire to visit a Danish family, which required her filling out a white card with various items of note about me, and if I had any preference as to the type of family I would like to meet. There were many Tourist Information Bureaus throughout Denmark. They provided a connection between a tourist who wanted to meet Danes and a Danish family who would like to have a tourist visit them.

I also inquired as to the whereabouts of a Youth Hostel but found it to be very far from the center of the city, and with the closing hours, I thought it best to acquire other lodging. I was directed to the railroad station next to the travel bureau in regard to lodging within the city. I was interested in private lodging so I might meet the people of Denmark firsthand.

I was asked the usual questions and given a slip of paper with the number 93 in the upper right-hand corner and was told to report back to the desk of the cashier's window when I saw my number flashed on a large neon sign in the center of the lobby. The number 90 was now flashing; it wouldn't be long for mine to appear. Number 91 appeared, but then they dropped to 88, 89, then 92. It seemed like a long wait, but finally, number 93 flashed on the sign. I was informed I could have private lodging at the home of Mr. and Mrs. M. Holm Jensen living at Ryesgade 27-B for eight krone, or $1.12, per day. I had to pay a service charge of 21¢ to the bureau for getting me the lodging, but this I gladly paid, and I was directed to their home and given a map of the city.

I returned to the tourist bureau to thank the woman who had helped me. She told me to stop in during the afternoon to see about my visit with a Danish family and also gave me literature on things to see and places to go. Before I left, I asked her if she could help me locate Eric Borchenious, my college roommate during my freshman year. The only information I had was that his father lived in New York, but he had once lived in Copenhagen with Eric, who was now thought to be in Denmark with the navy.

Leaving the tourist bureau, I boarded tram number 16, heading for the Jensen home, but again, I was informed I was going the wrong way. I was on the right tram but was going in the wrong direction. After setting myself straight again, I took a winding trip, getting off on Ryesgade Street.

The suitcase was heavy, and every so often I would stop to rest, each time asking where 27-B would be, each time being told to keep going. After what seemed like a mile, I found number 27, walked in, took the elevator to the fourth floor, rang the buzzer, and found I was in the wrong place. Instead of going down to the ground floor and coming up on the other side, the woman whose bell I had rang walked me through the attic and down to 27-B as I had come to apartment 27-A by mistake.

I was shown to my room, a nice one with a washstand of my own and a bath I would share with my hosts. My room had a bed, chair, dresser, table, and large double window. The apartment was located on the third floor, with a lovely balcony off the living room that overlooked the street.

The only trouble with the situation was that Mrs. Jensen could only speak Danish, and when she wanted to tell me something, she would have to phone her husband at work, tell him what she wanted to tell me, and he would have to tell me what she wanted to say as he could speak excellent English.

I was down to my last clean clothes. I soaked them while I went to the bakeshop three blocks away for some jelly rolls, cinnamon-sugar cake, and coconut macaroons.

Then I went to a shoe-repair shop for general cleaning of my shoes, polishing, and removing of tar, all done for 14¢ by a friendly old man who had so many shoes before him he didn't know what to do.

I returned to wash my clothes and take my first bath in eight days. Mrs. Jensen saw my wet clothes hanging up to dry in the bathroom and quickly called her husband, who informed me that his wife would see to it that they dried faster by taking them to the laundry room in the basement.

I then lay down to rest until 3:00 p.m. as I was very tired, having gotten little sleep during the previous night.

Awakening, I dressed and took a walk to the old section of the city, visiting the waterfront area, the market square, and city parks. Showers sent me under cover for a few minutes, after which time I walked to the tourist bureau, where I was given an invitation to dinner at 6:00 p.m. tomorrow at the home of Mr. and Mrs. John Svard. While I was planning my trip to Europe, I had clipped a newspaper article from *The Indianapolis Star* entitled "Danes Find Way to Meet Others." The article told of a program called Meet the Danes whose Danish families register at the local Tourist Information Bureau, telling about themselves and what type of visiting family or individual they would like to meet. They were matched up by a similar questionnaire completed by the tourist, and an invitation was extended by the Danish family for the tourist to visit their home. Having read this article, I availed myself of this program, which served as an introduction for tourists to meet Danish people firsthand. I was also informed that Eric was now in New York; the service director had called a Borchenious family in the city and asked for Eric only to be told he had been killed two years ago. Further questioning resulted in finding out that the Eric who was killed was the cousin of the person I was seeking.

I went into a barber shop for a haircut costing 65¢. Since it was now quitting time for the factories, traffic was heavy with many bicycles; one easily thought it might be Holland as the scene was typical of the place. I caught the right tram, number 16, to take me home, only this time the walk from the bus stop didn't seem nearly as far as I was home in eight minutes.

On the way, I bought two sandwich buns and three slices of ham, which would go nicely with the bakery goods I had in my room. I rested until Mr. Jensen came home from work, having stopped to see the doctor on the way.

Mr. Jensen was associated with a Danish firm that made Softis, a soft serve ice cream product similar to the frozen custard that one would find in our own country. Speaking with him, I was given advice on how to leave the city on Friday in order to make the best connections to Hamburg, Germany. For nightlife in Copenhagen, he suggested a visit to Tivoli, and dressing warmly, I was soon off into the cool night air.

The admission to Tivoli was 75 øre, about 11¢. I was amazed at the spectacle of what lay before me. Tivoli could best be described by saying it was a combination of all the amusement parks in the world put together. Three orchestras went from bandstand to bandstand throughout the park, and recreation of all types was available. All buildings were outlined in colored lights. I walked over the many paths among a general crowd of fifty thousand people. I took time exposures of various interesting patterns made by the lighted buildings, during which time I met a couple from California who were also trying out their camera on the beautiful sights.

One stage show was doing a pantomime with various dance acts, while within ten minutes the stage was converted for acrobatics. The performance included excellent talent. A most unusual sight to see was the use of periscopes by the people who were standing behind people too tall for them to see the show. It rested on a broom-like handle and could be adjusted to various heights to see over taller people standing in front of them.

TIVOLI

At eleven fifteen, a display of fireworks covered the lake area. I took time exposures, hoping the results would afford me with a duplicate picture of the sight I saw that evening.

Leaving the park, I bought some Softis and took the trolley home after a very enjoyable day in wonderful Denmark. It wasn't long afterward that I was sound asleep, thankful that I was again side by side with Lady Luck.

June 28—Rainy, Sunny, Rainy, Sunny, Rainy, Sunny, Rainy, Sunny…

I was gently awakened by a touch on my hand by Mrs. Jensen at 9:00 a.m. as she brought breakfast to me in bed. My, what service! On the tray were sweet rolls and buns for cheese sandwiches, orange marmalade, and a pot of tea.

After eating the filling breakfast, I turned over and slept until 1:00 p.m., whence I dressed and went to see an unusual ashtray suggested by Mr. Fielding in his book on travels. The ashtray was of ground glass, about six inches across and one and a half inches thick, with one's initials cut into the bottom, all this for only $6.

I left the store and walked to the dock area, hoping possibly to see the freighter *Royal*, which was due in Copenhagen, and then continued along the pier to where the British had a battleship and aircraft carrier on display. The freighter *Royal* was the ship I had boarded in Scotland for a possible experience as an assistant deck mate in order to cross the North Sea but would have taken me to Copenhagen instead of Norway.

Seeing many people going up the gangplank, I decided to follow them, not understanding what the sign read. I soon found myself in the center of a huge ship, 767 feet long, weighing thirty thousand tons. I walked onto a large circular disk some sixty to seventy feet in diameter. In a few minutes, we were brought up to the flight deck, where the jets were on display.

The demonstration of a mock rescue at sea with a helicopter proved very interesting as the man was pulled through a hatch while the copter hovered above.

I walked to the stern of the ship after examining the guns and jets at close range and was brought down into the center of the ship on another circular disk, like the one that had brought me to the flight deck.

After viewing a display of various military equipment, I walked down the gangplank and along the shore, through a park and to the old military quarters of the city. Many guardhouses stood around the three-hundred-year-old buildings. The fort itself had been occupied by the Germans during the last war.

Going into the shopping district, I bought a teaspoon for Mrs. Eckman, a friend of the family from Saint Louis, as she had asked me to bring one from Denmark for her. I climbed aboard tram number 10 and headed for home, where I washed and readied for my dinner date. I wanted to shave before going to dinner but found the current to be direct. My hosts would have to see me unshaven, but I was sure they would understand.

At six two I arrived at the residence of Mr. and Mrs. John Svard, who, according to Danish standards, lived on the first floor, but as you would count them in America, they occupied the third floor.

While dinner was being prepared, Mr. Svard and his son Jerry discussed the trip I was taking. At around six thirty, we were called to a dinner consisting of meatballs, boiled potatoes with melted butter, and cut lettuce. I needed several helpings to fill me before fresh strawberries were served with sugar and cream.

During the course of the meal, Pilsner beer was served, a good Danish beer. With beer in hand, we left the table to be shown the paintings Jerry had made. He was twenty-four years old and painted from inspiration alone. He planned on going to Boston in October in order to train as a textile worker, for the painting was just a hobby of his.

Soon we were discussing the German invasion of Denmark on April 9, 1940, and I was shown a book containing many photos from the day of the invasion to the day of liberation, May 5, 1945.

The street scenes were the same ones I had walked through today, only now they were rebuilt and no remains of the war prevailed. Mrs. Svard served tea and Danish sweets in the living room, the best I had ever tasted.

Mr. Svard helped me map out my departure from the city tomorrow, and I thanked the family for all they had done. Jerry drove me home as it was late and he feared I would become lost. I extended an invitation to him to visit me if he ever came to Saint Louis since he would be spending two years in this country in the Boston area.

Mr. Svard worked in a men's-hat store, while Jerry had just completed studying at Leeds, England. Though not a wealthy family, they did make my visit one of the highlights of Copenhagen.

The weather during the day was most interesting. It rained eight different times only to be followed by a deep-blue sky before the process would be repeated. My stay in Copenhagen had been a most wonderful experience. The people I met had become true friends and were most cordial at all times. After writing in my diary, it wasn't very long until I fell into a deep sleep.

June 29—Partly Cloudy and Windy

I was awakened at six forty-five as breakfast was placed in my room by Mrs. Jensen, my host in Copenhagen. After dressing, packing, and paying Mrs. Jensen, I was again on my way, taking the sweet rolls from breakfast with me for a midday snack.

I took tram number 10 and transferred at the Royal Theatre, taking bus number 41 to the end of the line. I hitched a ride to Glostrup, a town ten kilometers from the city. Here the highway was four lanes—with much traffic—Denmark's most modern highway, newly constructed Highway 1.

My next ride came from a farmer who sold minks for $300. He took me twenty-three kilometers to the city of Ringsted, where I was approached by three small boys who wished my name and address, collecting them for a hobby. I took a picture of them and was soon to be picked up by a furniture dealer who was moving his store from Copenhagen to Suro. He went out of his way to drop me at a choice location for obtaining rides.

At this point, I had some competition; a girl was also hitchhiking from the same location. She was picked up within ten minutes, though standing only forty yards from me, while I waited about forty-five minutes for my ride. During this time, two other boys had asked me for personal information, name, address, etc., for their collection.

My latest "taxi" was a furnace salesman, Mr. A. Christenson. We hadn't driven more than a few minutes when he stopped to pick up another hitchhiker, Peter Ekknud, a Danish boy who offered to share his lunch with me while we took the ferry across the water that separated the two main islands of Denmark. Peter divided his five sandwiches with me as we bought a pot of tea and ate in the snack lounge.

Since Jerry was going south, while I had to go east in order to reach Germany, Jerry departed, while Mr. Christenson took me through the green countryside, which was very flat and reminded me of Holland. Beauty, yes, but I would always remember the friendly people of Denmark.

I was left off at three twenty after coming the better part of 130 kilometers and waited at the intersection of Highway 1 and Highway 10 for a ride to Hamburg, Germany. The first two cars passed without slowing down, followed by a sightseeing bus. I had learned not to try to get a lift with one of them for they would charge you with the price of a fare.

The bus had stopped several hundred feet before me to let off two sailors, and now it had pulled to a stop about fifty feet beyond where I stood. I looked over my shoulder to see why it might have stopped so soon; all the people in the bus were waving from the windows, motioning for me to come over to the bus. Picking up my suitcase, I walked to the bus and climbed aboard, for surely, these people were not on an ordinary sightseeing bus. The bus had been chartered by the passengers, and they had asked the driver to stop and offer me a ride after seeing my USA suitcase.

There I was among eighteen Germans on their way home from an eight-day trip to Copenhagen, having come from the city of Flensburg, just inside the German border. They joked with me in their language and laughed at the USA suitcase.

Just then, a boy from the rear of the bus came to sit with me as he too had been picked up by these people. He could speak English very well. He introduced himself as Joachim Klebe, whose home was also in Flensburg, but he had been visiting Copenhagen for several weeks rather than being on the sightseeing tour.

We stopped at a roadside restaurant/hotel for tea, coffee, and cake. The German tourists had a gay time as I took their picture. They were happy people who enjoyed the offerings of life. Going into the restaurant, I asked an employee where the bathroom was, only to be asked if I wanted one or two beds. Before I could reply, I was shown a nice room for two as the manager thought Joachim and I were staying overnight, but we cleared up the confusion and were directed to the restroom.

The floor of the restaurant was of loose stone or small pebbles. Their food was very good, and the rest did us some good. Before we left, we were asked to sign the guest register.

As I was about to board the bus, I felt a fly resting on my face. I swung at the insect only to be stung by a bee, leaving a sting half an inch from my left eye. The manager applied salve, and the pain lessened, and I again boarded the bus.

I traveled to the border of Denmark as I related my intended plans for Germany to Joachim. Joachim invited me to spend the night with him at his aunt's home. Of course, I didn't refuse! Soon we passed through the German border and were shortly in Flensburg, now inside the sixth country of my three-week tour.

We said good-bye to our German friends and left on a local tram for his aunt's home. Leaving our luggage, we went to his girlfriend's home but were not in luck as she was working. Her mother took us to the flat rooftop for a good view of the city, which also afforded some good pictures.

Returning to his aunt's home, we had a dinner of six boiled potatoes with melted butter and two herring. This was a change for me! No cheese. I shaved for the first time in four days and went to a school where my friend taught fencing. I enjoyed the action and met some of his friends.

We left to visit a bar with true German atmosphere, where we drank beer and chatted for an hour. Taking a tram home, I noticed that the conductor alighted from the streetcar at each stop to help passengers step down to the pavement.

My bed for the night was a couch that opened into a bed. Another day had ended, another day of good luck and good fortune. As I was writing this account of the day's activities, I could hear the gay voices of people below my window, representing the Germans in a friendly and harmless manner, who would try to do everything they could for you.

Joachim, my host for the night, was twenty-four years old. His mother was Danish, while his father was German. Although he did not see fighting in the last war, he had many close adventures with military life. He was a fine boy and had shown me a good time in his old city—old, yes, but very quaint. We said good-night to each other as the bed and couch were quickly put to use.

HITCHHIKING THROUGH EUROPE DURING THE SUMMER OF 1956

June 30—Clear and Pleasant

At 9:00 a.m. we were awakened by the knocking on the door by his aunt. The room was very cold. I dressed hurriedly and was given a pan of cold water and a glass of water with which to wash and brush my teeth. Surviving the ordeal, I was served breakfast of jelly, butter, and rolls.

We walked to the bank, where I exchanged my Danish money and some traveler's checks for German marks. We walked to a sporting goods store, on the way passing some children who were playing during their recess period at school. Although it was Saturday, the children were in school as classes were held six days a week.

I bought a knapsack that was listed for twenty-five marks but was sold for fifteen since there were some rust marks on the metal. Joe said it was a very good buy; I called my friend Joe since it was easier to pronounce than Joachim. In packing the knapsack, we took everything out of the suitcase except my sheet sleeping sacks and pajamas. It was easy to carry an empty suitcase since my shoulders were now carrying all the weight. Walking was better too. After packing, I thanked his aunt and was asked for my address as a little girl had heard me speak of my sister Carol and wanted to write to an American and be a penpal.

We walked through the city and market square as Joe wanted to see that I got on the right road to Hamburg. I only had to wait five minutes before a boy of twenty-four named Peter Carstersen picked me up in his 1955 model German car. He was on his way to Hamburg to see his girlfriend, Elfriede.

We listened to music, stopping once to buy a bag of cookies. We were held up by a swinging bridge once and another time by a long train. Peter could not speak English, but we managed an interesting conversation.

He took me right to the entrance of the Hamburg airport, just another of my lucky breaks. However, I had just missed a PAA flight to Berlin. I was put on their waiting list for the 8:00 p.m. flight. It was now only 4:00 p.m.

I tried to get passage on BEA and was more successful in my endeavor, paying 115 marks for a 9:40 p.m. flight to Berlin and on to Frankfurt after my brief stay in Berlin. Having time to spare, I wrote a letter to Mother as I sat in the observation area of the airport. Then I went to a small store, where the owner was scrubbing the steps of the entrance before closing the store. I bought a liter of milk, a loaf of brown bread, and sliced cheese. I returned to the observation area to eat while waiting for my plane to depart.

In walking to the store I found I was walking on the cycling path that bordered the road, as the sidewalk for walking was only gravel and bordered the cycling path, which was paved. I watched the PAA flight leave and waited for my flight. Looking at my watch, I noticed it was eight thirty, with only forty-five minutes to wait before I checked in at the scales, but upon looking at the airport clock, the time was now nine ten! Evidently, my watch had stopped. Considering myself lucky to avert a mishap, I weighed in with forty pounds and went to waiting room B.

I boarded the plane at nine thirty-five and found myself flying in a sixty-passenger DC-4 plane within ten minutes. From the time the engines were gunned, it took twenty-five seconds to leave the ground. Our cruising speed was two hundred miles per hour at 3,700 feet. Within fifty-five minutes, we would be in Berlin.

The flight was smooth and pleasant; my only complaint centered on the fact the hostess would not let passengers sit in the last row of seats, which I considered the best for viewing as well as for safety.

At the airport in Berlin, I wanted to confirm reservations to Frankfurt upon my departure from Berlin, but the office was closed.

I went to the hotel counter and informed the attendant I had been staying in hostels and would like to obtain cheap lodging. She called a hotel and was told a room was available for four marks. Thanking her after being given the address and directions, I was thankful the hotel was only two blocks from the airport. The hostel in Berlin was located ten kilometers from the city limits, and the hotel was convenient and inexpensive. For this service, I paid the hotel-counter attendant fifty pfennigs (12¢).

I walked to the hotel, seeing many American servicemen dating the girls of Berlin since the service club was across the street. Reaching the hotel, I walked into a dark hall and up creaky steps.

A young girl came to meet me and carried my suitcase to the third floor, where I was shown a room for four marks. It was five feet wide with one bed against the wall and a small stool at the foot of the bed.

I was also shown a room with four times as much space, a washstand, two chairs, a table, a phone, a large window, a cedar closet, and a large bed with a night table and lamp. The price of this room was six marks. I gladly took this room and signed the registration papers. The owner of the hotel was a fat grandmother whose granddaughter helped with the cleaning. We talked until 12:30 a.m. and drank tea made by the granddaughter.

I was shown to the balcony, and as I walked past the table, her dog lunged at me, tearing my pants but just nipping my skin. Medicine was applied to the bite, and I was told they would mend the trousers. It was related that a soldier once hit the dog with a beer bottle, and since that time, the dog had been "on guard." The khaki pants I was wearing probably reminded the dog of the incident. It wasn't bad, and saying good-night to Granny and her granddaughter, I went to get a good night's rest.

Shortly thereafter, another person was shown the room for four marks. He offered three marks, saying the room was not worth any more. Granny stuck to her price, and the man left the hotel. I do believe today was *exceptional* as far as luck was concerned, and I hoped it would continue tomorrow.

July 1—Clear and Very Warm

I was awakened by the ringing of the phone in my room. I was told breakfast was ready as it was nine o'clock. I dressed and washed in a hurry so as not to be late for breakfast, which consisted of two fried eggs, six pieces of toast, jelly, butter, and a pot of tea, all this costing 66¢. Without the eggs, it would have cost 48¢, so I was far ahead to have the eggs as well.

I went outside to take a picture of the hotel before walking across the plaza to the Columbia House, the officers' club for the US Army stationed in Berlin. It was here one made reservation for the bus trip behind the Iron Curtain every Saturday, Sunday, and Wednesday. I was told the tour for today, Sunday, was filled, but I informed them I was leaving Berlin on Wednesday on the 12:30 p.m. plane and would have no other time for the tour. The receptionist suggested I return to the lounge at one thirty that afternoon to see if there were any cancelations but added I had a slim chance of making the tour.

I walked to the airport to confirm my reservations for the flight to Frankfurt on Wednesday then continued on to the Victoria Gardens, walking throughout the general area of my hotel, seeing large areas of waste and ruin. The building adjoining our hotel was a standing shambles; my hotel was once in that condition.

I returned to the hotel to rest until one fifteen before walking to the Columbia House, where I waited patiently for the tour guide to appear. When he did manage to arrive at one fifty, I asked him if I might join the tour but was told quite flatly there was no room. On second thought, he informed me to wait around to see if someone would not show up for the trip. In those few minutes, I was able to speak with the other tour guide, informing him I would be willing to sit on the floor of the bus since I would be unable to make any other tour.

To this suggestion, he agreed after listening to my pleas. At the same time, an army officer asked if a woman friend of his might also join the tour. Since there were two buses, the officer suggested the use of chairs from the dining room for the two extra passengers. This was allowed only if the officer would take full responsibility for the chairs to be returned to the dining room after the tour.

So now I had a seat; I was again fortunate in being able to talk my way onto the tour. We were briefed on the rules that would be in effect while in the Russian sector by Lieutenant Cook. I was the last to board the bus since my seat was next to the driver. I had the best seat on the bus, having a front and side window to look through.

We drove through Western Berlin past Teufelsberg, an artificial mountain of rubble made from the ruins of the shattered buildings covered with earth and laid out as a park, showing the Russians that beauty can come from the horrible taste of war. The name means "devil's mountain."

We continued on our way to the edge of the American sector. Here the West Berlin trolley stopped and the East Berlin trolley began, though both were on the same track. If one wished to go into East Berlin, he must pay an additional fare. Each sector had its own trolley system, own government, own police force, own water system, own phone service, etc.; in fact, one could not call from West Berlin to East Berlin directly. He must first call Frankfurt, where his call was connected to East Berlin, resulting in an expensive phone bill.

We stopped at the Russian Garden of Remembrance, where we viewed their various memorials to the dead. In each of the five sectors of plotted ground, buried were five hundred Russian soldiers who were killed in the last war. At the extreme end of the garden was a high monument, beneath which rested an additional five hundred soldiers.

Russian soldiers were as plentiful as flies in the area as it was Sunday afternoon, and they had little else to do. I was wearing a bright-red sport shirt and was a standout as far as being dressed was concerned. I did manage to take some pictures of their dress using my telephoto lens to avoid getting too close to them.

We continued on to Stalin Allee, the only street in the east sector rebuilt by the Russians. Many HO department stores lined the street. They were owned and operated by the government as there was no private industry to speak of. Behind this glorified false front were shambles of burned-out ruins, much destruction, and little for the people to be proud of. The people were dressed poorly; little gaiety was seen on the streets. One small-time circus operated by Busch was seen on a corner, but activity elsewhere was lifeless. It was hard to describe how the 1.2 million people of East Berlin lived and even harder to understand how they existed under such conditions. They occupied 158 square miles compared to the 3.4 million people of West Berlin, who occupied 186 square miles.

Our tour went through the backstreets; one was amazed at the complete destruction that still prevailed eleven years after the war. We passed through the Brandenburg Gate into the British sector and were able to contrast the mode of living. We were back in civilization. Once more we observed the scenes of gaiety and the abundance of people living for something—freedom—and as we passed the Kurfürstendamm, we could appreciate the willingness of a people to overcome their hardships. The buildings were new, representing the mode of new living. Peaceful yet bustling side streets were visited as we continued our tour. One thing to note in the British sector was the presence of a Russian war memorial that was hurriedly erected after the war, before the various sectors were defined. Today, the monument was guarded by two Russian soldiers, whereas formally, it was only guarded by one soldier. But one dark night he disappeared, never to be seen again. The presence of the second soldier was for the purpose of guarding the soldier who was guarding the monument. Quite confusing but nonetheless true.

We were taken back to the Columbia House, and the end of the two-and-a-half-hour tour through the forbidden land was now a vivid experiences. The price of the tour was twenty-five cents, whereas a bus tour with the German government cost anywhere from four to thirty marks, $2.00–$7.50.

I returned to my room, ordered a pot of tea, closed the curtain, and after drinking the tea, lay down to rest, which turned into a full night's sleep as it was now only 5:00 p.m.

July 2—Clear and Warm, Later Humid with Showers

I awoke at 8:00 a.m. after sleeping for fifteen hours, still dressed as I was when I went to bed the night before. I remembered waking several times during the afternoon and thinking of putting on pajamas, but I was too content to disturb my slumber.

I washed and went for breakfast of six pieces of toast, butter, jelly, and three cups of tea. Today I was to have a bicycle to aid in my sightseeing, but the bicycle was in the repair shop. I was to have rented it from a cleaning girl who came daily to the hotel, returning with it in time for her to go home. However, I first went to see a doctor about the bite on my leg but was told there was no infection. I next went to see about buying some tea glasses with wooden holders. Going to one shop, I was told to go to another across the street. Here the owner called two other shops for me and took me to the one personally to see that I got what I wanted.

Their cups were nice but were not what I wanted as they were plain wooden holders. I was given the address of the largest department store in Berlin, KaDeWe, and now set about renting a bicycle to get to this massive department store. It opened in 1905, being seven stories high, with sixty thousand square yards of floor space, selling 380,000 different articles. It was 90 percent destroyed in an air raid in 1943 and wasn't completely rebuilt until 1956. Surely, a store of this size would have what I wanted to buy! Going back to the hotel, I was told to go to the bicycle shop four blocks away. The shop only sold new bicycles and did repairing and could not help me. I then went to the officers' club to inquire if I could rent one from a serviceman, but all the personnel had motor vehicles.

I then went to a lot that had used cars and motorbikes; they too had no bicycles to be rented, and to rent a motorbike would require a Berlin license. Still not giving up, I went to the headquarters of the Sixth Infantry and asked the guards if they knew where I could rent a bicycle. They suggested a place in a remote section of Berlin that would have required half the day to reach.

I was about to give up when I passed the glass shop where the owner had personally taken me to another shop. She introduced me to her husband, who spoke English, telling him of my problem. He called two bicycle shops he knew of, but neither of them would rent a bicycle.

I was thoroughly downhearted by now and returned to the hotel. I explained the situation to Granny, and she assured me the cleaning girl's bike would be fixed tomorrow and I could rent it in the morning.

I then boarded a number 19 streetcar to head for the Kurfürstendamm, the well-known shopping center of Berlin. Going to KaDeWe, the large department store, I looked at the tea glasses that were silver plated with gold holders, but they had nothing in wood to hold the glass cup.

I next tried my luck at F. W. Woolworth but again had no luck but was told to go to a wood-carving shop nearby, where I might get the bottom holders in wood.

I could not locate the store, so I decided to ask at a furniture store, but they could not help me. The office of Air France was down the street, and a girl there was able to direct me to the wood-carving shop. My luck was none the better here. This venture had all begun because I was served tea at breakfast with this type of cup in the hotel. Leaving the wood-carving shop, I was told to try another store across the street.

Drudgingly, I dragged my weary body across the street and entered a small shop. Again I asked for a glass-topped and wooden-bottomed teacup. The woman went to the rear of the shop and brought out twelve or fifteen of them with two different markings. I bought six of the dark-stained wood bottoms and asked them to ship them home, being careful not to break the glass tops. The two women who ran the shop said they could understand my German and thought I was doing very well. They gave me three glasses of water and directed me to a bakery and the Brandenburg Gate.

I walked to the bakery and bought sweet rolls and cheesecake, then I proceeded among many war ruins and into residential areas. Whole blocks where homes and other buildings once stood now lay flat. It was a strange feeling to think that destruction could be so complete.

Nearby was a newly constructed modern structure that sharply contrasted with the remaining ruins. I emerged on June 17th Street and walked past the Victory Column erected in 1873. It was 220 feet high. The street was named for the day Berlin was liberated and was the most modern of streets in Berlin.

I walked through Tiergarten, a replanting of trees and shrubs in a once beautiful area laid to waste by the war, then proceeded on to the Russian war memorial in the British sector and finally came to

Brandenburg Gate, where the red Communist flag wavered from a pole on top of the gate.

Going on, I walked past the British-border guards, continuing along the border where a sharp contrast between the eastern and western sectors was noticeable. Huge piles of brick and shattered buildings formed only skeletons of what once was a beautiful Berlin.

I walked through parts of the east sector as part of a shortcut to Potsdamer Platz, where the British, American, and French sectors came together. I had been in the British sector but crossed into the Russian sector for two blocks in order to reach the American sector, passing the bahnhof (train station) and an arena-shaped building. I took bus number 24 to within blocks of my hotel and easily walked home.

I explained my hectic day to the hotel keeper concerning my endeavor to obtain the tea glasses. She offered to sell me six of her wooden holders for fifty cents each if I could buy the glass to fit the holder as there were many sizes, depending on the maker of the item. She directed me to another department store where I might buy the tea glasses that would fit her holders. I was told it was an eight-minute walk. Deciding to go right away, I discovered it was more like a fifteen-minute walk, and to make things worse, none of the glasses fit the holders.

A saleswoman, noticing I needed a shave, rubbed my chin and tried to sell me shaving cream and lotion. I was quick to say no to the purchase.

On the way back to the hotel, I bought for 24¢ three slices of cheese and a can of applesauce that I ate in my room before getting ready to attend the army theater at their recreational area. Arriving at the theater, I was told a coat and tie was the required dress. I hurriedly returned to the hotel and dressed accordingly, arriving in time to see the show. The movie was a weird film about humans changing into seedpods, reborn without emotion.

Leaving the theater, I inquired if I might go to the recreation building, where dancing and an American bar were located. The only requirement was a valid passport, I was told. Thinking it best if I shaved, I again returned to the hotel, shaved, and headed for the recreation building. My passport was checked by a guard, but things were just closing as it was 10:30 p.m. I began talking with Ron, a soldier from Wisconsin. He bought me two Cokes served with *ice*, the first drinks served to me in Europe as such. We talked until 11:00 p.m., during which time I was invited to meet him at the bar around seven thirty the following night. I thanked him, and leaving the center, I walked to the airport. A strange man approached me and offered to exchange money on the black market, but I turned my head the other way and walked back to the hotel. Guests were just arriving at the hotel. I offered to help carry their bags to their room before retiring for the night.

July 3—Cloudy, Rainy

I arose at eight forty-five to take a hot bath before eating breakfast of the usual. Today I was treated to stale buns at no extra charge! I returned to my room to wash my clothes and hang them up to dry before setting out with the cleaning girl's bicycle. I was told I was the first guest to wash his clothes in a hotel room and that it should not be done.

Hagar, the cleaning girl, had brought the bicycle for me to use during the day. I took my camera and took off to see Berlin the easy way.

I first went to see Teufelsberg, the mountain made from the rubbles of the shattered buildings that now was the site of a park. Teufelsberg meant "devil's mountain" and was about an eighty-meter-high rubble covered with dirt. Trees and plants adorned the site.

Having trouble with a loose lens on my camera, I stopped to have it tightened at a camera shop then headed for downtown Berlin, taking the main street, from which I branched off to the side streets to see the utter ruin that still prevailed. Ten years ago, Berlin was 80 percent destroyed; today it was well on its way to complete recovery, but manual labor slowed down the process. Employment was at an all-time high, which made for better all-around living conditions. Sidewalks were still made by laying brick by hand; concrete was mixed on the spot. Everything was done by hand. I drove the bicycle across the area of rubble and stopped to survey the scene about me. I thought for a minute that I was in another world; skeletons of concrete and piles of brick surrounded me. Foundations jutting from the ground in shattered shame stood before me.

I went on to a grade school to photograph the children at play in a fenced-off area. They seemed to be in a gay mood, considering what was around them. I continued on until I came to the Russian sector that jutted into the British and American sectors at Potsdamer Platz. I rode slowly through the street, not being stopped as I was in no man's land.

It started to rain, so I rode my bicycle on a winding path several hundred feet till I came to a low-type building standing in a weeded field. I was now in East Berlin. As I entered the side of the building, a sense of loneliness crept over me. Though I was in East Berlin, no one knew of my presence as there was no sign of life around. The structure sheltering me from the rain was a one-story motel-type building having thirteen rooms and a large bathroom, though all the fixtures had been stripped from the building. A long hallway connected the rooms, but its former use remained unknown.

I made myself at home while waiting for the rain to cease, for I had not brought my raincoat along. It was a funny feeling being all alone, knowing life once existed there and fighting prevailed. The wall around the building was marked with bullet marks and shell bursts.

I remained here until 2:00 p.m., almost a wait of two hours. Leaving the structure, I noticed that it was not only the fixtures that were removed but also the wiring, hinges, and window frames. All that remained was an empty shell!

Before leaving, I rushed across the field several hundred feet so I might take a picture of the building that had been my abode. I returned quickly to fetch the bicycle and head for the British sector, fearing that I had possibly been seen. Within a few minutes, I was again on "free soil."

I rode to the department store KaDeWe, where I bought bakery goods consisting of jelly rolls and pretzels. Then I bought some glass teacups for the wooden holders the hotel owner had given me. I had brought one of the holders with me, hoping I could match the glass with the holder, which I was able to do.

I returned to the hotel to pick up the other wooden holders so that they might all be sent home in one package. The saleswoman tried to help me with the correct pronunciation of German words as she wrapped the package.

Back at the hotel, I took my second bath of the day and dressed in a coat and tie for my visit to the Seminole Club of the Sixth Infantry. My passport was checked, and I was wished a pleasant evening by the guard.

A trio was playing as I entered the club, but Ron was not around. I asked a soldier if I could join him, ordering a beer while he ordered a Zombie. I found I was unable to pay for my drink with American money since the club only allowed payment with "script," American army money in bills.

The soldier was a green private from Maryland. He offered to buy the drink. Shortly after, Ron arrived and sold me some script, selling me $1.25 for five marks. He bought a round of beer while

I ordered some hamburgers. The bill for two hamburgers came to thirty cents; they were good hamburgers with lettuce and tomato to top them off. I offered to buy Ron a drink, but he wouldn't allow it since he worked at the club and received all he wanted for nothing. Ron Bayer, the soldier befriending me, came from Beloit, Wisconsin, where he worked in a J. C. Penny store. We talked for several hours as we continued to drink good American beer. Try as I might, I could not spend the entire $1.25. Ron took back the script, giving me two marks for what was left. At the bar, canned Budweiser was sold for 25¢. A carton of American cigarettes was sold for $1.20. Uncle Sam was taking good care of his boys.

I then thanked Ron and returned to the hotel to wash some clothes before dropping off to sleep, concluding a very interesting day in Berlin.

July 4—Warm and Partly Cloudy

I had the best of intentions of sleeping until nine thirty but was awakened at eight forty-five by a duet of weird music playing below my open window. Two men were playing a violin and an accordion, hoping people would toss coins from their windows. I felt like throwing an old shoe but controlled myself long enough to contribute an American penny.

I went for breakfast of two fried eggs, nine pieces of toast, butter, jelly, and a pot of tea. I paid my hotel bill and returned to my room to pack my knapsack. I was asked to sign the guest book, and bidding the hotel keeper, her granddaughter, and the cleaning girl good-bye, I walked to the airport and checked my luggage on the scales at forty pounds.

I boarded Pan American flight number 175 to Frankfurt and seated myself next to a window of the sixty-passenger plane. At twelve thirty-five, we left on the start of a rough journey. The air pockets were very noticeable; we had to keep our safety belts fastened for the entire trip. Lunch consisted of cold cuts, cheese in a packet, lettuce, rolls, sliced cheese, marble cake, and coffee.

Our blue sky had left us as we were now in the middle of a huge cloud bank. They were very thick and quite dark. Our speed was 350 miles per hour at six thousand feet. The hostesses were very nice compared to the rude treatment I received on the BEA flight.

I arrived in Frankfurt at two ten, from which I took the PAA bus to the center of the city, where I checked my baggage. I bought Mother some steak knives and some bakery items for myself. I bought a train ticket to Hanau, as was suggested, then boarded the train to sit on wooden seats for the twenty-three-kilometer ride. In Hanau I walked from the station to the main highway, where I began hitchhiking again. Within five minutes, a car stopped to take me to a main intersection on the other side of town, from where I received a lift after waiting one minute. I was picked up by a Puerto Rican named Lewis, a sergeant in the US Army on his second tour of four years.

He took me to the city of Aschaffenburg and left me on the far side of the city limits, where I had only a seven-minute wait before I was picked up by Lewis Cerdini from the town of Rimpar located eight miles north of Wurzburg, my destination for the night. He could not speak English, but we were able to make ourselves understood. We stopped at a roadhouse, where we bought a pot of coffee and four jelly rolls. He insisted on paying the bill.

We continued on to Wurzburg, arriving there at around seven thirty. He asked someone where the Youth Hostel was located and dropped me off a short distance from it. Upon inquiring at the hostel, I was informed there was no room for the night. I was, however, given the address of Hotel Hosplz no more than a hundred yards down the street. Here I was shown to a lovely room with a washbasin, chair, table, closet, and very soft bed. The price of the room was six marks ($1.40).

I went to the dining room for a huge bottle of cold beer (70% of a mark, 0717¢) and a bowl of thick soup (90% of a mark, 22¢). Music was playing. I felt very good, having been lucky throughout another day.

I took a walk around town and returned to the hotel at nine fifteen. I talked to the owners of the hotel until eleven as they helped me with my German pronunciation and vocabulary. Their son would come to the United States in October. He was very encouraging, saying it wouldn't take long for me to learn his language.

Today I knew I was nearing Southern Germany. The hay wagons were blocking the highway, either being pulled by animal, tractor, or people. Then, too, the towns were old, narrowing the highway down to a narrow street that twisted and turned. The people dressed in farm clothes and were seen working in the fields from early morn till sundown.

My trip was progressing so nicely that it seemed like a thousand dreams all bundled into one. What happened from day to day was a combination of things and experiences that were hard to believe could happen to one person. Travel was such fun if luck and good fortune were with you, but most of all, it would mean more to you if you knew the guiding light and hand of God were with you, for He was my guiding light, my Pilot through the foreign lands.

July 5—Warm and Pleasant

I awoke at 9:00 a.m. after a very restless night. The bed just did not suit me for one reason or another. I dressed and went to the dining room for hot rolls, jelly, butter, and a pot of tea for 1.90 marks (46¢). I asked directions to Rothenburg and took pictures from the hotel window before setting out for my destination.

I walked through town and over the Main River to find I was now on the road to Stuttgart. It was very warm. A drink of lemonade proved refreshing. I was forced to again cross the Main River, only on a different bridge, as I had walked to a castle thinking the road I wanted ran alongside the castle grounds.

I stationed myself on a corner, and in fifteen minutes, a sergeant in the army for twenty-six years stopped to take me about two kilometers. Here I waited for an hour until a Special Services civilian of the army associated with the PX and his wife stopped for me and offered to take me as far as they were going. I was invited to their home for lunch, and it wasn't long before ham sandwiches, pea soup, olives, onions, tomatoes, sardines on bread, and tea were served. For dessert we had pineapple pie and milk.

The wife painted ties for her husband. I was shown her collection and told I could have one. I chose a white tie painted with various colors, seemingly very beautiful, unlike any I had ever seen.

I was taken into town after they packed a snack for me. I bought two notebooks as I had filled one with my activities. Next, we went to a camera shop as I was having trouble with the shutter. I was advised to go to a camera shop in Rothenburg. I was taken to the edge of town and given a copy of the *Stars and Stripes*, the daily army newspaper, having been treated like a king by this family.

I read the paper as I waited for a lift, which came within ten minutes. I was picked up by Serhard Koschel, a former tennis star, one of the ten best in Germany between 1936 to 1943. He was driving a German convertible, taking me forty-eight kilometers to Rothenburg, a medieval town with a great amount of history. I gave him my address so that his fifteen-year-old daughter could write my sisters. He took me right to the hostel; it was only four hundred years old, the only place I could find to sleep for the night. The only remaining lodging in the hostel was in the attic, on some cots, where the overflow of students could sleep. I was on the fourth floor, directly under the roof.

A new hostel was being built since the four-hundred-year-old structure seemed to be on its last leg. Lodging for the night cost 12¢. It was the same price if you were lucky enough to have a bunk bed that occupied the other floors. I was given some blankets and made my cot as comfortable as could be expected.

I went into the center of the town, which was all medieval and quaint. I went to a camera shop to be told my camera was in need of repair, which could not be done for several days. The price of a new Exakta would be 645 DM. However, this shop had none for sale, but the girl working in the shop took me to a smaller shop, where I was shown the only one in stock. It was a beautiful 1956 model; the

American price in Germany was $161. I decided to buy the camera, knowing the price in the States to be close to $300, and since my other camera was broken, I would be unable to take pictures of the remaining days of my trip.

I returned to the hostel for supper consisting of a large bowl of stew (24¢). At the table, I met four German boys who were also eating the stew. The stew was mostly old vegetables, which didn't taste too good, but since I was hungry, I ate what I could.

The four German boys accompanied me into town, where we walked on the old wall surrounding the town. As we walked, we sang the "Happy Wanderer" while one of the boys, named Fritz, played his harmonica. The wall was quite thick and surrounded the entire town, except for a small portion of the town that bordered on a high cliff, which was not accessible.

We returned to the hostel and made ready for the night. We had to climb four flights of stairs that were worn off on the edges, enough to cause one to break his neck in a fall. The attic was cold since there were broken windows at both ends of the battered old building. Before going to sleep, I mapped out my plans for the following day and prepared for the 10:00 p.m. lights-out. The noise of the many students ceased shortly after the lights were turned off, and I was able to get some sleep, though I was uncomfortable on the hard cot.

July 6—Windy, Warm, and Pleasant

I was awakened at 6:30 a.m., partly from the light of the sun, partly by the various noises of the other boys, partly because of the coldness of the room, but mostly due to being uncomfortable on the hard cot. I did manage to remain in bed until seven thirty before dressing for breakfast of three rolls for four cents and jelly for two cents. This was the extent of my breakfast!

I took a picture of the German boys and of the four-hundred-year-old hostel after obtaining permission to leave my suitcase at the hostel while I went into town for another walk around the wall, taking care not to bump my head on the rafters of the overhanging roof.

At the main entrance to the town were gaily dressed boys and girls in the costume of the olden days. They were posed for a movie scene that had one of the girls slapping a boy after he tried to trip the girl with the stock of his rifle. This was being filmed for TV, but where it was to be shown, I was unable to discover.

I greatly enjoyed my tour of the town. I returned to the camera store to check on the operation of the existing camera. The new camera was sold for $153.67 and the leather case for $7.86. I bought both for $160. I left my broken camera to be sent to Dresden, Germany, in the Russian zone, to be repaired. They were to send it to my home in Saint Louis when it was fixed, and I would send a check to pay for the expenses of shipping and labor upon my returning home.

I walked to the hostel and assembled my belongings. A road junction five hundred meters away was the next place in which I tried my luck for a ride. After a fifteen-minute wait, a US Army truck stopped, and I hopped aboard to occupy the wooden benches with six other soldiers. They were on their way to Crailshelm; all they could do was complain about army life. Though the ride was bumpy, I was thankful to be on my way again.

I was left off twenty-two kilometers from Dinkelsbühl. It wasn't long before I had a ride taking me thirteen kilometers to a small town, where I again found myself on a highway that was more like a country road. I sat down to eat the snack that was packed the previous day by the American couple, Mr. and Mrs. Bielawski from Ochsenfurt, who had given me the hand-painted tie and served an American lunch.

Shortly, a car with two salesmen stopped and took me to Dinkelsbühl, where I was left off at the railroad station. Being behind schedule, I decided to make train connections to Balingen as it was now twelve forty-five. A train was due at twelve fifty-one, but I discovered we had to go north in order to go south. In thirty minutes, I was back in Crailshelm, where the next train was due at 2:44 p.m. The conductor told me the train was first going to Ulm before going to Stuttgart, and it would be best for me to take the train going directly to Stuttgart at five eighteen, which would arrive only eleven minutes later than the one going first to Ulm. This sounded like a sensible suggestion, and checking my baggage, I went to a small store for a half-liter of milk, four rolls, and a dish of ice cream.

I walked through the small town and inquired as to the quality of frames for my glasses. I was told of a store in Balingen, where I might purchase the best brand. I returned to the railroad station to wait for the train, and in the course of waiting, I met six servicemen who had just been released from the jail. They had served two months for drunkenness after getting into a brawl on a train shortly after arriving in Germany with the Sixth Airborne Division. The six of them had only the equivalent of 12¢ among them; it was easy to see they were depressed with army life. One soldier had only four days to serve before he would have been discharged when he was arrested.

At five ten I inquired what track my train was coming in on, only to be told that the five eighteen was no longer running. Needless to say, I was boiling mad! To further raise my blood pressure, I was told that if I wanted my money back, I would only be able to obtain it in Balingen. The stationmaster marked my train ticket as such, and I left the station quite peeved at the outcome of things. Of all the dumb tricks to happen to me, the conductor should have known if a train was still running or not.

I unchecked my baggage and walked to the highway headed to Stuttgart with a mark of determination. In less than five minutes, I was offered a ride but was only taken twelve kilometers. Shortly after, I was offered a ride to where I was conveniently dropped off on the edge of the city, at the base of a steep hill.. Again, within minutes, I was picked up by a florist in a Volkswagen bus. He was on his way to Ulm, fifteen kilometers to the south but bypassing Stuttgart.

On the way we stopped for coffee and rolls before arriving in Ulm at 9:05 p.m. We went directly to the railroad station in hopes that I could get a train to Balingen. I was informed a train was leaving at nine thirty-one, only it was going in a roundabout way, going first to Plochingen and then to Tubingen. It was the only train leaving, so I bought a ticket but was running low on marks and was befriended by an American man standing in line also, who exchanged two of my American dollars.

I hurriedly said good-bye to the very kind florist who had befriended me. I felt bad as I had forgotten his name and address as I boarded the train with one minute to spare. Within the hour, I changed trains and found myself sitting beside Manfred Kaun, a twenty-four-year-old boy from Kempton, who asked me to visit him if I came near his town.

I arrived in Tubingen at 11:42 p.m. but had to wait until 4:44 a.m. for a train that would take me to Balingen. The railroad station was deserted except for a bearded bum sitting on a wooden bench in the waiting room, who made known his presence by a series of loud snores.

I stretched out on another bench for some needed rest only to be awakened an hour later by a policeman who wanted to know if I needed a hotel for the night. I informed him I was waiting for the 4:44 a.m. train, which evidently met with his approval, for he allowed me to remain in the waiting room, but not so for the sleeping bum. He was awakened and marched off with the policeman; meanwhile, I struggled to get back to sleep on the hard bench.

July 7—Warm, Clear, and Humid

I awoke at 4:00 a.m. after a very restless and uncomfortable night on a wooden bench in the railroad station of the town Tubingen. I bought a ticket to Balingen and boarded the train, reaching Balingen at six two. On the way, the Hohenzollern Castle was a standout on the mountain as we passed quite near the place the Hahn family had visited the year before.

Once in Balingen, I received my refund on the train ticket bought the day before and also bought a ticket to Endingen, a small town that would put me within walking distance of Rosswangen, the German village I was to visit, as it was the birthplace of my grandfather. Our family had been there only last year, but the true warmth and primitive living of these people who had so little yet did so much for others could not keep one away for long.

It was only a five-minute train ride from Balingen to Endingen and a three-kilometer walk from Endingen to Rosswangen. I had left Balingen at 6:34 a.m., and after the short ride to Endingen, I found myself walking up a sloping grade, but with my goal in sight, I tried not to become tired.

Halfway there I came upon a man working on the road. He stopped me and asked if I wasn't Joseph Hahn. I told him I was, and he replied he was a Butz, a relative of Elfriede Butz, a girl I had met last year at a dance. He put my knapsack on his back and the suitcase across the handlebar of his motorcycle and took them to the Effinger home, the place where I was to stay while visiting Rosswangen, while I walked on into town by myself.

I approached the cemetery and entered the town, bringing back fond memories of my previous visit. I felt funny walking through the town all alone, but few people were around as they were working in the fields. It was now 7:00 a.m.

As I came to the Effinger home, I was met by Juhlean, my grandfather's sister. She put her arms around me and hugged me as I was shown into the house. Little Anna came running toward me with the mail that had come—five letters, three from home and two from Grandma and Aunt Lizzie.

A pot of cocoa and some pretzels were served as breakfast as I sat down to rest and read the mail. What a breakfast—at 7:30 a.m. too!

I was shown to my room, which turned out to be their living room, in the house of Joseph and Elise Effinger. Dad's cousin and cousin by marriage. I washed and then rode a bicycle to get the package of clothes sent from England to lighten my load. It had been sent to Elfriede Butz's home along with a letter telling her when to expect me.

Arriving at her home, I was met by her sister Theresia and then her mother, Josefine. Elfriede and her other sister, Agnes, were working in the field. After telling them it was good to see them again, I left, saying I would return later in the day.

The Butz Family of Rosswangen, Germany
after a hard day of working in the field.

Back at the Effingers', I unpacked and rested until Joseph, Elise, and the others returned from the fields. I gave baby Berhardt the doll I had won on the ship and gave little Anna some bubble gum and candy.

At eleven o'clock, I went to see Elfriede. I was given the rest of my mail, after which we talked and drank wine before taking a walk into the field, from where we could see the surrounding countryside and Rosswangen, nestled in the valley. It was nice being together again. We could not spend too much time with each other as she had to be at a wedding that afternoon.

I returned to the Effingers' and worked in the fields under a very hot sun until six o'clock, before we all returned to town. I drank a bottle of Sprudel (fizzy soda water) and then went to see the Butz family. I talked with Theresia and Agnes as Elfriede had not returned from the wedding in Balingen. I helped them in the field next to their house until nine o'clock.

The Effingers were having dinner at nine o'clock, and I hurried so as not to be late. Dinner consisted of two bowls of soup and four fried eggs that were made to perfection. They were going through so much trouble for me; I constantly told them to make me the food they normally ate, but this went unheard, for someone was always making something American style.

These people literally worked twelve to fifteen hours a day and had little to come home to before they were again in the fields. I was sleeping in Elise's bed, while she was sleeping on the floor with a blanket and feather covers, which further made me feel like I was an *inconvenience*.

Thanking Elise for dinner, I returned to the Butz home via bicycle for brandy and fresh wine, which we enjoyed until the hour became late. Since none of us could understand the English and German spoken by the other, the need of an English-to-German and a German-to-English dictionary was necessary.

The short ride to the Effinger house, without the aid of a light, on the bicycle was difficult only in regard to seeing that I did not hit a manure pile, as these were formed in front of each house to provide a means of fertilizing their fields. This was done by having the downspout from the roof drain water through a pipe, allowing it to seep through the manure and into a well beneath the manure. In the spring, this rich mixture was pumped into a "honey wagon" and spread on the fields. A "honey wagon" is a large wooden barrel (aid on its side with small holes to allow the mixture to drip onto the field when pulled by oxen, after the barrel was placed on a cart.

And so ended another day.

July 8—Clear and Very Warm, Possibly Hot

I awoke at eleven forty-five and had lunch of noodle soup, meat, gravy, noodles, sliced apples, salad, sliced cucumber, and dessert of strawberries and pudding. This was served in the old house, as the entire family ate together.

In the afternoon, I went with Elfriede to a shady place in the field, where we played badminton. We then walked through the dark woods to a berry patch and onto the top of the sloping hills, where one could have an excellent view of the valley.

We arrived at her home at six thirty. I was invited to stay for dinner, which consisted of bread, butter, various cold cuts, and cold cider. Not having told Elise that I was invited for dinner at the Butz home, I returned in time to have another dinner with her. This dinner consisted of hot soup and a large bowl of fresh strawberries and a bottle of Sprudel.

Franz and Rosalie Effinger, Dad's other cousin and cousin by marriage, had asked me to visit them, but they were still in the field, picking strawberries, at this late hour. When it became so dark that it was impossible to see, then and only then did they come inside their home.

Rosalie served strawberries and Sprudel as unexpected guests arrived. We sat and talked until 10:00 p.m., and although my German was not too good, I was told that what I said was understood.

I returned to the Butz household, where I had left my camera, and then came home for a restful night. The experience of travel was beginning to show its effects as the weary traveler was taking shorter steps.

The blanket that was on the bed was filled with feathers and provided nearly a foot of cover. The bed was a welcome sight to fatigued Joe. I was tired.

July 9—Warm and Pleasant

I was up at ten for an adequate breakfast of three eggs, bread, butter, and large pot of cocoa. I straightened up my room, unpacking a suitcase that had only been partly done when I arrived.

I wrote a letter home and rode a bicycle to the post office then continued on to help work in the fields with Franz, Rosalie, and big Anna. I raked, pitched hay, and even drove the tractor. We worked until the two wagons were filled with cut hay. Returning to the house, I packed a box of heavy clothes to be sent to Saint Louis, which would lighten my load.

Franz Effinger preparing to load his wagon with recently cut hay. The town of Rosswangen can be seen in the distance. This picture was taken by Joe on his 1955 trip to Rosswangen, Germany, and was given to an artist to be painted and framed as a gift to his parents on the celebration of their 25th wedding anniversary on June 1, 1957. The painting now hangs in the living room of Joe and Nubia as a remembrance of his visits to the birthplace of his relatives.

I began mapping out a route of travel to Vienna and, from there, back through Italy and Switzerland when I was called to the door by a constant knocking and ringing of the bell. To my surprise, I found little Anna and six of her friends standing before me, asking for *kaugummi*. I gave them each a piece of the bubble gum they were trying to ask for and asked them to pose for a picture. When the gum became soft after it was chewed, the children pulled it into long pieces. They were having quite a time. The children saved the wrappers and funnies as I watched them from my window.

I returned to the task of mapping out a route, but it wasn't long before the doorbell rang again. This time word had gotten around town that I had bubble gum, and most of the children were gathered outside. Joseph Effinger was now home from work and explained to the children that I would come to the school during recess period in the morning to give away some more gum.

Elise had prepared an evening meal, but I could only eat a small portion as I had eaten with Franz and Rosalie at 5:00 p.m. They had asked me for dinner when they returned from the field but were soon to return and work until dusk.

Going to the Butz home, I wrote several American poems and let the girls translate them into German. The radio was on, and we listened to good music.

Leaving here, I saw the carpenter whom I had met last year; we talked briefly before I went home to pile my dirty clothes by the door. Elise wanted to soak them now and wash in the morning. I told her I would wash in the morning, but she insisted on doing it for me. Thanking her in advance, I climbed into bed without the thick blanket and was soon asleep.

July 10—Warm and Partly Cloudy

Elise awoke me at eight fifteen, but I managed to remain in bed until eight forty before arising for breakfast of four eggs, honey milk, bread, jelly, and a piece of breaded veal.

I gave my dirty clothes to Elise as she insisted on washing them. Meanwhile, I walked to the school with the bubble gum given to me by Mac Brown, the filling station owner back home, and some of the taffy my sister Janet had given me. As I neared the school, the children crowded around, knowing what I had for them. Mac Brown had asked me to give bubble gum to the schoolchildren as he had heard the children of Germany had a great desire to blow bubbles and stretch the used gum.

As the noise of the school yard gave way to their eagerness, the schoolteacher appeared in the doorway. I asked her permission to give the children the gum, thinking that it might possibly be best for her to give the gum to the children. She instructed them not to chew it in the school as I distributed the whole bag of gum and taffy. Eager eyes beamed, and shouts of "Bitte" (please) and "Kaugummi" filled the air.

The children formed in front of the school, and I took a picture. The schoolteacher hurriedly combed her hair to be in the other pictures.

I then went to see Hans, the carpenter, whom I was to meet at 11:00 a.m. for a trip to Balingen, as we had talked the night before and suggested I go to Balingen with him instead of going on a bicycle as I had planned.

We made the trip to Balingen in his new Volkswagen. I was left off at Metger Optic, where I purchased new glass frames, glasses, and had my eyes tested. The price for this was 65 DM, $15.60.

I then went to Volks Bank to get some marks for my traveler's checks, after which I walked to a nearby park to rest. I had made arrangements to see Elfriede at work and had some time to spare. While resting on a park bench, I noticed a couple dressed in black with some flowers, the man in a tall silk hat, and a priest carrying a prayer book walking beside them. Thinking that a wedding was scheduled during the afternoon, I didn't pay too much attention.

However, in the process of sitting in the park for half an hour, I saw many women dressed in black pass by. I became curious and followed one to a church, where the wedding was just about to begin. It was an old custom for people to dress in black for a wedding. I entered the graveyard surrounding the church and listened to the music while admiring the beautiful flowers.

I left for Elfriede's office and stopped to buy some pretzels and jelly rolls on the way, arriving at her place of business at 1:30 p.m. I was given a bottle of Sprudel as we talked in the back-office room. She combed her hair and was ready to leave as she had asked to have the day off, explaining to her boss that I was coming to see her from America.

We walked through town, stopping at the Thum Hotel for a few drinks on their patio. Before leaving, Elfriede excused herself to go to the restroom, during which time I paid the bar bill. When she returned to the table shortly thereafter, I suggested we leave as it was getting late. She reminded me to pay the bill, but I told her it was better to leave without paying. Well, she wouldn't budge from her chair. I got up and started to leave, but she continued to remain seated. I slowly left the hotel to see if she would follow me, but after I had gone a good distance, she went inside the hotel to check with the manager to see if I had paid the bar bill.

Elfriede and her car in front of her office.

Elfriede at town fountain, ready for a Sunday drive.

Laughing quite heartily over this, we walked to the park, where we sat and talked until five o'clock, and then returned to her office, stopping for two more jelly rolls and a piece of cherry crumb cake.

The clouds had formed very quickly, and rain began falling as we waited for a bus that would take us to Rosswangen. To our surprise, Joseph, the man at whose home I was staying, was the bus driver. It was now six ten as the time had passed quickly. Joseph would not let us pay the bus fare, which was fine with us.

The evening meal consisted of buttermilk and bread, but I was shortly given a substitute of meat as I could not stomach the buttermilk—not a favorite of mine.

I went to see the Butz family and walked with the girls before the rain sent us back to the house. We listened to American music and drank wine and cognac until it was time for me to make my way through the dark streets to get home and climb into bed.

July 11—Cloudy with Rain

I awoke at nine thirty and found breakfast waiting for me. I again had breaded veal, four eggs, honey milk, bread, and butter. Finding time to write some letters, I informed my family and Grandma just what I had been doing. It wasn't long until lunch was prepared by Anna as Juhlean joined us for egg soup, apples, and fresh doughnuts.

Because I was feeling a cold coming on, Anna rubbed my chest with Vicks salve, and I lay down for an hour's rest. I awoke to rewrite my expense account and study my maps until Joseph and Elise came home from work.

We had dinner of assorted meats, tomatoes, and cut lettuce. I then went to pick up Elfriede to bring her to the Effinger home for a farewell gathering. When I arrived at her home, all the lights were out, and it led one to believe no one was at home. Elfriede answered my knock and led me to the living room, where strands of colored lights were turned on.

On the table were four glasses and colored lights as centerpiece. At one end of the table, small green peppermint leaves were arranged to spell "Auf wiedersehen," which meant "until we meet again." We drank cognac and then two glasses of wine as Mother Butz, Agnes, Theresia, and Elfriede were dressed in their best clothes.

I thanked them all and said, "Sorry for not being able to remain longer," and Elfriede came with me to the Effinger home, where Anna, Franz, Rosalie, Joseph, Elise, little Anna, and baby Berhardt were waiting for us. We talked and talked, having many good laughs. We were served a green drink (quinquina) and then beer as we continued our merrymaking until 11:30 p.m. *Quinquina* is a green wine that contains tree bark with quinine in it and is normally served as a before- or after-dinner drink.

I thanked everyone for all they had done for me during my visit as they would be gone in the morning, having to be at work by seven o'clock. I walked Elfriede to her home, where she kissed me and gave me a red rose, wishing me a safe journey. She also asked if I wouldn't send her some American stamps for her collection. Elfriede had pulled me to the corner of the living room for our good-night and good-bye kisses as she reminded me her mother would be looking through the large keyhole to observe our fond good-bye. She must know her mother well!

I returned home, dodging mud puddles, and hurriedly retired for the last time in Rosswangen. It has been a wonderful experience and one I should not easily forget. What happy people these poor people were!

July 12—Cloudy, Clearing, and Warmer

Elise awoke me at eight thirty and served a wonderful breakfast of breaded veal, three eggs, rolls, honey, and honey milk. She then helped me pack as my clothes had all been washed and ironed. I was given some gift soap, which they sold to the people of Rosswangen. Elise had been more than a mother to me; my socks and pants had been mended, and my shoes were shined every day. What a worker she was, hardly taking any time for rest!

Outside it was cloudy, but there was no rain. I went to see Johnan, who lay in bed, quite sick. Johnan was my grandfather's brother, who remained in Germany with her sister Juhlean, as his other brothers and sisters came to the United States. I took a time exposure of him and one of Juhlean at his bedside, whom I asked to sit still but who excitedly waved her hands as the time exposure was being made.

I shook hands with Johnan, knowing I would never see him alive again. I felt funny as I was presented a bouquet of flowers by Berhardt and little Anna as my suitcase and knapsack were placed in a small handmade wooden wagon. Elise, Anna, little Anna, and Berhardt were to accompany me to Endingen, where I would begin hitchhiking again.

Juhlean had tears in her eyes as she too sensed she would never see me again, as she was eighty-three years old and Johnan was eighty. The group posed for a picture before we left. The wagon was pulled through the town while Elise pushed the baby carriage with Berhardt. Little Anna rode her bicycle as she had come home from school to see me leave.

We slowly made our way to Endingen and headed for the highway that led to Rottweil. As we neared the highway, Anna saw a car coming and suggested I try for a lift. I raised my USA suitcase and indicated I wanted a ride, and to my amazement, the car stopped.

I hurriedly crossed the highway as I had flagged him down from the wrong side of the road. As I put my suitcase and knapsack into the car, Anna and Elise crossed the highway and wished me a safe journey as well as told me to convey their greetings to the relatives in Saint Louis.

The driver stopped in Rottweil so I might mail the package of heavy clothing to the States and continued as far as Schwenningen, where he lived. In a few minutes, I was offered a ride to the city of Donaueschingen, where I was left in the center of town.

I walked until I became tired, hoping to get a ride, for it was difficult to obtain rides within a city. People gazed at me, more out of curiosity from the suitcase with the USA in large letters and my height more than for anything else.

Within fifteen minutes, a Volkswagen with two women stopped, but the car was loaded with packages, and I was sure there was no room for me. She had pulled to the side of the road and remarked she couldn't leave one of her boys standing along the road. All her belongings were stuffed in the front trunk, while the remaining items were piled on the roof rack. I climbed in the backseat, after which the remaining parcels were piled on my lap. The driver's name was Lillian Sheppard from Los Angeles. She had some friends in Saint Louis by the name of Mallinckrodt, who were in the chemical business, living at 16 Westmoreland Place.

When she came to a fork in the road where she was turning, she stopped and began halting other cars at a narrow passageway, trying to get me another lift. The road was so narrow only one-way traffic could proceed, yet she succeeded in asking several people, but all of them were going in the wrong direction.

After her unsuccessful attempt, she gave me a bag of apricots, and I was soon to be walking along the road with some German boys who were also hitchhiking. I shared the fruit with them as one of the boys carried my suitcase. We walked to the edge of town, where getting a lift would be easier. At their suggestion, the three of us did not stand together as getting a ride would be easier if we were separated.

As they walked along the road, a car with four people stopped for me. It had not been more than a few minutes when I was picked up by these people who looked like Germans. I began speaking German to them only to find that they were speaking English. My suitcase was stood on end in the front seat with two women. As things turned out, these people were from New Jersey and were now on their way to the Bodensee at Konstanz, near the German-Swiss border.

I had not planned on going this route but thought it would be exciting to go through Switzerland on my way to Austria. They were very lovely people, and we talked and joked about me taking them for Germans when I entered the car. On the other hand, they thought I was a German boy when I approached the car since I was speaking German. They had not seen the USA suitcase.

They were going to a factory in Konstanz and unfortunately left me in the center of the city. I asked a policeman the way to Bregenz and a route out of the city. He suggested I take a city bus, and walking me to a bus line, he waited to tell the conductor where to let me off. Wasn't that nice?

Alighting from the bus, I inquired at a BP filling station the way to Bregenz and was directed along a main road only to find myself at the Swiss border. Here I showed my passport and continued on foot. I stopped at the edge of town to eat a sandwich Elise had packed. A car stopped but wasn't going to Bregenz for another hour; they would, however, pick me up if I was still waiting for a ride when they passed again.

Two minutes later, Doc F. Peter from Berlin and his wife from Switzerland picked me up and took me to Arbon. He related he had been captured during the last war and was a prisoner of war in Texas for a year.

As I left them, I was given a ham sandwich and also informed that they had gone out of their way to drop me at a good location so I might obtain a ride easily. There I was on the highway again.

My sixth ride of the day came in a few minutes as an old man took me to Rorschach and left me beside the Bodensee. It was a beautiful sight, but cloudy weather made photography poor.

After a train had blocked traffic for a while, the cars once more appeared on the highway. A car traveling fairly fast stopped one hundred feet ahead and motioned for me to get in the car, but at the same time, another car stopped for me only a scant ten feet from where I stood. I chose the latter car driven by Olaf Rohmer from Lindau, Germany. I was taken to Bregenz while finding time to stop for pictures along the way.

In Bregenz, Olaf tooted at a man in a sports car who had passed him a few minutes previously. To further get his attention, he passed him and tooted some more, finally making himself understood, that he wanted the sports car to stop. Olaf went to the man and asked if he wouldn't take me as far as he was going, which turned out to be Feldkirch. It was only thirty-five kilometers away, but I'd never been so scared in my life! His six-month-old sports car zoomed along between 120 and 150 kilometers (seventy-two to ninety miles per hour) along the country roads, possibly slowing to one hundred kilometers when we went through towns. I was indeed thankful to arrive safely in Feldkirch.

I began hitchhiking in town but was told it would be better at the city limits. I had to walk on a narrow highway to reach the edge of the city and was shortly picked up by a family from Innsbruck, Austria, who could only take me to Bludenz as they contracted business there.

Again I walked to the edge of town, hoping for a ride. Soon a car driven by a young girl stopped for me, but she was going in a different direction. I was now 150 kilometers from Innsbruck, and it was early evening. As it became dark, a car occupied by three civil engineers from Innsbruck stopped and offered to take me along to their destination.

This was my tenth lift of the day. These men had been working on a power project in Western Austria and were now on their way home. We headed into the mountains and were met up with dense fog and bad weather. At the top of the pass, we stopped for cognac and continued on only to find much better weather. A rainbow shone brightly, and we stopped on a lookout curve to photograph the spectacle.

We continued on to a small village, where we had two beer for one DM 24¢ and a bowl of soup for 15¢. As I had no Austrian money, the three civil engineers paid for my food and drink. It was only an hour's drive to Innsbruck, and the driver, Walter, left Fred and his friend, Paul Stritz, the only one who could speak English, off with me in the center of the city. Paul walked with me to the Gasthof Sailer Hotel, where I found a room with double beds and a washstand for $1.04. I thanked Paul and went to the room located on the fifth floor, eighty-eight steps from the ground floor, and was soon sleeping and getting some needed rest, for it was now midnight and I had come a good distance in one day.

July 13—Warm and Clear

I awoke at 9:00 a.m. and washed in a hand basin after fetching water from the hallway faucet. Then I dressed and took pictures of mountains from my hotel window. I went to the bank and then walked into an old section where one year ago, I had also made my journey. I strolled down Maria Theresa Street to the Inn River, where I saw an art truck from Vienna. I waited for the driver to return in hopes I could obtain a ride to Vienna, but he wasn't leaving until next week. I was, however, welcome to ride to Vienna with him then.

I next saw a young woman from Vienna parking her car, and when I asked her for a ride, she replied it would be two weeks before she returned home. You might wonder how I could tell a car was from Vienna. Well, my clue was the large white *W* on the license plate that indicated the car was registered in Wien, the Austrian spelling for Vienna.

I asked another truck driver for a ride but again had no luck, so I returned to the hotel. On the way I passed a sausage shop and bought two ham sandwiches on a bun for five cents each. I gave the man five shillings (20¢), to which he asked if I had any smaller change since he didn't have the correct change. He gave me one shilling but still owed me some money, so he gave me two pieces of candy to make up the difference.

My hotel bill was 26.80 or $1.07. I paid this amount and headed for Highway 1, the highway that would take me to Wien. I was walking through the main section of Innsbruck and just crossing a street when I saw a car with a big white *W* pulling away from the curb.

Without thinking twice, I hurried back across the street and walked slowly in front of the car and stopped alongside the vehicle. The window was rolled down, and I asked if they were going to Vienna. The driver said no. I then asked if I could ride with him as far as he was going. He replied he was going to Salzburg on business and would be unable to take me along.

Not wanting to give up, I then told him I was lost in the city and would appreciate directions or a ride to the outskirts of Innsbruck. The two men looked at each other and said, "Get in." The back door of the four-door Opel Sedan was opened, and I was again on my way. I had only expected to go to the edge of town, but not a word was said, and I soon found myself breezing along the countryside. Salzburg was 153 kilometers away, and I knew I would soon be there. I really talked myself into getting this important lift.

My lift—or rather my *forced* lift—was being "offered" by a Dr. Walter Gatterer and his friend, who were with the Hass Tapestry Business. Their firm had furnished the opera house in Vienna. We rode quite fast, but I was still informed of the interesting sights along the way. Since the doctor was going into Salzburg proper, he suggested I get off at the border near Berchtesgaden, where all cars must stop. He thought it would be a better place to obtain a ride from rather than along the highway.

He asked the border police if I could wait at the border; furthermore, he told them to try to get me a ride to Vienna, which I didn't find out until later, for at that time I saw a policeman talking to a man who had just stopped to have his passport stamped. Both came toward me. The man asked where I was going and replied he could only take me to Linz. Asking if I was alone, he then motioned me to follow him to his car. I thanked the border police of Germany and climbed into the car with Lt. Gil Hall and his wife from Maine, who was now stationed in Livorno, Italy.

They were on their way to Linz to visit friends and to adopt a baby. We also traveled at a good speed, bypassing Salzburg and covering the 118 kilometers to Linz with little trouble. Midway, we stopped for a rest and a glass of beer, while their dog, Penny, also found time to relax. Before leaving, I bought four sugar rolls in a bakery.

Mrs. Hall took over the driving. Of course, we were now going slower, but it wasn't long before we arrived at a fork leading to Linz or Wien, the place where I was to be left off, and as we stopped, an American car from Virginia struck a motorcycle, knocking the driver some twenty feet to the ground. We rushed to the scene, where I took some pictures as a crowd quickly gathered to offer aid and assistance.

I left Gil and his wife after thanking them and soon found myself interested in the happenings of the accident, the first I had seen while on this European trip.

After the police and an ambulance came, I stood by the roadside, hoping to catch a ride with a car from Vienna. One car with a *W* was parked nearby, but they were not going to Wien, only to Linz. I rode with them to a better intersection. After a thirty-minute wait, during which time a small group of boys stood around me and did nothing but stare, a car similar to our Crosley stopped, and I was taken three kilometers by a young woman of twenty-five to another big intersection, where outgoing cars to Vienna would be passing. I thanked her and headed for the main corner.

There stood two Austrian boys who were trying to hitch a ride. As I approached, a truck stopped for them. I took over the spot occupied by the boys, hoping I would have as good a fortune as them. To my surprise, the boys were left off down the road and walked back to where they had stood. I wasn't about to move!

They gave me a dirty look and stood twenty to thirty feet in front of me. I had a few nibbles of a ride where a car would slow down but no one would stop. After forty-five minutes of unsuccessful hitchhiking, the two boys nodded heads and walked down the highway, leaving the busy intersection all to myself.

Luck was no better until a small green car that had passed a few minutes before made a U-turn, passed me on the other side of the street, made another U-turn, and pulled alongside my suitcase. There were three people in the car, and I could see no room for me or my belongings. The trunk was not large enough for my suitcase, but my knapsack was able to fit there.

I sat in the front seat with the suitcase on my lap. Two women sat in the back of the small car. The woman who talked the most was Jenny Kopriwa; her brother-in-law was doing the driving. They only took me twenty-five kilometers, but most of the time, we hovered behind an American Buick with eight colored men. My driver kept tooting and waving at the men, hoping they would stop so I might continue to ride to Vienna with the colored men, but I did my best to discourage their efforts, not wanting to hurt their feelings for what they were trying to do. I kept saying "I don't think there is enough room for an extra passenger," but my friends kept tooting and waving. Once we managed to pull alongside the Buick, luckily, my Austrian friends were not understood by the Buick driver.

The colored men thought we were playing games for they laughed at us and waved as we followed them along the highway. It wasn't long before we arrived at the town where my Austrian friends lived. I was told I could remain overnight with them, but since they were leaving at 5:00 a.m. for a trip into the mountains near Salzburg, I thought it best to decline the offer.

They parked the car at the side of the road, and all stood on the highway, waving cars with a *W* to a halt. Each one would be asked to take me, their American friend, to Vienna as it was important I reached Vienna that night. Most of the cars were crowded, but I wondered what people thought of these people as they motioned for drivers to stop. Drivers first might have thought we had car trouble, but it wasn't long before they got the idea the whole bunch of us was crazy or we were out to rob them. Jenny showed the most interest as she ran alongside cars, yelling, "Hello, hello."

This whole operation was taking place on a hill, and fearing an accident, I suggested I try the old way of hitchhiking, which had proved quite adequate in the past. As time dragged on and we were getting nowhere, my fifth suggestion that I try to hitchhike finally convinced my friends I might be right. I thanked them for their trouble and watched them drive into the town a short distance away.

It was now 6:30 p.m., and I was still 192 kilometers from Wien. I had made up my mind to stop for the day if by seven o'clock, I had not been picked up. At six fifty, however, almost as if a dream come true, a large sedan stopped. There was the *W* staring me in the face from the license plate, and I hurriedly placed my suitcase in the backseat as the driver, Franz Diemat, a tailor, said "Nach Wien," which meant "to Vienna."

Soon we were on our way. Everything had worked out perfectly for me, as for the first time, I realized it was Friday the thirteenth! I relaxed and listened to music. Trains stopped us twice, but the destination was now much closer to reality.

When we were seventy-two kilometers from Wien, Franz suggested a coffee break. We stopped at a roadside café for Meinl Espresso—much too strong for me—but I drank it since Franz was buying. In my 1955 trip to Europe, I had met aboard a ship Thomas Meinl, the son of Julius Meinl, owner of this well-known coffee company, who had given me his business card. I always felt obliged to purchase his brand of coffee even though it was too strong for my taste buds.

Returning to the car, we washed the bugs from the windshield and continued on to Vienna. I had informed Franz I was to stay with Dr. Walter Hynek and family, but since this was nowhere near his home, he drove me to a café in the center of the city and called them, telling them where to pick me up. I thanked Franz and spoke briefly with Dr. Hynek on the phone, saying I could come to his home on the tram, but he insisted on meeting me at the café and said he would pick me up shortly.

As I waited for Dr. Hynek to arrive, I drank beer and read *Life* magazine. Within fifteen minutes, the doctor joined me in a cup of coffee and insisted on paying for the drinks, my third bought drink of the day.

We arrived at his home and met his wife, but their three children were sleeping, as it was now 11:00 p.m. His charming wife, Elfriede, made me a dinner of fried ham and eggs while I took my first bath in ten days since I left Berlin!

The three of us talked while I ate the delicious dinner. We then sat in the living room and drank gin until 2:00 a.m., which found us all feeling quite well.

My room and bed were quite inviting, and I headed there for a *gut schlaf* (good sleep). I had traveled from Rosswangen to Wien in a day and a half—quite a distance—and I had pieced one piece of luck to another with the net result that I had reached my destination!

July 14—Warm and Partly Cloudy

Elfriede woke me up at nine thirty for breakfast of scrambled eggs, which were served in a quaint style, on a table set in the shade of the trees overshadowing the driveway. Dr. Hynek, whom I shall now proceed to call Walter, came shortly, and we greatly enjoyed the good cooking. They explained that most of the breakfasts and lunches during the summer were served in the driveway (patio), which was located next to the kitchen.

I straightened up my room and met their three children, Edda, Eva, and Erika. Elfriede (the mother), Walter, Erika, and I went shopping at the market square for fresh fruits. We stopped to buy some pickles, which were sold like one would expect to see candy sold in America. We walked through the square, eating the pickles like it were an everyday item or common snack. The square had many small huts were people sold their wares. This was quite in contrast to our supermarkets and was very interesting as people came to the square with large shopping bags and handled everything, trying to get the best product.

We next went to a bakeshop located on the narrowest street in Vienna, in one of the oldest sections. Continuing on, we had a general tour of the city and returned home around noon. Walter called the restaurant where a waitress I had met the year before worked. He inquired if Frauline Traute Zellinger was there but was informed no one by that name worked there; he was, however, told that a Traute Zellinger worked at the restaurant. Boy, the person who answered the phone certainly didn't use her head!

Walter spoke with Traute on the phone and informed her I was now in Vienna, staying with them, and that I would like to see her. Furthermore, Dr. Hynek extended an invitation to Traute for dinner at the Hynek's home, to be followed by dancing in the nearby village of Grinzing for tonight.

She accepted the invitation and said she would be at the Hynek home at seven o'clock. I then spoke with her and tried to explain why I was unable to arrive in Vienna when I had planned, for she had come to the Hynek home the previous week, thinking I was in Vienna, as I had written I would be there at that time. When she heard no further word from me, she took it upon herself to locate my whereabouts. I had anticipated arriving in Vienna somewhere between the eighth and twelfth of July. It was now the fourteenth, and Traute had taken a two-day leave from her job, thinking I was in Vienna. We were glad that things were straightened out, and we looked forward to seeing one another that evening.

Dr. Hynek told me that Traute's mother was a patient of his, and she had paid a visit to his office, asking about me also, and extended an invitation for dinner for me after I arrived.

Walter and I walked down the street to the wine gardens on a hill overlooking Vienna. From this vantage point, a good view of the city was obtained, and the huge wheel (the Wiener Riesenrad, which means the "Vienna giant wheel") could be seen. More about this structure later.

Returning home, I was then taken on a personal tour of his garden consisting of many fruit trees and berry bushes. His neighbor lived in a $200,000 home served by seven servants. The gate to his driveway worked by remote control, as did various other items within the home. The fence in front of the house was made of frosted glass.

The Hynek home was plain and simple but adequate for his family. His income was not great, but they enjoyed their freedom. The doctor excused himself to do some work in the study while his three daughters again accompanied me to the wine gardens. This time I took some pictures of the interesting sights.

Lunch was served when we returned to their home, and again, a delicious meal was set on the table. In the early afternoon, Walter slept while I sat in the garden and watched his daughters play in the neighbor's swimming pool. Iced tea was served shortly, and Elfriede's parents came for a visit. We enjoyed the pleasant breeze while relaxing in the garden.

Elfriede pressed my trousers and coat while I washed and readied for Traute's arrival. I was waiting when she rang the gate bell at seven o'clock sharp. I accompanied Edda to the front gate to greet Traute; we talked in the living room and took a walk in the garden while dinner was being prepared. I gave her some postcards of Saint Louis, which she had asked me to bring her in one of her letters.

We returned to the house, and I showed her the map of my travels. She had come right from work on the tram and looked quite nice. It wasn't long before Elfriede called us to dinner of fried ham and *gurkensalat* (cucumber), all of which was very tasty. We enjoyed several bottles of beer before dessert was served as we found many things to talk about.

As previously arranged, we left to go dancing at the Musil, a nightclub in Grinzing. Here we shuffled about until we found a good table near the dance floor and ordered a round of gin fizzes. I danced with Traute, but the floor was very crowded, and the floor was quite small. This was overshadowed by the good music and Hungarian interludes. Many old people peddled roses in the nightclub. The club was formally located in the Russian sector, but since the Austrian liberation, it as well as other nightspots were now modern and beautiful.

Walter danced with his wife and Traute, and another round of gin fizzes was ordered before we left the friendly atmosphere at eleven thirty. We walked Traute to a bus stop after Dr. Hynek bought her four long-stemmed roses. It was a common thing to put one's date on a bus or tram after a date if she lived on the other side of the city, which was the situation in this case.

The three of us now walked home and talked of our wonderful evening of song and dance. Oh, what a time I was having in Vienna! All the people were so nice and friendly that I found I was not anxious to leave this fair city.

I had arranged to meet Traute on Monday at 11:00 a.m. in the center of Vienna, at a place convenient to both of us, as she was taking off from work. With this and prospects of a trip into the mountains tomorrow with the Hynek family in mind, I bade them good-night and went to bed.

July 15—Warm and Pleasant

We had planned to arise at 6:30 a.m. to make a trip to Mariazell, where Edda would be the guest of a friend for a week, but somehow, none of us arose until nine o'clock. Then, too, Walter had trouble starting the car, and to top it off, he wanted to wash it also as he did not believe in taking a dirty car on the highway. In fact, every morning except one, Walter washed his car before he went to work! The standing joke of the family was that the car trouble developed from Walter's excess washing.

Elfriede packed a snack for the trip, and after breakfast of scrambled eggs in the shade on the driveway, we took the dog to her parents, filled the car with gas, and were on our way to Mariazell.

We headed south to Graz but turned off the main highway to take a scenic trip through the mountains. We enjoyed a good weather and finally stopped at the small town of Heiligenkreuz, where an old monastery still existed. We toured the grounds and entered the old church, which displayed old Roman architecture. In the courtyard, an old fountain still supplied the people with their water needs.

We continued on the journey that would take Edda to her girlfriend for a week's visit, which constituted the reason for the trip. Soon we stopped along a small stream and spread our blanket on the soft grass and unpacked our lunch, for it was now early afternoon. We had sandwiches and fresh fruit. I took the opportunity to show the girls how to make an orange sandwich, which I had learned from the Dutch girl on the voyage across the Atlantic. Walter took a picture of us relaxing as we enjoyed the fresh air.

Going on, we entered a wooded area called Walstern, a virgin forest that was most beautiful. We stopped several times for better views of the scenery. A slight admission was charged to enter the park, but it was well worth the price. The admission was three Austrian shillings (12¢), but the funny thing was that this toll was collected by a small boy about five years old who operated a log gate; it was such a struggle for him to open the gate, yet he was doing his job.

We arrived in Mariazell at one thirty and ordered Wiener Schnitzel and beer in the hotel restaurant where Edda would be staying as guest of the hotel owners' daughter. All seven of us rode to a nearby lake, and on the way, I saw my second accident between a car and a motorcycle, though this one was not serious.

The girls changed into their swimming suits in the car and went for a refreshing swim while the "old" folks watched. After their short dip, we returned to the hotel. The women chose to go shopping, while Walter and I went up a mountain in a cable car. A delightful view of the valley and mountains could be seen as we slowly made our way to the zenith in the cable car similar to the one we rode in last year in Innsbruck.

Reaching the top, we climbed some stairs inside a monument and went heavenward until we reached the top, landing where a platform with a raised telescope gave us a clear picture of the mountains in all directions.

You could see the ski runs, and we were told the fastest time was two minutes, while it had taken us seven minutes via of the cable car. I took pictures of Walter in his white cap, as he wore it to keep the wind from blowing in his ears. It was the same type of white cap worn by doctors while they were operating on a person, and for him to wear it in public seemed quite silly.

We returned to the hotel, where I had another beer and ham sandwich before visiting a church eight hundred years old. It stood in the center of town and was a main attraction; the inside was redone and presented itself in various outlines of cut glass and mirrors. Personally, it was one of the most beautiful I had ever seen.

Leaving for home, we waved at Edda and her girlfriend, who was coming to Canada in September to study for several years. We came home via a different route, going only 148 kilometers, while coming, it had taken 153 kilometers. The whole trip was 186 miles, and what a wonderful trip it was.

Back at the Hynek home, we sat and talked while drinking three glasses of good Vienna wine, and finding myself fit for a good night's rest, I went to bed.

July 16—Pleasant and Sunny, with Brief Showers in the Afternoon

Mrs. Hynek knocked on my door at nine thirty and informed me my bath was ready, and much to my surprise, I found she had filled the tub with warm water. After a refreshing bath, I went downstairs to be served a breakfast of eggs, rolls, jelly, and Ovaltine.

Mrs. Hynek insisted on pressing my pants for she thought they looked too wrinkled for me to see Traute with, so after a ten-minute wait, I was ready to board tram number 38 to meet Traute at the Ringstrasse, the center of Vienna.

Eva and two of her friends walked me to the tram stop, and on the way, we passed a post office. I asked for three air letters and gave the man a handful of thirty coins, but I was told that I only had enough money for one air letter.

The old, rough, and ready tram came swinging down the tracks as if it were coming apart. Their streetcars were either coupled in two or three sections, and one section might well be swaying to the left while the other was leaning in the other direction. I took the tram to the end of the line where I was to meet Traute at eleven o'clock. I arrived on the corner where the Votivkirche was located, the famous church that had two similar steeples. This was not far from the Hotel Westminster, where we had stayed the previous year.

Traute arrived only a few minutes late, and I promptly took some pictures of her near the famous church. We walked through the

Ringstrasse on to Burggarten, the Rat House, the famous University of Vienna, the also famous opera house, Saint Stephen's Cathedral, and past the Vienna Volksoper, where our family had seen an opera last year.

We were now only two blocks from her aunt's home, and as we were invited for lunch, we hastened our pace as we were tired from our long walk. It was now 1:00 p.m., and after meeting her mother and aunt, Wiener Schnitzel was served. An excellent dinner it was; it was explained to me that the biggest meal of the day was usually served at noontime, which accounted for the fact that this meal seemed to be more than filling. Possibly, they were treating their American guest with the true Austrian hospitality.

I drank two bottles of beer with the dinner and was served fresh fruit as dessert. It was difficult to make myself understood as none of the older people could speak English, and Traute didn't know too much herself.

I offered to help with the dishes but was told to remain seated while Traute and her aunt did the chores. It wasn't long before I fell asleep on the couch for an hour's rest. I was awoken to be served strawberries and a very black coffee, which was quite strong. I was asked what I wanted to do, to which I replied I had a great desire to visit the Prater, their amusement park. I also expressed a desire to ride the Wiener Riesenrad, the huge Ferris wheel that towered over Vienna.

Before leaving, I took some pictures of Traute, her mother, and her aunt in the garden. We walked to the office where Traute's cousin worked, and then the four of us journeyed by tram to the Prater. We enjoyed rides on the Geisterbahn (ghost train) and a roller coaster. We sat in an open café for a refreshing beer and pretzels while talking among ourselves.

The wheel was our next objective. The huge structure normally had thirty cars, each holding twenty-five people, but at present, they were using half of the spaces designed to hold a car since business was not as brisk as it used to be. The fare was five shillings for a complete revolution, which took fifteen minutes. I had been under the impression that the wheel moved faster and was disappointed to find that the person riding the wheel only made one complete revolution. The giant wheel was 212 feet tall, and as I previously said, they had taken off half the cars. In reality, the cars were called gondolas, and when the structure was built, it was designed for thirty gondolas and indeed did operate with thirty gondolas until the war heavily damaged the wheel. When it was reconstructed after the war, only half the original gondolas where replaced, so there was a large space now seen between the gondolas as it operated daily with fifteen, each gondola still carrying a capacity of twenty-five people.

I took Traute on another roller coaster (12¢), and then we were treated to a spook and ghost house trip by Mrs. Zellinger. Next, we rested and had another beer in a garden café for half an hour. Our next stop brought us to the house of mirrors, where we had many laughs before we boarded a tram for the trip to her aunt's home.

I did display good American manners on the tram as I offered my seat to an elderly woman. Back at Traute's aunt's home, we were served an evening meal around nine o'clock of hard boiled eggs, cold cuts, salad, potato salad, and sliced tomatoes. Tea was served with the dinner, and for dessert, sliced bananas and strawberries with cognac were served.

I thanked them all for the wonderful day and the excellent food. Traute and her mother boarded the same tram with me as we both had the same transfer point. They saw that I safely boarded the right tram as we transferred, and it was only twenty minutes before I arrived at the Hynek home, where I spoke briefly with Walter before retiring for the night.

July 17—Cloudy with Light Rain

Again I was awakened to have a refreshing bath, my third in four days! Walter was already at the breakfast table, waiting to enjoy the bacon and eggs his wife had prepared. Leaving the dishes, Elfriede and I then took the tram to the Ringstrasse and visited the famous Demel restaurant to buy food for a dinner party she was giving. We also enjoyed a raspberry dish while waiting for Walter to meet us, but he wasn't there when we finished. We left word we would come back as it was my desire to buy a needlepoint purse for Mother.

We went to a very fine shop Mrs. Hynek knew of, where she could get a 10 percent discount. The first purse I looked at had a price tag of 6,500 shillings, which would be around $250. I was told my taste was very good and proceeded to pick one from the shelf for 8,000, only $307.70. Some of these purses took twenty-two weeks to make, and quite often, one's eyes went bad from doing the delicate work.

Finally, I saw some costing 2,800 or $107.70, and with the discount, it would only cost $96.70. We decided to talk the matter over with Dr. Hynek in the Demel restaurant, where he was now waiting. He suggested we look for cheaper purses and then make a decision about them.

Our next stop was at Mem Parfumerie, where we saw some purses with needlepoint on only one side of the purse. Also of fine quality were some compacts with a needlepoint cover. The lady was very nice and agreed to put the items away until tomorrow, when we would let her know one way or another.

I did buy a wine-drip catcher and two pins for my sisters as well as a display box of wooden matches that were over a foot in length, displayed in a wrought iron holder, which would adorn the living room by the fireplace. These items were wrapped, and we headed for home and soon were eating a lunch of potato soup, stuffed green peppers with rice, and meat covered with a tasty sauce.

I now lay down to rest until 4:00 p.m., when we were invited to the home of nearby friends. A girl from Dublin, Ireland, was the housekeeper, as the wife was having a siege of TB. The name of these friends was Mr. and Mrs. Fritz Götzl. The invitation came about through Eva, who mentioned to one of the Götzl children that I liked to play ping-pong.

Before leaving for their home, I called Traute and made arrangements to visit her mother and father tomorrow between the hour of 3:00 and 4:00 p.m. Then Eva, Erika, and I walked ten minutes to the home of Fritz Götzl. The home was built in 1860 but only last year was completely remodeled. Entrance was gained by passing through a glass gate that was always locked. To enter, you had to press a buzzer that would ring in the house. The person answering the buzz would pick up a phone that would ring at the gate, and the visitor, or whoever might be at the gate, would have to identify himself. Another buzzer in the house controlled the gate lock, which would allow someone to enter.

The lawn far surpassed most American lawns; in fact, the entire home was a beautiful spectacle. I was met by the youngest Götzl boy, Christian, aged six, who promptly asked, "Joe, where is your horse?" Somehow he had the impression that all Americans were cowboys.

I was shown inside the beautiful home and met two of the other three children and the housekeeper. Tommy was twelve and Nike was fifteen, while their good-looking housekeeper, Pauline, was twenty-two. She had been with the family for the past three years as housekeeper and nurse. Being Irish, she was dressed in green and was quite nice looking. It was good to speak to someone who could speak good English for a change.

Tea, sweets, Ritz crackers, stick pretzels, and fresh fruit were put on the table. We talked for a while and then played ping-pong with Eva, who was only thirteen but was very good at the game. The scores of the games were 23–21, 21–16, and 21–10.

We had to play in the garage as it was raining, and our fun ended shortly as Mr. Götzl came home from work in his 1956 Mercury. I introduced myself and was handed a glass of vermouth as we went on a tour of his lovely home. It was equipped with all the modern conveniences one could imagine. Electric buttons controlled the glass gate, and a microphone from the gate to the house let one identify himself; then there were buttons in all the rooms for maid service, which flashed upon an indicator in the kitchen and gave the location of the person requesting a servant to come.

A spacious yard with very old trees presented themselves as part of a beautiful home. These people were most hospitable, and it was difficult to leave, for we were to be at the Hynek home at seven o'clock but didn't come home until 8:00 p.m.

Even with this, we were not late, for the doctor had invited two of his friends to dinner, which wasn't served until eight thirty. Dinner consisted of Mrs. Hynek's own specialty. We were served plum brandy before sitting down for dinner, and with the beer I drank with the main course, I began to feel the effects of drinking too much.

We sat in the parlor, where we were served coffee and ice cream. I was asked to compare Austrian ice cream to American, as the kind served was Vienna's finest. Another doctor arrived, and we continued drinking the good wine. I had three glasses as the discussion centered on finding a Viennese girl for me.

Becoming tired, I excused myself and tried to get some sleep. Flies were buzzing about the room, and I stood guard and swatted them down with marked success. In a few minutes, Mrs. Hynek came rushing into the room, thinking I had fallen out of bed, but when she saw what I was doing, she burst into a sidesplitting laugh.

July 18—Warm and Sunny

I arose at around 10:00 a.m. but remained in bed until noon for I needed rest. Walter and Elfriede had returned from an operation at his office and prepared another bath for me. Elfriede had to be her husband's assistant this week as his regular nurse was on her vacation.

We had an excellent lunch in the shade of trees by the driveway again, and then I took tram number 38 to Traute's aunt's home, arriving there at three fifteen. I had partly become lost but was in the general vicinity of her home when Mrs. Zellinger came running after me. Papa Zellinger had taken the day off from work, and they were a little disappointed when I informed them I could not stay for the evening as I had plans to go with the Hyneks.

Traute had gone to work at 8:00 a.m. instead of eleven so she could leave work at 4:00 p.m. instead of seven. Her aunt had prepared a nice lunch of ham sandwiches and jelly bread. We had our choice of either hot or iced tea, the latter being almost unheard of in Europe. The hot tea was indeed hot, but the iced tea was only cool tea because it was left in a bottle under a running faucet in the hallway fountain. I had noticed this bottle under the fountain when I came but had no idea it was for making cold tea. You see, ice was rarely used in drinks. The climate did not merit the use of ice in drinks; in fact, the beer served was seldom very cold.

Fresh strawberries and wine berries were also served. When Traute arrived, we all walked to the Türkenschanzpark, where we slowly walked through the beautiful grounds, seeing ducks and swans making themselves at home on the ponds. I took pictures of our group and walked to the tram that would take me to the Götzl home. Mrs. Zellinger insisted on coming with me as far as my transfer point and boarded the tram with me. I waved good-bye to Traute, her aunt, and her father, who were all very nice to me.

When I first saw Traute on Saturday, I asked her if I had any mail as I had used her address as a mailing point. She replied, "Yes, one." I asked her to bring it with her on Monday, but she had forgotten, and also on Wednesday, she had forgotten to bring the letter, so as I left Mrs. Zellinger, I asked her to please remind Traute to bring my letter to the restaurant where she worked and I would pick it up tomorrow.

I transferred to tram G2, and it wasn't long before I arrived at the Götzl home. It was now seven o'clock, and Eva and I played ping-pong before we said good-bye, as they were eating and we didn't wish to bother them.

I returned home to dress for a visit to a wine garden nearby as we had arranged to meet the Götzl family there. We were shown to a lovely table in the open wine garden that also had roving musicians. We ordered some wine, and a most delicious wine it was—right from the barrel and very cold. Mrs. Hynek had brought cold cuts and rolls along for a *blotter*, and we thoroughly enjoyed ourselves amid the highly atmosphered wine garden.

As we finished one glass—and a large glass it was (a quarter of a liter)—we were given more and more. We ended up drinking four glasses (one liter), or 1.0567 quarts, apiece, which left us all feeling quite gay. You might say we were all feeling good as we finished the third glass!

The musicians traveled from one table to another, playing pieces on request. For our table they played "It's a Long Way to Tipperary" and "The Stars and Stripes." We left after our fourth glass of wine as Pauline accompanied Walter, Elfriede, and me to Kahlenberg, a nightclub on top of a similar-named mountain for dancing and a good cup of coffee. The evening was a most enjoyable one and one I'd not soon forget. Everyone had been so nice to me, and I had made so many friends I almost hated to leave.

We dropped Pauline off at the Götzl home and shortly arrived at the Hynek home. It was now 1:00 a.m., and it wasn't hard to encourage me to get some sleep as I did feel a little tipsy.

July 19—Partly Cloudy, Warm, and Humid

I awoke at 9:00 a.m. to have breakfast with the family and was then off to the city as both Walter and his wife had business with a lawyer since they recently purchased their home. Of unusual interest was the fact that while their home was unoccupied after the war, a man and his wife had broken down a door and made their home in one of the back rooms. These people continued to live in the Hynek home and could not be evicted. They had bricked up the door that led to the main part of the house and used a side entrance. The Hynek's ended up paying for electricity and water bills as there was only one meter. Austrian law prohibited evicting a family in such a case as this because of some funny technicality.

After a forty-five-minute wait for a fifteen-minute conference, we went to Ruttner, a small shop where Mrs. Hynek often went shopping. There staring us in the face was a beautiful needlepoint purse on display in the window for one thousand shillings. We went inside and asked to have it taken out of the window for a closer inspection, and after deciding to buy it, we also purchased a compact to match the purse as well as some needlepoint pins for Grandma and Aunt Lizzie.

We received a 10 percent discount on all items purchased and then went back to Mem Parfumerie, the store we had visited two days previously, and told them not to hold the purse we had picked out any longer. Here, though, I did buy two ashtrays, a pencil tray, and a letter holder.

Our next stop took us to Saint Stephen's Cathedral, where we were thrilled by the beauty of the old cathedral. Mrs. Hynek commented on the eerie catacombs beneath the church, and to her surprise, I asked if we could visit them. The next tour began at noon, which was only five minutes away, and it wasn't long before we were descending the stairs and passing through an iron door. It was quite cool in the passageway. Our guide explained to us there were two sections, an old and a new. The new had the caskets of the recent cardinals of Wien, having been made cardinals by the pope, whereas the older section of the catacombs was at a lower level. In the old section, we viewed a chamber where five thousand people were piled in the 14th century. It was a ghastly sight to see bones, bones, and more bones. Skulls were also visible and looked quite dry. In another chamber were piled only leg bones, all neat and orderly, one on top of the other, as high as the roof of the chamber.

One would feel funny with nothing but bones of thousands of people around you. Above us was a chute where the caskets and people were passed down to the lower chambers to rot away. We slowly ascended from the dark depths and emerged along the cathedral into sunlight and clean-smelling air.

I was then taken to the café where Traute worked and went to see her for the last time. I asked Traute where I should sit, and she said, "Come." I followed her and found myself in the kitchen. The manager stormed at me, and I was shooed out in a flurry of loud words that I could not understand.

I was led to an outside balcony, where I ordered a beer and ham sandwich as I was sitting at a small table in the shade. The Hotel Westminster was only a block away, and just being in the café where we had eaten the year before brought back fond memories to me.

I drank the refreshing beer and ordered another sandwich. I now asked Traute for my letter, which she was to bring. She replied she had them downstairs and would give them to me when I left.

I was most surprised when she asked if I would give them back to her and politely said no. I paid my bill of 16.20 (65¢), quite high compared to what I had paid for similar purchases. Traute gave me three pieces of mail, the same ones I had sent her during our course of correspondence. Evidently, the dumb girl thought I was asking for my own letters, the ones I had written to her during the past year, not any new mail that had been sent to her for me.

I could hardly keep from laughing as I returned them to her and then tried again to ask if any letters were sent to her but that were addressed to me. She replied, "Oh, no," which left me somewhat disappointed, but I finally understood. I shook her hand and said goodbye to a girl who acted quite strange. She seldom talked and usually only when spoken to; she was very hard to get through to as she lived in a complete daze. Possibly, this was why she was only a waitress.

I walked to see the hotel we had stayed in last year (Hotel Westminster) and then boarded a tram to take me to the transfer point where I might catch tram number 38 and return to the Hynek home. However, while I was waiting for number 38 to come, a G2 came and I took it instead and shortly arrived at the Götzl home.

I rang the bell to the glass gate, and in a few minutes, a buzz sounded and the gate swung open automatically. After explaining to Pauline my experience of the morning, we sat down, and I was served three sandwiches of Swiss cheese, three apricots, and a glass of milk.

We walked through their garden, which was quite beautiful. I took some pictures and asked if they would take some of me *leading a life of leisure*. They suggested a picture of me in typical Austrian dress; Niki found some of her older brother's lederhosen (leather shorts) and a typical jacket and hat. Mrs. Götzl dropped a pair of long stockings and a brightly colored scarf from her window as she was watching what we were doing.

With a complete change of clothes, I was shown to Mr. Götzl's study, where I changed clothes and experienced some difficulty with the leather shorts but finally managed to pull them on. I tied a scarf around my neck and put on the jacket and hat and pulled the knee socks into position and presented myself as an Austrian boy.

Pauline, Niki, and Mrs. Götzl nearly died laughing. The girls wanted to change into Austrian dresses, and while they were changing, I walked through the garden.

The maid was looking out of the kitchen window and informed Mrs. Götzl that *a strange man was walking in the backyard.* When I turned around and she saw who it was, she laughed so hard she began crying and asking apologies for laughing at me.

A small table was placed in the garden with beer bottles and fresh fruit to adorn the scene. Pauline and Niki sat around the table with me, while Mrs. Götzl took pictures of the happenings.

We had a great deal of fun cutting up and pretending to drink the bottles of wine that we held high. I certainly looked like an Austrian boy and played the part well.

Pauline, sensing I was hungry again, served me a bowl of cornflakes with bananas and cream. Remembering that when the Hynek's had dropped me at the café, for me to have lunch with Traute, it was 1:00 pm, and I had said I would return to their home to be with the children, but had instead come to the Götzl home. I thought it best to inform the Hynek's where I was by telephone. This we had tried to do, but to no avail as the Hynek's phone was busy.

Finally, Eva called to inform the Götzls that Joe had not come to the Hyneks' home as yet since he was still visiting a girl in a café. Niki, who had answered the phone, said, "Yes, I know. He's eating with her right now. In fact, he's eating cornflakes and sitting in our dining room."

I left the Götzl home at five thirty, but not before I had been invited for dinner at seven o'clock. On the way home, I bought postcards and stamps at a small "Tobak" shop and hurried home to write the cards and get ready for the dinner date.

Eva wanted to make me something to eat before I left, and I could not talk her out of giving me a grapefruit and four slices of cheese on bread. I'd taken such a liking to the Hyneks, especially their children, whom I had taught to sing such songs as "My Hand on Myself" and "Around Her Leg She Wore a Yellow Ribbon," which they either sang or whistled constantly.

I returned to the Götzl home at seven ten and met the family in the garden, only to be bothered by many insects. Dinner was served at seven thirty, consisting of two Hungarian dishes, different but quite delicious.

One custom I'd noticed in all Austrian homes was that you ate one item of food at a time. This was more easily understood if I told you that only one item of food was put on your plate at a time. If you wanted to eat potatoes, you would take a serving of potatoes and eat them before you put something else on your plate.

Also, after the main course was served and as soon as everyone was finished, the head of the house would make a suggestion to leave the table and adjourn to the parlor or living room. Here dessert and coffee were served while the dining room table was being cleared. Of interest might be the comment concerning their coffee, which I found to be quite strong and only good with a pint of cream!

We mapped out a possible route to Switzerland for me while eating an excellent dessert of fruit covered with sugar-baked dough. We drank wine and talked while listening to an album of Bing Crosby before I returned to the Hynek home, as they were expecting me home early, as they wanted me to visit with their company who happened to be from Saint Louis.

These guests were Mrs. Pollack and her three children, who lived off Mackenzie Road, not far from our home. I was given their phone number and address and given an invitation to their home upon my return to the States.

I bade my Saint Louis friends farewell and thanked them for the invitation. Being quite tired, I wanted to retire, but Walter insisted on telling me some of his jokes, which were worthwhile staying up to listen to.

July 20—Partly Cloudy, Warm, and Rainy

I awoke around 10:00 a.m. and enjoyed the usual breakfast with the family. They went on a tour while I wrote some letters and generally loafed away the morning. They returned in the early afternoon, and lunch was served, after which I returned to my room to finish the letters.

Eva showed me some *Donald Duck* comic books printed in German. His nephews were called Trick, Track, and Truck but still got into as much mischief as their American friends better known to us as Huey, Dewey, and Louie.

At 3:00 p.m., Pauline called and reminded me we had a prearranged shopping date to buy the Hynek family a plant as a present from me for the wonderful things they had done for me on my visit to Vienna. I walked to her home, and we took the G2 tram to downtown Vienna, where we took another to the outskirts of the city not too far from the Götzl home, but since the streets ran into the center of Vienna like a web, it was difficult to travel with public transportation to the suburbs. To get from one suburb to another, one must first go into the city and then go out on another line in order to reach one's destination. To sum up the public transportation problem of Vienna, it might be said that the most direct way to get somewhere was to *go in a circle*.

We entered a small flower shop, and immediately, my eyes fell upon a plant about forty inches high and quite spread out. It was priced at sixty shillings ($2.40). Other plants were priced higher, but this looked the best, so I bought it. The name of the plant was *Aralia balfouriana*. It was carefully wrapped and brought to the Hynek home by the two of us and placed in my wardrobe as a hiding place, as it was to be given to them later. The only ones who knew about the present were Pauline, Erika, and her grandparents, Mr. & Mrs. Dworak, who were sitting in the garden when we brought the plant to the Hynek home.

They promised not to say anything, and we sat down with them to eat fresh fruit in the garden until a storm forced us inside the house, where we continued to talk until the Hyneks arrived.

Pauline was asked to stay for dinner along with four others of the doctor's friends. Mrs. Hynek worked in the kitchen while I kept Walter occupied in the study, during which time Pauline placed the plant in the living room.

Mrs. Hynek was the one to discover the plant and was overjoyed at receiving it. They carefully unwrapped it, watered it, and placed it in front of their living room window.

I dressed for dinner and met the guests, who were being served wine as I entered the room. It wasn't long before we sat down to a fried chicken dinner with fresh lettuce, sliced tomatoes, and cucumbers. After three pieces of tasty chicken, a large portion of salad, a bottle of beer, and some crusted bread, we quickly adjourned to the living room for chocolate-covered cream cake. We continued talking and consuming wine in large quantities until 10:00 p.m.

Leaving his guests for the moment, Walter took his mother- and father-in-law home and also drove Pauline to her home as I accompanied them. Pauline discovered she had forgotten her key, and everyone was sleeping, so no one could release the lock of the electric gate.

I climbed over the tall fence and opened the gate, but now we couldn't get into the house. We yelled and rang the house bell; Walter turned on the outside lights and threw pebbles at the windows, but no one awoke to let Pauline in the house.

Our last chance was to awaken the partly deaf maid, who occupied a first-floor suite. Pauline pounded on the window until the maid was awakened; though half-scared from the turmoil, she opened the back door, and Pauline was home at last.

After thanking Pauline for taking the time to shop for the plant, I returned home with Walter, and saying good-night to his guests, I went to my room for my last night's stay in old Vienna.

July 21—Clear and Warm, Later with Rain and Cool

I awoke at seven thirty and found myself going back to sleep until eight thirty. I dressed and packed before having a breakfast of eggs, ham, sausage, and a large bowl of blueberries. I took a picture of the Hynek family with the plant I had given them and loaded my belongings into the car. Elfriede presented me with a small cup and saucer as a remembrance gift that I had admired the previous night.

I thanked them for everything and kissed Mrs. Hynek while receiving one from Eva. Erika went with her father to take me to the southern edge of the city, but we had only gone one block when I remembered I had forgotten my maps.

After getting started again, we drove through the city, and Walter stopped so I could take a few pictures before proceeding to the outskirts of Vienna. I waved good-bye to him and began the task of hitchhiking again at 11:15 a.m. It had been such a wonderful week, and much had been done for me; it had not gone unappreciated, and the last thing I was told was that I was welcome at any time.

Within five minutes, I was picked up by Mr. Bleyuert Omer and his wife, who took me about twenty miles, where I again only had a short wait before a small car driven by August Wipoel, a lawyer from Vienna, stopped and said, "I'll only be able to take you fifteen kilometers, but if that will help, you're welcome to come along." I told him fifteen kilometers were better than none and climbed in the left side of his car.

We drove without saying very much before he asked where I was headed. I replied, "Italy and then Switzerland." August then informed me that he was meeting a friend in fifteen kilometers who was driving to Italy that same day, as the two of them were going to the island of Grato between Venice and Trieste. I was welcome to come along if there was room and if his friend didn't mind, since his friend was doing the driving.

August took me to the extreme edge of the city, where he was to meet his friend, and left me at a grass triangle, sort of a fork in the road, where outgoing traffic would pass. Meanwhile, he returned to his friend's home and packed the car while I waited at the edge of the city for them to return. It was twelve twenty when I was left off, but August said he should be coming back around 1:00 p.m. and I should wait for him. I lay down to rest and ate two of the sandwiches Mrs. Hynek had given me.

A policeman was patrolling the highway on foot and stopped to talk, explaining his function of being on foot instead of in a car. It was cheaper for the government, for one thing, and then two, each officer had a certain section to patrol. He could stop a car by holding up a red flag, and if the car didn't stop, he would write down the license number and turn it in to the headquarters. He was also able to come to the aid of people in distress. Austrian people knew a policeman patrolled each ten miles of highway, and if they came upon an accident, it wasn't a long ride to pick up a policeman to bring him to the scene.

At 1:00 p.m., my ride had not come. I became worried and wondered if he might have played a joke on me. However, at one thirty, a Fiat came along and stopped. August and his thirty-one-year-old friend, Anton Unban, also from Vienna and son of a wealthy nut-and-bolt factory owner who employed 1,100 people, had room enough to take me to Italy with them.

We were making a good time, and the scenery was unmatched anywhere in Austria as we climbed into the mountains. As we climbed higher and higher, we ran into a storm, causing the roads to become quite slippery, and since the tires were worn, it was decided to stop and buy new ones. The first garage we came to had only one tire, so we bought a bag of pretzels and continued on to the next town, where again we could only find one tire to fit the car.

In Villach, twelve kilometers from the Italian border, we were told to go to a garage that would be opened if we mentioned the name of the friend who had sent us, since it was after 6:00 p.m., and the garage was normally closed.

We returned to the filling station and had a snack of wieners, bread, and beer in the café operated by the station attendant. Two lovely girls waited on our table, and we smiled constantly at them.

We continued on our way, but within ten kilometers, we discovered we were driving on a flat tire, as one of the new tires had a pinched tube. Being quite upset over this incident, we nonetheless changed the tire and found a garage nearby to repair the tire before continuing on to Italy.

The sun was setting over the mountains in a most beautiful manner as we came to the Italian border and passed through customs.

I slept on and off until we arrived in Udine, but after this city, I slept until we arrived in the small Italian village of Cervignano, where Anton asked for a room for me as they were going on to their destination. There was no room at this hotel, but we were directed to another that turned out to be a restaurant bar, but there were rooms available for four hundred lire (70¢) in this multipurpose building with rooms available on the second floor.

I thanked Anton and August, who had taken me 560 kilometers (330 miles), and was shown to my room by a good-looking Italian girl. It was a nice room, but the noise from outside and downstairs was terrible. Also, a fight was being televised, and most of the townspeople were watching it at various taverns, as the taverns and bars all had TV sets and very few people owned them.

There was a knock on my door, and I was informed I must pay for my room in advance. The girl could not speak English, which caused some trouble, as I had no Italian money and only 18.30 Austrian shillings. The price of the room was either four hundred Italian lire or twenty Austrian shillings. Since I had neither, I gave the girl a $10 traveler check and received a five-thousand note and three one hundred notes as change.

There were two beds in the room, one too small in length but two feet off the floor, while the other was long enough but was on the floor and consisted of a mattress and blankets. Since I could stretch out on the bed on the floor, and since it was more comfortable, there was little doubt in which bed I would sleep. I wrote in the diary and began a restless night in a very noisy town, only after making sure the door was locked. For the first time on the trip did I have fear of what might happen and felt restless.

July 22—Clear, Warm, and Beautiful

I was awakened at 3:30 a.m. by a busload of Italians singing and playing music beneath my window. This continued until 4:00 a.m. as I had gotten up to watch the proceedings. I had never seen so many people taking about nothing. Jabber, jabber, and more jabber at three thirty in the morning.

I went back to bed and slept until 7:00 a.m. and then *rested* until seven thirty when I found it was useless to try to rest any longer. I washed and dressed in my lucky clothes and headed for the highway to Venice, one kilometer away.

HITCHHIKING THROUGH EUROPE DURING THE SUMMER OF 1956

I arrived at the highway at 8:15 a.m. and had a fifteen-minute wait before a small van-truck driven by an Italian man and his wife stopped. My suitcase was put in the rear end, and I climbed in after them; it was quite warm in the back end as there was no air circulating. Various odds and ends consisting of a baby's high chair, dust mops, and brooms littered the area where I tried to relax.

As long as we kept going, everything was fine, at least when we didn't hit bumps, but when we had to wait ten minutes for a train, the heat became unbearable. The couple could not speak English, which led me to see why confusion reigned. I was taken thirty kilometers and dropped off after pointing on the map where I wanted to go since they were turning off the main road. I thanked the couple the best I could and began the task of trying to get a ride to Venice.

It wasn't much of a task, for within two minutes, a car came along and stopped. As I saw that the license plate indicated the car was from Switzerland, my hopes were raised. The driver was Ernest Bass from Basel, Switzerland. He was a buyer for warehouses and was returning from a twelve-day vacation in Yugoslavia.

He had left Trieste at 6:00 a.m. and was on his way to another lodge of his in Southern Switzerland. He could speak many languages and seemed quite nice. Since he was going on to Switzerland and I was behind schedule, I decided to bypass Venice and take the scenic route to Treviso and Vicenza. All along the highway were rows of trees bordering the flat Po Valley, which made Northern Italy appear quite picturesque.

We continued on and related our various travel experiences to each other. We arrived in Verona at 11:45 a.m. and headed for the old Roman arena, which was built two thousand years ago, where gladiators once performed and where the Christians were placed with lions. The arena was massive and truly a beautiful structure. Today, operas were presented in the arena during the month of August.

We sat at a sidewalk café across the street from the arena and drank coffee. Ernest had an espresso while I enjoyed a cappuccino, a most delicious drink. I was experiencing my first Italian coffee and greatly enjoyed it.

I took some pictures of the arena, Ernest, and the pigeons before driving to the San Zeno church, which was begun in the ninth century but not finished until the twelfth! It was a beautiful church with reliefs depicting both the Old and New Testament on the outside wall. These reliefs were started in the first Romantic style and finished in the first Gothic style. The reliefs were one of the first we could find in the Christian world. The outside door was covered in bronze, also in relief. Two lions stood guard outside the door carved in a crude style of early Venetian living.

We continued on to Brescia, where we stopped at a café for lunch. We were waited on by men in tuxedos, which was quite a change for both of us as Ernest was dressed in shorts and sported sandals as footwear. I drank a bottle of Italian beer and had a dish of ravioli and then a dish of tagliatelle, both of which were very good.

We drove to another café and sat underneath a Mussolini-style arch for another cup of coffee. On we went to Milano, during which time I was invited to visit Ernest at his lodge near Lugano. I refused for fear of making me later than I was on my scheduled trip, and then there was the possibility I would have difficulty leaving the remote location.

We had been on the Autobahn since Brescia, and I was soon to say farewell to Ernest as our ways were to depart. As I was about to be on my own again, he suggested continuing on to Domodossola as that would be better for me. In so doing, he would be going about one hundred kilometers out of the way, but since he was in no hurry, the extra driving would not be too much of an inconvenience for he enjoyed my company, as we had become good friends.

Ernest, a bachelor of forty-eight, insisted on doing this for me, and it wasn't long before we were in the Lake District. We were driving along the shoreline of Lake Maggiore, having seen two accidents on the Autobahn, neither of them serious, but we took it easy as we entered the valleys and neared the mountains.

We stopped in Arona for another cup of coffee and relaxed at a table overlooking the lake. The Lake District was very crowded at this time of the year as people could have a vacation without too much expense.

We arrived in Domodossola at 6:15 p.m. and found lodging for 750 lire ($1.32) apiece at the Hotel Milano. I had now been with Ernest for nine hours and had come 550 kilometers for another day's travel of nearly 330 miles. We checked in at the hotel and washed up before walking through the town that had once been one of the Germans' last strongholds in their retreat from Italy.

We walked to a small inn, where Ernest bought a bottle of Barbera red wine and ordered a plate of salami and some rolls for each of us. A group of Italians came in, singing loudly, and were well received by the owner. They were all in gay outfits and were doing a good bit of celebrating.

We then went to a standing bar for our fourth cup of Italian coffee of the day. The cup was quite small, but the quality of the coffee was very good. The coffee was strained through a slice of lemon, which gave the coffee some of its unusual taste.

On the way back to the hotel, we viewed a race among the waiters from the various hotels and cafés of the town. They were making a circular tour through the town to see who could win a race while balancing a filled tray. I had never seen anything like this, but the townspeople cheered their favorite onto the finish line.

I sat in the lounge of the hotel to write in my diary, while Ernest read the newspaper and asked various guests to take me to Switzerland tomorrow if that was where they were headed, but no one offered to have me as passenger. At 10:00 p.m., we retired for a restful night.

July 23—Clear, Warm, and Beautiful

I awoke at six thirty and was washed and dressed by seven. I then packed my suitcase and carried it to the main lounge, where I discovered Ernest had paid the hotel bill. We walked to a café and had a typical Italian breakfast of bread rolls and coffee. Ernest also paid for this and then took me to the edge of town, where I would have a better chance for a ride into Switzerland.

I thanked him for all he had done and found myself looking for a ride at 7:50 a.m. There were few cars coming along the road. I was anxious to get into the mountains as it was a beautiful day.

When I still found myself without a ride at 9:00 a.m., I walked toward town, where the cars would not be going so fast as there was no speed limit in most European countries, and when cars hit the open stretches of road, they went along at a good clip.

Boys with large baskets strapped to their backs were delivering bread on bicycles to the restaurants in the town, having just come from the bakery. One car stopped for me but could only take me two kilometers, so I refused the ride, hoping I could do better where I was standing.

I had been unsuccessful in getting a ride in two hours and forty minutes, as it was now ten thirty, when a small Volkswagen stopped. The car was from Denmark, but when the driver saw I had a knapsack behind the suitcase, he replied, "I'm sorry, I'm afraid we don't have any room."

I began a sob story—that I had been waiting since 7:50 a.m. and was desperate for a ride as I was due in Switzerland that evening and asked him if he could help me in any way possible.

The driver was Paul Kragh from Skoelskor, Denmark. He was traveling with his daughter, Ingra, and after rearranging the trunk and rear seat, I climbed into the car for a trip that would bring me to the mountains of Switzerland.

It wasn't long until we crossed the border at the Simplon Pass. Since we had to have our passports checked, we also took time for coffee and wine, my friends from Denmark drinking the coffee.

We continued on to the summit of Simplon Pass, taking twenty minutes to explore the top and photograph the mountains. Ingra and I walked to a small lookout, where a huge eagle of stone was erected.

We returned to the car and began our descent, stopping halfway down for a picnic lunch. This consisted of a bottle of red wine, sausage, cheese, and rolls, which we ate while sitting on a bench overlooking the Rhône Valley.

Parked in front of us was a sedan from Belgium, and I decided to ask them if they were going to Lausanne, to which they replied yes. I asked if I might go with them and showed them where I was headed on the map. They said they had no room, but I rearranged the backseat and sat down to show them there was ample room. They were just about convinced there would be room when they asked about my suitcase. I showed it to them, and immediately they said, "Oh, no!" This was their answer, and they had not even seen my knapsack!

I thanked them anyway and walked back to the bench for a cup of coffee with my Danish friends. We washed the dishes and were soon on our way to Brig.

The trip down to Brig was very beautiful and impressive. Arriving there, I filled up the canteens with cold water from a public fountain while Mr. Kragh went to the post office.

Before we left Brig, we exchanged the money we had for Swiss francs. We continued on, and I was left off near the town of Leuk as Ingra and her father were going into the mountains to Leukerbad, where they planned to do some climbing. I was left off at 3:50 p.m. and stationed myself along the only road to Aigle, my next destination.

It was very discouraging as the minutes dragged into hours and I did not get a ride. I was so close to my destination, considering how far I had come in two days, that I hardly noticed a yellow convertible pull to a halt beside me. It was driven by a Mrs. George Placzek, an instructor at the Institute for Advanced Learning at Princeton, New Jersey.

Her child and another hitchhiker were in the backseat, as they were on their way to Sierre, a town twelve kilometers away. I informed her that I was expected to arrive at a Swiss chalet that evening and asked of the possibility of taking a train. She then took me to the railroad station in Sierre, where we found the next train to Aigle was due at 6:30 p.m. and would arrive in Aigle at 7:40 p.m. From Aigle I could get a train at 8:09 p.m. to Ollon, arriving at 8:18 p.m.

These plans met with my approval, and we walked to a sidewalk café near the station, where my American friend bought me half a liter of wine and left me to wait for the train

I made the above connections without difficulty and found myself getting off a streetcar-like train consisting of one car at eight eighteen (just as promised). I still had a long climb to the chalet as it was located on top of a mountain, and the last bus for the day had long since left the station. The chalet was located in the village of Huémoz, which I thought was a six-kilometer trip but which turned out to be a full ten-kilometer journey.

The climb was a steep one, and I soon became tired. I had hoped a car or truck would come along, but only a jeep passed my way but did not stop. It was nearly dark, as it was now eight forty-five, when I heard the drone of a motor coming from below. I turned the USA on my suitcase outward and stood in the center of the road to stop his travel.

The approaching car had to stop or run over me, and seeing me wave my hand, the driver of the Volkswagen pulled to a stop. Inside the small car was a man, his wife, and their ten-year-old child. They motioned for me to get in the backseat, and we continued on into the mountains to the town of Huémoz. Conversation was limited since they were from Brussels, Belgium, and could not speak English.

They left me in the center of town, and I thanked them in English and German, hoping they would understand my appreciation for the ride. I asked a young lad where the chalet of Reverend Schaeffer was by showing him the address I carried and was led some three hundred meters to its location on a sloping hillside.

Thanking him, I climbed the terrace only to find the chalet dark. I opened the front door and entered a dark room, which caused me to retrace my steps and walk to the rear of the chalet. Here I saw lights and climbed the stairs to knock on the door, hoping to find someone at home.

I was greeted by Dorothy Jamison, the friend of Ruth Abrahamson, who had told me of the Schaeffers. Mrs. Schaeffer then came to the door and informed me I was just in time for dinner, though it was now nine o'clock. All the guests had just sat down at the table, with Dr. Schaeffer sitting at the head. Other guests included Isaac Moore and his sister Doris from Georgia; Mrs. Jamison and Dorothy from Los Angeles; Mr. and Mrs. H.R. Rookmaaker and their three children from Amsterdam, Holland; Dan Russell from Florida, a student in Lausanne; and Evelyn Unna, formerly from Stratford, England, and now from Hamburg, Germany.

I quickly washed and sat down to dinner of corned beef hash, a salad of split tomatoes and cream cheese, and a large serving of lemon pie, which was the best lemon pie I had ever tasted.

After dinner and while still at the table, Dr. Schaeffer took his Bible and read from John 3, after which he spoke for thirty minutes on taking Christ as your Savior. I was filled with great inspiration and felt relieved that I had now reached my destination, a place where I would feel quite close to God for five days and where any questions or problems could easily be discussed with Dr. Schaeffer.

I had always thought I was a Christian and had God as my Savior, but as he spoke, I began to wonder if I had ever really seen the Light. At the close of our worship service, Evelyn was asked to select a hymn for us to sing as it had been one year since she accepted Christ as her Savior. We closed with a brief but meaningful prayer, and then all helped clear the table and wash the dishes.

It was now 11:00 p.m., and we dressed warmly as we were taking a walk to an impressive point overlooking the valley a short distance away. Below we could see the lights of Saint Maurice, and although it was quite late, no one bothered about the time. We all felt close to God and talked freely with Dr. Schaeffer concerning personal problems.

He had a quiet manner of speaking, one that built one's confidence in him quickly. We walked slowly back to the chalet, arriving there at about 1:00 a.m., but our conversation did not end there, for we continued talking long into the early morning hours.

The Schaeffer family was a family working for God. They had four children, Priscella, nineteen; Susan, fifteen; Debbie, eleven; and Frankie, four. The family lived in Saint Louis from 1945 to 1948 then spent some time in Philadelphia and now resided here, doing the work of Christ.

Susan had had rheumatic fever and was slowly recovering, while Frankie had had polio and had recently received a brace for his leg. This somehow didn't seem right, for this family had given its all to Christ, and yet through the hardships, their spirits remained high.

Tonight there were nineteen at the chalet, while some had decided to find lodging in another chalet nearby. The task of getting people to accept Christ as their Savior was a task achieved by the entire family, truly a Christian family sent to do the work of Christ.

They overcame any and all difficulties that came their way and had changed many lives, turning their thoughts from the broad way of the sinful life to the narrow way of the godly life.

Before coming to the mountain chalet, they had lived in Saint Maurice, a small village on the other side of the Rhone River that was 100 percent Catholic. Dr. Schaeffer had often spoken the true word of Christ and, in so doing, had changed the religious feeling of one of the men of the village, which in turn resulted in a rash upheaval. The Schaeffer family was forced to leave the village of Saint Maurice, and through prayer and determination to remain in Switzerland, they were able to buy this chalet from gifts and contributions sent to them by many friends. So now the work of Christ went on in a never-ceasing manner.

The girls came to the living room to make the sofas into three beds for Isaac, Dan, and me. It was while the beds were being made that Priscella explained the family struggle to remain in Switzerland and informed me of the events of their life.

As we turned out the lights at 3:10 a.m., I found myself struggling to get to sleep after a hard day, having been on the go for over twenty hours.

July 24—Clear and Warm

I slept until 11:00 a.m. and dressed in time for a late breakfast that was served on the balcony overlooking the Rhone Valley. The sun was shining brightly as we sat around the table for a typical European breakfast of bread, jelly, butter, and tea or coffee. The beauty of the mountains covered with snow added to the richness of color and beauty that surrounded us.

Plans were made for a hike up the mountains as some of the guests had expressed a desire to do some climbing and also take in the beauty from an advantageous position. It wasn't long before a lunch was packed and a group of six took off in a car for a nearby service station so a flat tire could be fixed while the climbing party began their mountainous journey. As we walked, the road narrowed to the size of a trail, and it was not long before we were alone on the mountainside.

We passed several small buildings that looked like old barns, and we were informed that they served as storage areas for weapons in time of war.

We continued on up the steep slope and stopped halfway up at a place called Chammossaire, where we decided to rest and have our picnic lunch. Priscella offered grace, and we sat down to enjoy ham, pork, and jelly sandwiches with a peach for dessert.

It was a filling lunch and served to strengthen our bodies so we might reach our destination, the top of the mountain and Bretaye. Here we found small huts and many animals belonging to the peasants. The huts were shabbily put together, and the people were far from clean. This was in sharp contrast to the scenic beauty and the tourists who had either climbed the mountain slopes or come up on the cog train. Of particular interest were the actions of a group of children who had just come to the top on the train. They were Swiss children but evidently came from an urban area, for they swarmed over the mountaintop as though they had found something new.

Three ski lifts originated in this area, and following one down a sloping trail, we came to a beautiful lake nestled among the trees. The lake was one of four within the immediate area.

We stopped for a drink at an inn alongside the lake, but they were sold out of everything except beer and wine, and asking for that would not have been the thing to do under the circumstances.

We decided to return up the slope on the ski lift, and one by one, we entered the swinging chairs, and while still moving, the safety bar was closed and we were swung out into space and over the trees.

Reaching the top, we were able to have a nonalcoholic beverage, and after a brief rest, we began our homeward trip at 5:40 p.m. We walked to the edge of the steep slope and began our journey over steep and rough terrain. We could hardly hold ourselves back at times and often found ourselves running down the grassy slopes, holding back as best we could when rougher ground appeared.

We met an old mountaineer, eighty-one years of age, who was looking after his herd of animals. As we left this interesting old man, it was not long before we reached more gentle slopes. We had enjoyed our hike as the weather provided a good view of Mont Blanc, the highest mountain in Europe. It was 4,810 meters high and could easily be seen from our vantage point forty-five miles away. Another famous mountain that we could see today was Les Diablerets (3,222 meters high). There was much snow visible, and the mountain trip was truly a wonderful day to remember.

We arrived back at the chalet at seven o'clock and sat down to enjoy an excellent dinner of tomato juice, chicken à la king, cauliflower, and Mrs. Schaeffer's homemade pie.

Tonight, Dr. Schaeffer had to teach a Bible class, as he did every Tuesday night, and we all journeyed by car to a home near Villars, where other people also gathered to hear the Word of God. We did not sing hymns since we were having our worship in an apartment-type home. There were about thirty people who gathered in the small quarters to listen to the message of Dr. Schaeffer. It was 9:00 p.m. when he began, and as he finished each sentence, he would pause so another man could repeat the sentence in French for those who did not understand English. After the French translation, the message was further translated into German for those who could only understand German.

The blinding power of the group was quite evident and very inspiring. As the message of the evening continued, I began to wonder if I were only a true Christian in name alone. I wondered if I had taken God as my Savior, hoping I had but not sure in my own mind if I had. I could only satisfy my doubt through a personal conference with Dr. Schaeffer, and I hoped for the chance to come before too long.

The evening worship was over at 11:00 p.m. Tonight's message concerned the reasons why people had not taken Christ as their Savior. It was his belief that too many people try to attain the level of Christ or try to reach His Summit, whereas they should remain below this level and seek His forgiveness.

After a closing prayer, tea and cookies were served, but we lingered and spoke with many of the people, finally leaving for the chalet at midnight.

Since the chalet was still overcrowded, I again was asked to sleep on the sofa. While we had been away, the beds had been made for us, and it was only a matter of minutes before I was in bed. I was puzzled or slightly shocked at the overall atmosphere of the chalet. I was further determined to find myself and answer pressing questions I knew must be answered if I were to know if I had taken Christ as my Savior and, in so doing, would attain everlasting life. It was one o'clock when I went to sleep.

July 25—Clear and Warm, Very Beautiful

I was awakened at 4:30 a.m. by Isaac Moore, who was just coming to bed after having a conference with Dr. Schaeffer. I went back to sleep and awoke at ten thirty to have the usual breakfast. We bade farewell to Isaac and his sister. He was stationed with the Army Security Agency in Germany and had come to the chalet after hearing of its existence from some friends.

I now moved my clothing upstairs to a room and was glad to learn I would not have to sleep on the sofa anymore. The morning mail arrived, and I received some news from home.

I helped Dr. Schaeffer store excess blankets in the attic and then began cutting the lawn as I wanted to help out as much as possible. It wasn't long before we were called to lunch, and looking at the table, I wondered if we were feeding an army. Mrs. Schaeffer had made sixty sandwiches for eight people. There were thirty pork and thirty lettuce-and-tomato sandwiches served with refreshing iced tea. Returning to the chores of the lawn, I had nearly finished when John Donson, a twenty-five-year-old opera singer from Milano, Italy, arrived. His home was in England, but for the past year, he had been in Milano with an opera group and had made several trips to the chalet, having accepted Christ several weeks ago.

John was my new roommate, and during our first chat together, he told me he had been a Christian for twenty-three days, this having been his third visit to the chalet.

Pris, John, Frankie, and I went to town for bread and soup, and on the way, John related how shocked he had been on his first visit and knew that he had come to the right place to accept Christ.

We returned to the chalet in time for afternoon tea, after which I typed a letter home to the parents.

Mr. Rookmaaker, the man from Amsterdam, a historian on art and museums, had planned to show some slides tonight, but his slides were too large for the projector owned by the Schaeffers. I was asked to make an improvised box through which the slides could be shown and gladly did so. Mrs. Schaeffer then called for me to take a wagonload of trash to the city dump, which was all downhill. I had Frankie and Debbie as passengers on the trip down but encountered difficulty in convincing them I would be unable to pull them up the hill.

Dinner this evening was roast beef and boiled potatoes with brown gravy, and dessert was a delicious chocolate cake with one-fourth-inch-thick icing.

After doing the dishes, we all went to the main lounge, where Mr. Rookmaaker gave a lecture on art and told how some artists actually swore at God's creations in their paintings, presenting slides to stress his point. His presentation was most interesting and lasted until 11:30 p.m.

I went to my room and looked through the guest book, but before Dr. and Mrs. Schaeffer went to bed, they came by the room to say good-night.

It was then I asked him the question that had been bothering me. I told him I hoped I was a Christian but wanted to be sure that I was and that I had really taken Christ as my Savior.

We went to his study, and he read several passages from the Bible, and then after talking over the passages, he set about asking me four questions. I was trembling inside, never feeling this close to God, almost as if I were talking directly to Him. The four questions asked me were as follows:

1. Do you believe God is who He says He is?
2. Do you believe you are a sinner worthy of condemnation?
3. Do you believe Jesus died the way it is written in the Bible?
4. Do you believe Christ died for you personally?

I was able to answer the first three questions easily, but I had to struggle with the last question because I had always believed that Christ died to save us all. Now with further understanding of Christ and His dealings with man, I accepted Christ as my Savior and, in so doing, assured myself of everlasting life because God had said "He that believeth in the Son hath everlasting life."

I felt very funny inside and was trembling a great deal, knowing I was now closer to God than I had ever been before. I was aware of a richer realization, having Christ as my personal Savior. I was then asked to pray to God, thanking Him out loud, and as we both bowed our heads to pray, I found words difficult to speak. As I finished, Dr. Schaeffer prayed for me as no one had ever prayed for me before. I began to cry but could not hold back the tears. I felt so good.

Thanking Dr. Schaeffer, I returned to my room to explain what had just happened to me to John Dobson, my roommate for one night. He was very easy to speak with and said he was the only one in his family who was a Christian and related the terrific struggle he was having trying to win his parents to the side of Christ.

As I went to bed, I lay awake and thought of my great experience. I felt so wonderful now having Christ as my Savior and possessing everlasting life. It wasn't long before I was sound asleep.

July 26—Clear, Warm, and Again Beautiful

I arose at ten thirty, dressed, washed, and walked to the balcony of my room. Here I sat down for breakfast with John and Dr. Schaeffer. The usual was served, and we soon found ourselves involved in a discussion concerning prayer. We talked for over an hour and then continued our talk in the garden under a large birch tree so the table could be set for lunch.

It was a very inspiring discussion relating to the problems man was confronted with in his life cycle. The two problems we discussed were the "deterministic man" and "the one and the many."

Baked fish and boiled potatoes were served for lunch with string beans and a lettuce salad. For dessert we enjoyed pineapple upside-down cake, and as we finished, we had another thirty-minute discussion followed by a closing prayer.

I returned to my room to write a detailed letter home informing them of my great experiences. I then found time to rest until tea was served at 5:30 p.m. An added attraction served with the tea was buttered bread sprinkled with sugar.

We were suddenly startled by the screams of Frankie as he had fallen from a chair and split his head open, not that the family didn't have enough troubles already.

I helped Pris set the table for dinner and then sat on the lawn chair to continue reading the guest book. Everyone signed the book and was asked to write a few lines concerning their visit. I was not alone in experiencing greatness at the Schaeffer chalet.

Just when Frankie had settled down and the bleeding had stopped, he tripped on his brace and opened the cut even more. He was rushed to a doctor for medical treatment.

After their return, I asked the doctor when the time to ask forgiveness of sins was. His answer to this question was "Right away, and be specific with your sins."

Dinner was served at eight forty-five. Mrs. Schaeffer had made a rice dish and had split open tomatoes and filled them with hard-boiled eggs. Dessert was a home-baked cake topped with ice cream.

John Dobson departed the chalet to catch a train while Dr. and Mrs. Schaeffer conducted a Bible study, as each of us read two passages and then joined together for the singing of two hymns. Pris was asked to play the Messiah for the group on the record player, while the words on a sheet of paper were read to obtain a fuller meaning. Before leaving the group to retire for the night, I spoke briefly with Dr. Schaeffer and then walked onto the balcony, where I found time to be alone for a prayer to God.

The moon shone over the mountains, and all was peaceful and quiet in the valley below. I felt so near to heaven, and all godly things seemed so at hand. I was ready to enter the kingdom of God at any time.

July 27—Clear, Warm, and Beautiful

I arose at ten thirty and took my first bath in a week. The last one I enjoyed was in Vienna. I dressed and ate a few pieces of bread and jelly for breakfast and decided to finish cutting the lawn. It was warm, and I was working slowly, but I finished the job before lunch.

Finding some spare time, I pressed my pants and shirts, which had been washed with the family laundry, and then sat in the sun to read the Bible.

Before we ate lunch, the bench we sat on had to be repaired, but this only took a few minutes, and before long, we were eating stuffed tomato, lettuce, sausage, milk, and apple Jell-O.

We had a small devotional as several chapters were read from the book of Romans. We again sang two hymns, and Susan offered a prayer. It was now 3:00 p.m., and I asked the Schaeffers to pose for some pictures so I might better remember my experiences.

I found time to play with Frankie on the lawn and pulled a mushroom from the ground and told him his mother was serving it for dinner. He looked at me with curious eyes and replied, "God doesn't like you to tell lies." This was just a small example of the complete and overpowering faith these people had in Christ.

I found a relaxing place in the sun and tried to read the Bible, but the warm sun was too much for me, and I was soon asleep.

The girls had gone to Villach for groceries and newspapers of the tragic shipwreck of the Italian liner *Andrea Doria*. They returned at 6:00 p.m. with three newspapers of the tragedy. A prayer was offered for those people who were on the two ships and for those attempting rescue work.

I was helping Dr. Schaeffer clean up the yard when a car turned into the driveway. We were greeted by three servicemen who were also in the Army Security Agency, though they did not know Isaac Moore, the soldier who had left several days before. They had left their army post at 8:00 a.m. and had driven all day in order to reach the chalet by nightfall.

Dinner was ready, and we sat down to enjoy oxtail soup, potatoes, veal, and a tossed green salad. Instead of an evening devotion, the showing of slides on Hinduism and the missions of India and Syria were presented.

These slides were shown to us by a woman who had worked in these countries trying to teach children Christian living. She had some heartwarming experiences to relate and some interesting slides to further explain the living conditions in these countries.

Later, Dr. Schaeffer talked with two of the servicemen, while Pris and I read more accounts of the shipwreck in the army newspaper, *The Stars and Stripes*. Pris went on to relate how her brother Frankie had come down with polio while they were coming across the Atlantic Ocean on their way to Europe. It had only been a blessing that he had been able to walk, and this was due partly to the use of a brace. With it being late and I being tired, Pris and I said goodnight and turned in for the evening.

July 28—Partly Cloudy and Warm

I slept until ten thirty and met the others on the balcony for breakfast. Since I was leaving today, I was asked if I had any questions. The one that came to mind was how I would explain to other people why I was so certain of being saved by Christ. We discussed this question in the garden while the girls prepared lunch.

Lunch was served on the balcony, and after a passage was read from the Bible, I was asked to request a hymn. The songbooks were passed around the table, and we all joined in on one of my favorites, "Softly and Tenderly." We left the table at three thirty, and for the first time, I had anticipations of coming home.

Most of the people were going into Villach for shopping, but I elected to remain at the chalet and pack. I did, however, ask Pris to bring along five packages of cream soup, which I wanted to take home. It was Knorr potato soup and was *outstanding* in taste and texture.

I began packing, but before I could finish, Evelyn asked me to walk to the post office with her. Upon returning, I finished packing and then played badminton with one of the servicemen while the girls made a barbecue for dinner.

We continued playing badminton until we broke the strings in both rackets. I found time to have a last-minute talk with Dr. Schaeffer, a personal talk that should help me in an important decision in life. Before we joined the group again, he prayed for me in a very personal way.

We were called to roast our hot dogs over the fire as we decided to have a casual supper. A bowl of salad, lettuce, and tomato and iced tea were also served.

I was due to leave on the train from Ollon around 8:45 p.m. and would have had to take the late-afternoon bus to the village had not one of the servicemen offered to take me in his car to the station. This gave me several more hours time with the Schaeffers and also allowed me to have an evening meal. As I was about to leave, Dr. Schaeffer called on me to give a prayer for the group, which was followed by an eight-minute prayer by Mrs. Schaeffer.

It lasted so long I thought I might miss the train, but after giving the Schaeffers $20 to *cover* my expenses, I was able to depart for Ollon at eight twenty, but not before I shook hands and thanked everyone concerned.

We reached the station just as the one-car train was leaving, and climbing aboard, I thanked the servicemen. Reaching the next town, Aigle, I purchased a ticket to Paris for 45.70 Swiss francs. Since 2,501 French francs were needed to purchase a maritime ticket from Paris to Le Havre, and since the exchange rate was better in Switzerland, I decided to exchange my remaining Swiss francs and enough American money to have the desired amount of French fancs for my train fare.

The train to Paris was fifteen minutes late, but after boarding the train, I found a compartment occupied by only two other people who were getting off in Lausanne. Thereafter, I had the compartment to myself, except when four campers invaded the car for an hour's ride.

I pulled the shades down so as not to be disturbed, and after being checked by the French custom authorities, I stretched out and slept quite well for the night.

July 29—Cloudy and Windy

I awoke at five thirty to find a French soldier sleeping in the compartment. He could speak English and offered to help when he learned I was not familiar with the city of Paris.

The faint rays of dawn shone down upon the slums of the famous city. It was not a very pretty sight as we pulled into the Gare de Lyon station at 6:05 a.m.

I had been given a metro ticket for the Paris subways by Brigette, a girl who was working at the Schaeffer chalet. She had neglected to use it on her last visit and had given it to me when she learned I would be in Paris and could easily use it for travel.

As I showed the soldier my metro ticket, he directed me to the subway station, as he was going there also. The subway was very warm and stuffy, and there were not many people this Sunday morning in the normally crowded passageway.

A large map of the subway system was printed on the wall, and my route of travels was pointed out to me. Thanking the soldier, I boarded the metro and transferred at the Columbia station. It was not long before I arrived at the Saint Lazare station, having been able to use the metro ticket in transferring from one train to another.

I inquired at a ticket window for someone who could speak English to help me but had no luck. The old people working in the ticket windows could only speak French. I decided to try the British Tourist Information Bureau.

Here a woman directed me to a ticket window, where I bought a first-class ticket to Le Havre for two thousand francs. I was surprised since I had been told the fare was 2,501 francs, and inquiring again at the tourist bureau, I discovered I had neglected to buy a maritime ticket.

The woman from the tourist bureau accompanied me back to the ticket window and explained to the ticket salesman what had happened. I now had to buy a supplement, but this salesman could not sell me one for I had to purchase supplement tickets at another window.

At this window, I was able to get a supplement to my original ticket, but the combined fare on both tickets now amounted to 2,521 francs! This amount was twenty francs more than should be charged, and I informed the ticket salesman that the purchase price should be 2,501 francs, not 2,521. I refused to pay the additional price, acting on principle alone, for I had originally explained to the ticket salesman where I wanted to go.

A British officer overhearing my troubles gave me the additional francs. I thanked him and explained the whole situation to him. One other reason for me being unable to pay an additional twenty francs was that in exchanging my Swiss francs for French francs, I had only gotten 2,501, the exact amount of francs I would need to reach the ship by train.

I sat in the waiting room until 7:45 a.m. and then boarded the first-class train that would take me on a nonstop trip to the port of

Le Havre. It was raining as the three-car train pulled from the station at eight thirty-three, but before we had left the city, the sun was shining.

I occupied a compartment with two German brides and a French girl, Simone Vitrant, from Nancy, France.

We arrived at Le Havre at ten fifty as the special boat train pulled alongside our ship, the *Ryndam*. It was very similar to the *Maasdam*, the ship that had brought me to England from America.

I was assigned cabin 408 on deck B and had a second table seating at a round table, as I had requested. I received three letters that brought me up-to-date on the latest news from home.

My roommate was Ludwig, a German boy from Nuremberg. He was coming to the United States to become a mechanic.

I was very hungry, having gone without breakfast, and decided to ask the chief steward if I could eat lunch at the first seating for today only. He replied there was no reason for anyone to be hungry on his ship and gladly permitted me the privilege of eating early.

I had not eaten since 7:00 p.m. of the preceding day and therefore found little trouble in putting away three sirloin steaks and all the trimmings.

A weather bulletin had gone out for rough seas, so I took a seasickness pill and went to bed while riding out the trip to England. I tried to fall asleep, but the channel was a raging fury. I found myself thrown into the air as the ship would get tossed in the waves, but I managed to remain in bed until we reached quiet waters and awoke to find that around 80 percent of the passengers had gotten sick in crossing the English Channel.

I took a walk around the decks and then dressed for dinner. I found myself at a table for six and introduced myself to Joe, Mary Dillion, Simon Benenson, Edith Wedan, and Emmy Herzog.

We enjoyed a lovely chicken dinner and then went to see the movie *While the City Sleeps*. Returning to the Palm Court, where

I hoped to meet someone for dancing, I immediately cast my eyes upon two girls standing in the doorway. I looked them over and asked the more attractive of the two to dance. Her name was Doloros Dean from Lawrence, Kansas; her friend was Barbara Walker from Connecticut, and as Doloros and I began dancing, Barbara excused herself.

Doloros was a very striking girl who had been to the Middle East for the past six months. We found conversation quite easily and joined a group of friends and sat to talk while we were not dancing.

I walked her to her cabin and thanked her for an enjoyable evening. She was one of the nicest girls, I believed, I had ever met. Saying good-night, we made arrangements to meet after breakfast tomorrow.

I returned to my cabin and talked with Ludwig for a while before turning the clock back an hour and getting some needed rest.

July 30—Cool and Pleasant

I awoke at nine thirty for a breakfast of eggs, toast, honey, and milk. I met Doloros and walked around the deck as we viewed the shoreline for the last time. We were informed of a boat drill at 11:00 a.m. and went to our respective cabins to wait for the alarm.

The drill was well attended, and we were eager to learn what to do in case of an emergency. This was due no doubt to the recent shipwreck of the *Andrea Doria*, for usually, many passengers took boat drills lightly.

I hurried downstairs and rushed to the barber shop for my first haircut since June 27, and I paid only 35¢ for a very good job.

I met Doloros and went to the sports deck for some deck tennis until it was time for lunch. After lunch, we got a bridge game together in the Palm Court and finished out the afternoon with a few more games of deck tennis. We enjoyed the fresh air and found time to meet new friends our age.

I returned to my cabin and took a shower and dressed for dinner. Chicken was again served, and the people at our table became more familiar with one another.

Tonight's movie was *The Harder They Fall*, and after watching this, we went to the Palm Court for dancing until twelve thirty. Doloros and I drank beer before saying good-night and going to our respective cabins. She was a lovely girl, very intelligent but slightly older than me, and at the age of twenty-five, she was looking to older men, but since there were few other Americans on board around her age, I might as well avail myself to the situation. As I was quite tired, it was only minutes before I was fast asleep.

July 31—Cool and Cloudy

I was up at nine fifteen for breakfast and then looked for Doloros. She was sitting in the Palm Court, reading a book, but it wasn't long before we had found a third and fourth for bridge.

After lunch, I entered a bridge tournament that began at 3:00 p.m. and was over around four thirty. I held good cards and ended with 2,630 points but did not win any prize.

I asked Doloros to go for a walk, but she was resting since she had been invited for cocktails by the captain at six thirty. We did agree to meet in the Palm Court at 9:00 p.m.

After dinner, I retired to the Palm Court, but the captain had now invited those at his cocktail party to be his guest in the Palm Coort, so as yet, I could not be with Doloros.

Around 10:00 p.m., after dancing with other girls during the evening, I asked Doloros for a dance, but she was obliged to return to the captain's table. I carried on these visits until 11:00 p.m., at which time the captain excused himself, and Doloros and I could be together.

We danced until the music stopped playing, which was after 1:00 a.m. I asked her if she wanted to take a walk around the deck, but she said that she was tired and was going to bed.

Somehow I did not believe her and walked down the hall to wait to see what would happen. Within three minutes, her cabin door opened, and she walked down the hall with a coat and scarf around her for her deck stroll.

I was quite upset at this, not because she did not want to walk with me, but because she had lied to me. If she wanted to take a walk by herself, that was her business, but she could at least tell me the truth. She had not seen me, nor did she know that I knew she was lying.

I went to the bar and met Joe, the man who sat at our table. We had a drink, and I told him about Doloros.

Girls are just like streetcars; if you miss one, another one will always come along.

I said good-night to Joe and returned to my cabin for a good sleep.

August 1—Cool and Clear

I awoke at nine fifteen and had a light breakfast, then I went to the library to read and write. Also in the library was Simone Vitrant. I invited her to sit with me while we wrote letters and talked for over an hour.

We took a walk around the deck and then availed ourselves to some deck chairs at the stern of the ship. Before going to lunch, I asked her to come dancing with me in the Palm Court that evening.

After lunch, I played bridge with Joan Frey; Simon Benenson, an elderly Russian antique dealer from New York; and Doloros, as the game was prearranged the day before. Simon was an excellent bridge player, having won the tournament on the United States liner going across the Atlantic.

We played three rubbers, changing partners after each rubber. We finished at five thirty, but at Doloros's suggestion, we went to play deck tennis. Joan accompanied us, and we easily found a fourth player, and an exciting and closely contested game was had.

I was somewhat surprised at the change in Doloros, and as we walked to the stern of the ship to view the playful porpoises, I asked her to meet me in the Palm Court at 9:00 p.m. for dancing.

As I walked to my cabin, I was sorry I had asked her and hoped she would not show up or would find some excuse for not being there.

After dinner, I decided to walk with Edith Wedan, the Austrian girl who sat with us at our dining table. She was twenty-two years old and was a very lovely girl, but for some reason, I had not given her much attention. We walked to the stern of the ship, and again I sat and had a long talk with a member of the fairer sex.

She told me how lonely she was as she had few friends and knew only those sitting at her table on the ship. She would be living in California for a year before returning to Vienna to complete her schooling, as she was studying to be a doctor.

I talked with her until 9:30 p.m. and embraced her as I tried to convince her that once she reached California, she would have friends. She suggested we go to the Palm Court for dancing, but she evidently sensed my uneasiness and suggested I go alone. She knew I had been associating with Doloros but did not know of Simone.

I then told her of the mix-up that was shaping up fast as I was to meet Doloros at 9:00 p.m. and meet Simone there for dancing as well, and now if I came with Edith, I did not know just what would happen.

Since it was now nine thirty, I thought perhaps that Doloros would have given up waiting for me, and with this in mind, I ventured to the Palm Court. Doloros was nowhere to be seen, and as I turned around to leave, I saw Simone standing behind me. We talked for a few minutes, and at my suggestion for a walk, we went through the lounge and bar.

I thought I was getting away from it all, but upon entering the lounge, my eyes fell on Doloros, Joan Frey, and Barbara Walker. I saw Doloros at the same time she saw me, and both of us turned our heads away at the same time.

Simone was not aware of this incident, and we continued through the lounge and out to the promenade deck. I was really on a spot now. I was with Simone, Doloros was in the lounge, and Edith was waiting for me to take her to the Palm Court for dancing.

Two young men came along and began talking with us as we stood at the ship's rail. One was a medical professor from Saint Louis University. After we talked for a few minutes, the suggestion was made to go to the bar for a drink.

We made it there safely without being detected and were about to buy a drink when I turned around and saw Doloros walking past the entrance to the bar. I turned my back on her but had the surprise of my life when fifteen seconds later, she came up to the bar and said, "Well, good evening!"

She went on to say that she had waited for me at the Palm Court until nine thirty and then had left for the lounge with some friends. I quickly replied that I had been sick in my cabin and had laid down to rest from eight forty-five until nine thirty and then had set about to look for her, having come to the Palm Court, but being unable to find her, I met the French girl Simone and then had seen her only minutes before in the lounge. Boy, what a mess I was in!

We left the bar together and entered the lounge, only this time Simone was waiting for me. I continued on through the lounge and headed for the Palm Court with Doloros, but at the entrance stood the Austrian girl Edith. As we passed her, I nodded my head and said, "Hello."

I had finally settled down with one girl for the evening. I was glad all the confusion was over, at least for the present.

The Palm Court was filled with bingo enthusiasts, so we went to the card room to play the game of Patience. It was a new card game for me, but it was something to occupy time until the dance floor was cleared.

We were able to dance at twelve thirty and joined a group of young people.

Since the clocks were set back one hour again, there was time for an hour's dancing and fun making.

As the evening came to a close, I decided to again ask Doloros if she wanted to go for a walk, and hoping for the worst, I was surprised to have her reply. "Yes." Well, I didn't know what to think of things. Here I had tried to make excuses to be with other girls, and now she was willing to be with me. I guess I never will understand women.

We walked to the rear of the ship, where we sat in the cool air and talked for ten minutes and then returned to our respective cabins for needed rest.

August 2—Clear, Warm, and Pleasant

I enjoyed a good night's rest and had breakfast at nine thirty, then I met Doloros and sat in deck chairs to get a suntan. Joan Frey had agreed to carve a turtle out of a bar of soap and offered it as a prize to the winner of a bridge game. The foursome would consist of Doloros,

Joan, Simon Benenson (the cute Russian who enjoyed the game so much), and me.

We hoped that Simon would win the game and agreed to switch partners after each rubber. We had talked of the contest the previous day and suggested that there should be a prize for the winner, and since Simon had always won, he was quite excited to learn that a prize would be given to the winner.

The turtle was expertly carved from Ivory soap and appeared quite realistic. Joan received many compliments for her work, and we looked forward to the afternoon bridge game.

We played deck tennis until one fifteen and then returned to the deck chairs to relax in the warm sun. At 4:00 p.m., the foursome gathered in the Palm Court for the bridge tournament.

We informed Simon there was a prize for the winner and settled down to a serious game of cards. He proceeded to win quite handily as he was on the winning side for each of the three rubbers. Once, Doloros and I went down five tricks, while vulnerable, doubled, and redoubled! This cost us 2,800 points.

We presented the prize to Simon, and he was overjoyed that anyone should spend three hours carving a turtle from a bar of soap for him. His face beamed with excitement as he displayed his prize to his friends.

The young people then went to the sports deck to play some deck tennis. We played seven games of the intriguing sport and played until it was time to dress for dinner.

After dinner, I met Doloros in the movie lounge, but since there were no more seats, we adjourned to the card room for another round of Patience. We finished up the card-playing with several games of Hollywood Gin Rummy.

We then went to the Palm Court to end the evening on the dance floor and sat at the stern of the ship for forty minutes, talking over each other's trip. I walked her to her cabin, and another wonderful day ended.

August 3—Cool and Foggy

I awoke at nine fifteen, and after a light breakfast, I filled out my declaration form for the United States government customs. I had to stand in line for ten minutes to hand it in, but with this chore out of the way, I was able to be with the girls while they filled out their forms.

I returned to my cabin to catch up on writing in my diary and expense booklet. This occupied my time until 12:30 p.m.

I went to the sports deck and found Doloros (Dee) and an Englishman named Peter talking together. Peter was born in South America but now lived in Georgia.

Before going to lunch, I addressed a postcard to Edith, wishing her a good trip, and signed by "the captain." I put this on our table and waited until our gathering came to the table for lunch.

Edith discovered the card and willingly showed it to all of us. She believed that the captain had actually sent her the greeting. The card was not meant to deceive her but to cheer her up, and this did achieve results.

After lunch, I had made plans with Joan Frey to play bridge with Mr. and Mrs. Roeske from Wausau, Wisconsin. I held remarkable cards, and Joan and I were champions for the afternoon. The Roeskes were lovely people and extended an invitation for me to visit them and go skiing on Rib Mountain near their home.

It was 6:00 p.m. when the game broke up and we dressed for dinner. I was to meet Dee afterward and receive her itinerary, but she decided to attend the movie, so the scheduled meeting was postponed.

Later, Dee, Simon, Joan, and I gathered in the card room for some more bridge. Simon brought his pet turtle along, which had now lost three legs and his tail. He asked Joan to "repair" the wounded animal so he could show it to his wife back home.

Turtle or no turtle, Simon was not lucky at cards tonight. He lost two rubbers, and with Dee playing quite well, we easily managed to take top honors.

Simon offered to buy us all a drink, and for the first time on the entire trip, I had Seagram's Seven and 7-Up. Before this, the drinks had been served with sparkling water or some other mixer that I did not care for.

The four of us went to the Palm Court and joined another young group. I was feeling in an active mood and asked Joan, Edith, Simone, and Dee to dance. The music stopped playing at 1:00 a.m., but our attention was now occupied by the drunken tactics of Mr. Craig, a Canadian passenger who had too much to drink.

I walked to the rear of the ship at 1:30 a.m. with Dee, and we talked until two forty. I was invited to visit her in Lawrence, Kansas, sometime in August. Our discussion centered on morals and the beauty of English women. Then I walked her to her cabin and thanked her for the wonderful evening.

Clocks were turned back thirty minutes, and I decided to head for the bar, where I met Edith and two Scottish girls. We had a drink and then returned to our cabins. My roommate, Ludwig, was still roaming the ship; this was most unusual for him, but I had seen him earlier with a German girl, and he was probably having his first shipboard romance.

I was just going to bed when he returned. We stayed up and talked until three thirty before we finally went to sleep.

August 4—Clear, Sunny, and Cool

I awoke at ten o'clock but couldn't stay awake, so I remained in bed until ten forty-five. I looked for Dee but could not find her. I walked around each deck and finally knocked on her cabin door only to learn she had just left. It wasn't long before I found her in the Palm Court, and she was able to give her itinerary and other helpful information.

We went to the sports deck, where we met a Dutch flyer by the name of Jerry. The three of us alternated playing deck tennis until lunch.

Today I brought a cut flower for Edith and placed it in her drinking glass. She was very pleased with it. Lunchtime was always the time for fun with our table. I enjoyed pork chops and two ham-and-cheese sandwiches.

Afterward, I met Jerry, and we went to the curio shop, where I bought my sister Janet some perfume and our home minister, Reverend Friz, some cigars.

We then went to the sports deck to bask in the sun and carry on a conversation between games of deck tennis. Dee came to the sports deck with another fellow, but we did not bother her but waited for her to come over to us.

We knew we were getting closer to land for fishing schooners were within sight of the ship. They were armed with harpoons on the bow.

I suggested that Dee buy us beer as she owed me one from yesterday's bridge game, so the three of us went to the bar and were bought a glass of beer.

She excused herself from our company, and Joe, the one who sat at our table, came along and started a discussion on flying. Jerry, the Dutch flyer, was born in Java and was trying to become a US citizen so he could be an air force pilot. We talked until 7:00 p.m. and watched the sunset on the ocean.

I took a shower and dressed for the farewell dinner of filet mignon. I was hungry after a hard day and ate three of them, two bowls of soup, french fries, tomato salad, lemon ice cream, and compote of apricots and plums. To top this off, the men at the table had bought two bottles of wine, one white and the other red, and by the end of the dinner, we were all feeling quite gay.

After dinner, Jerry and I waited for Dee and Edith to join us for dancing in the Palm Court. The dance floor was very crowded, and Edith did not join our crowd. I went to look for her but could not locate her. Meanwhile, Jerry danced with Dee.

Edith was to have had a blind date with Jerry but evidently backed out at the last moment. I continued to look for her as I took little side trips to various sections of the ship where she might be hiding.

I finally found her and convinced her to join our group. I introduced her to Jerry, and we sat down for a drink. I danced with Dee and Simone until one thirty but also had fun entering an "orange dance" with Dee. The object of this game was to balance an orange on a couple's forehead while dancing together. The strain was too much for us, and the orange slipped to the floor.

Another funny incident of the evening occurred when I danced near the orchestra and had my coat caught in the accordion.

Edith, Jerry, Dee, and I walked outside and sat in the deck chairs. We were able to see several falling stars and the Milky Way as a clear sky prevailed.

Later, we went to the lounge, where we talked until 3:45 a.m. Here I told Dee what I had done to make the homesick Edith feel better, as Edith and Jerry had excused themselves for a few minutes. Dee told me I was a thoughtful and considerate person, to which I replied it was the way I had been brought up.

We could not understand the actions of Edith for she excused herself every few minutes for periods of fifteen to twenty minutes.

I guessed we would never know her reasons for leaving us so often, but she did some crying and appeared quite upset. I walked Dee to her cabin at 4:15 a.m. and went to my cabin for a very short night of sleep.

August 5—Clear, Cool, Foggy, and Then Clear

I was up at ten thirty and, after dressing, went to the baggage room to declare unbought items that I was considering purchasing after I arrived home. On the wall of the baggage room was a large map that showed all the countries I had visited. I bought a similar one for 25¢ so I might display it at home.

I went to the sports deck, but finding no activity, I decided to visit the bridge of the ship. Here I was given firsthand information on all the equipment by the first officer of the ship. The automatic pilot was explained to me as well as the operation of the sounding devices, radar operations, and the closing of the watertight compartments.

Our group was told how the recent collision of the two ships might have occurred. This also proved to be very interesting. As our group was about to depart from the bridge, another group was arriving. To my surprise, Joan and Dee were among the people on this tour.

I waited for them to complete their tour, and then we all went to the sports deck, where we took a sunbath until it was time for lunch. It was so cool we had to borrow a woolen blanket to keep warm when the sun went behind the clouds.

The final bridge game of the trip took place after lunch. It was scheduled for 2:30 p.m., and by three thirty, we had completed three rubbers. My biggest thrill came from bidding six spades and making seven!

I talked with Barbara Walker in the Palm Court and found her very interesting. She was a bookbinder, sculptor, painter, and costume and jewelry designer and had four parents, had lived in three states, was eighteen years old, and had just spent the last year in Italy getting experience in her talents.

After teatime, I took a walk around the many decks of the ship. I walked over to the first-class side of the ship and walked through their lounge. I just wanted to see how the "stuffed shirts" lived since there were only forty-four first-class passengers.

Finding a ping-pong table, I asked someone to play, but while playing, we were told by the steward that the table was reserved for first-class passengers only. However, since no one was using the facilities, I saw no reason for not playing, and we continued our game after the deck steward left.

I returned to my cabin to rest and pack before dressing for dinner. We sat down to a delicious chicken dinner for the last time we would all be together. Joe invited Dee over for a glass of liquor, and we all adjourned to the Palm Court for dancing and community singing.

Tonight was also talent night, and Joan Frey sang three lovely songs. Other talent included sketch drawing and various dances. The funniest event occurred when a French woman who had been telling everyone she was a movie star took the spotlight. She looked like someone from the silent movies, and with her long red hair draped over her face, she created quite a sight.

We danced until 12:30 a.m., during which time Simon bought us a drink. I danced for the last time with Dee and Simone and met another girl, Jackie from Minnesota, who had traveled by freighter from Manila before boarding our ship.

I walked Dee to her cabin and asked her if she cared to go for a walk. She replied no, but again, I waited to see her come and go for a walk alone. She was a nice-looking girl but deceitful in her mannerism. At this point of the voyage, I was thoroughly disgusted with her and now wished I had spent more quality time with the nicer girls on the ship. I returned to my cabin and hit the sack.

August 6—Rainy

I was up 9:00 a.m. and finished packing before going to breakfast. We were traveling very slowly now and were not due to dock until 12:30 p.m. I went to the prom deck to see the city of New York, but the sight was hazy, and with the rain coming down, the idea of looking at the shore was forgotten.

At 11:00 a.m., the immigration authorities came on board, and we were hurriedly checked and received a landing card. Time was passing slowly now, and we were anxious to dock.

I went to the dining room for lunch at eleven forty-five and enjoyed two juicy steaks. I wanted to eat as much as I could since I did not know when I would be eating again.

I walked to Dee's table and wished her a good homeward journey and also said good-bye to Joan and all the other friends I had made.

Simon, the Russian, had asked me to carry a large parcel for him, which I gladly did, but the fact that we had to stand for an hour and a half before disembarking did not make any of us happy.

It was 1:30 p.m. before we were permitted to get off the ship and proceed down the gangplank. I had my knapsack strapped over my shoulder and carried my suitcase in one hand and Simon's parcel in the other.

I checked in at the customs' table and was inspected by an officer. He looked over my belongings and my declaration list and wished me on my way, saying, I could not have brought too much back with me since I traveled so lightly.

I turned around and met Adalie, a relative of ours from New York. Mother had written her I was coming to New York, and she offered to help in any way and was to take me to the Newark Airport for my flight home.

We walked to the area where her son Robert was waiting and then proceeded to her car. She wanted to show me the sights of New York, but my plane flight was at 5:00 p.m., and I suggested going directly to the airport, where we could relax and talk during the remaining hours.

At the airport, I checked my baggage in at thirty-eight pounds, and then before sending them to be loaded on the plane, I asked if I could take something from my suitcase. The inspector handed my suitcase back to me, and while he was busy with another customer, I unloaded some ten pounds of articles from my pockets and stuffed them in the suitcase as I didn't want to go over the forty-pound limit without paying a penalty.

I handed the suitcase back to the inspector, and he sent it right on down to the loading area without bothering to reweigh it.

Adalie, Robert, and I sat in the airport waiting room and talked over various things since it had been some time since they were in Saint Louis. I tried to tell them as much as I could about my trip, but there was too much to relate in such a short time.

We waited for the hour of 5:00 p.m. to approach, and at four forty-five, we walked to gate 12, where I said good-bye to the distant relatives who had been so nice to me and, thanking them, boarded the plane that was to take me home.

I sat in the rear of the plane and watched us taxi down the runway at five two, but we were unable to take off for forty-five minutes due to *air saturation*, the existence of too many planes wanting to land and take off in the immediate area.

After the long wait, we took off for Baltimore and landed there one hour late. The plane was refueled, and we headed for Washington,

DC. We again hurried our stop, trying to make up the lost time, and were soon on our way to Louisville, Kentucky, for a short layover.

On the flight I ate three roast-beef sandwiches and drank some tea. We were due in Saint Louis at ten thirty-three but didn't arrive until 11:05 p.m. I was so excited as we approached for the landing. Saint Louis looked so large as we flew over its many lighted streets. Out of the darkness, our plane suddenly seemed to settle on the large runway at Lambert Airport.

I was the first passenger off the plane, and in a few minutes, I saw Janet and Carol waving to me. Mother and Dad were right behind them, and they had that pleasing look on their faces as if to say, "Well, you did what you said you were going to do, and we're so proud of you."

We walked to where Grandma and Aunt Lizzie were waiting for their first glimpse of the *determined hitchhiker*. I greeted them warmly, but they were laughing at the way I talked, but that didn't bother me for I was glad to be home once more.

We drove to 5810 Kingwood Drive, where we gathered in the living room and I presented some gifts. Excitement prevailed into the wee morning hours as we talked and related experiences that happened to me as well as the ones that happened around home.

Many days were ahead, and many stories would be told, so it was to bed with us all and a restful night enjoyed at the grandest place in the world, home.

And thus my trip to Europe has ended.

This story would not be complete without mentioning the following two experiences that occurred—first, right after my returning home and, second, some nineteen years later—that closed the door on this wonderful travel experience!

Experience 1: Shortly after Arriving Home

I had arrived home on Monday August 6, 1956, and the family was eager to engage in conversation about my wonderful journey. I had my thoughts on my girlfriend, Carol Ratjen, from Chicago Heights, Illinois. I had lovely gifts and had yet to meet her parents, so against my parents desires, I planned the coming weekend trip of three hundred miles to see my love and relate the experiences of my trip.

Carol had planned dinner at the Pump Room and a play for our first night together, which was all first-class! I had been invited to stay in their home for the weekend. Sunday, after lunch, we retired to the living room for conversation, during which time I gave Carol some gifts from Europe—a sweater, purse, and jewelry were some of the items. Everything was going well, until I suggested Carol visit us in Saint Louis to better acquaint herself with my sisters and parents, as I had only begun dating Carol several months prior to my departure. She avoided an immediate answer to my invitation, but later, when we were alone, she informed me of her attraction to a new boyfriend in my absence and declined the invitation; needless to say, I was in a state of shock and could not believe she let me come to Chicago without informing me and that she accepted the expensive gifts and then told me of her new relationship! The rest of the visit was now dampened, and departure on Monday gave me a lonely trip home. I wished I had taken my parents' advice to stay home for a while and dreaded the confrontation with them when I would tell of my rejection. The lesson learned: listen to the experience of your parents, who love you and know better. This experience was the *only* negative impact on my wonderful trip to Europe in 1956.

Experience 2: Do Not Despair—My Most Wonderful Mother Made All Things Better, but I Had to Wait Nineteen Years for a Blessed Event to Occur

My birthday is January 24, and my fortieth would occur in 1975. We were celebrating Christmas in December 1974, and I was given a surprise gift to cherish forever. While I was on my European trip you had just read, you probably noticed I mentioned mailing letters to the family via aerograms every several days. In fact, I sent twelve letters explaining in great detail what I had done, whom I had met, and to keep them abreast of my travels and not to worry. I thought nothing more of this correspondence until December 25, 1974, when as an expression of love, Mother and Dad presented me a gift from the heart, as they had saved these twelve letters and given me a scrapbook of these twelve letters typed exactly as I had written them and included the date they were received.

I have enclosed these typed letters as a fitting ending to a wonderful journey and wish to share with those of you who have enjoyed reading about my hitchhiking experience in the summer of 1956. I hope you have enjoyed reading my adventure as much as I have enjoyed putting these experiences together, truly the greatest accomplishment of eighty years of my living.

—Joseph E. Hahn

An Introduction to the Twelve Letters and My Parents' Cover Letter to Me as Given on Christmas Day, December 25, 1974

Dear Joe:

We had fun reading these letters from 1956.
    There were many things that we did not remember. We decided to make a copy of your twelve letters you sent us. You surely had some wonderful experiences which we know you'll never forget.
    We're very proud of you and as you stated in your letter from the chalet that "God is Always With You."
    A most Blessed Christmas and much happiness with your family in the coming years.

Lovingly,
Dad & Mother
(The following letters are typed exactly as they were written.)

Letter 1

(This letter was received Saturday, June 16, 1956.)

R.M.S. Maasdam
June 9, 1956
HOLLAND-AMERICA LINE

Dear Mom and Dad—

All is going well with me. As you can see, I made the ship. I was on the ship by 9:20 a.m. I had arrived in N.Y. at 6:45 & called the Stocks & Elizabeth around 7:15.

I have a lovely room, small but quite adequate for my type of living. No sea sickness as yet but we've had lovely weather.

Received telegram from Carol and your sweet card for which I thank you.

The sea has been most calm and we've had sun every day but two. The swimming pool was opened, but as yet I haven't tried it out.

There are ten persons at our table and they have varied set of personalities, coming from all parts of the world.

There is a wonderful Dutch girl from Winterswijk, a woman from Oklahoma, a dentist from Scotland, a Frenchman (about my age) a French woman (42) who lives in N.Y. a prof. of Modern Languages at Cornell and the two daughters & son of a family from Bethlehem, Pa.

I shall disembark in the morning of June 13 at Southampton.

This ship is one from heaven—having all modern conveniences & large recreation rooms, a palm court for dancing that would make most of our night clubs look sick.

June 11—Yes, the ship is a good one. I'm glad I'm well on my way.

Yesterday I played ping-pong with the Captain of the ship. He just looked like another officer, but later found out he was the Captain.

Also took very interesting trips to the engine room & the Bridge. Speaking of Bridge reminds me to tell you I'm playing 2 to 3 hours a day and doing quite well.

The food on ship is great. I've got a second setting which allows me more sleep in the early hours of the day.

I'm going to scribble out a few post cards today and then call it quits on writing except to you and Carol—but only when I have time.

I met a Mr. Blattner from St. Louis who runs a bar down on Shendoah (spelling) in South St. Louis. He is quite a good singer.

Nothing to complain about now and only good things to tell you, so you should not worry.

One week is now past and the others shall pass quickly also.

June 12, 1956. Well, England is in sight and the beautiful day makes for great anticipation of what shall come. I've never seen such beautiful weather for a crossing.

I've met a Mr. & Mrs. John Shortall from Boston who brought a car across with them (a Cadallic) and they disembark at Southampton tomorrow. They are going within 20 miles of Preston & I'm promised a ride if they are not too overcrowded.

Last night was the Farewell Party and it was full of fun and excitement. The life on a ship is so wonderful I wouldn't mind crossing back & forth each summer.

Everything is <u>still</u> going fine & no hitches have developed. The meals have been superb & filling.

The friends I've made have been countless.

I'm about to pack as I've washed out all dirty clothes and they are now drying.

Today the SS United States passed us like we were sitting still, but we've been going 21 miles an hour.

Well, I must close for now but am thinking of you always,

Love,
Joe

Letter 2

(This letter was received June 18, 1956, from Preston, England.)

June 14, 1956

Dear Mom, Dad, Janet & Carol—

I received your letter this morning & wish to thank you for it. The reason you didn't hear from me is that there is no daily mail service from the ship. Now to tell you all the latest happenings.

We docked early in Southampton & I had a breakfast & packed some sandwiches for my trip north. Please prepare yourself for some tales of fascination—well here goes.

I took a taxi from dock to Winchester & hit the truck route. I waited 15 seconds for 1st ride which was in the cab of a brick truck. He took me to Newbury. My next ride came along in about a minute; he was an Irish Naval Tailor & he took me 23 miles. My next ride came in about 20 sec. I was picked up by two American Soldiers from Chicago & N.Y. who were delivering a transformer north. The big truck could hardly make it through the winding streets. Rode with them for an hour & then was picked up after waiting all of 1 1/2 minutes by a gravel truck driver.

My next ride was from Mr. Norris, a man in produce business, who dropped me off in Stradford, the hometown of Shakespeare. He even drove by the statue so I could photograph it.

My next ride was with a married couple on their way to Birmingham. Here I was shortly picked up by the Nichols family & brought further north.

My 9th different ride was with a steel driver from Hull, England who took me to Litchfield. Here he stopped & hailed a moving van from Manchester for me, which took me only 35 miles from Preston. The moving VAN was driven by Sid & Bill & was loaded down. I ate my sandwiches on the long trip North—which was my 10th ride. I was left off in heart of Manchester & waited only 2 minutes only to be picked up in pickup truck & had to sit in rear of it with my suitcase as we went through rush traffic.

My 12th ride was in a confectionary truck which took me to Bury. From there I was picked up by 2 men driving another produce truck & was dropped off at their garage.

I was only waiting a few minutes to be picked up by a couple on a date. They only took me a few miles. My 15th lift came from a businessman on way home from work. He dropped me 8 miles from Preston.

The very next vehicle to pass by was a Fire Dept. Service truck that had been delivering hoses to Manchester & who was headed for Preston.

I told him the street, I wanted & he went out of his way & dropped me off 3 houses from where Eric lives. It took me 10 1/2 hours & 16 rides to go from Southampton to Preston—380 miles as I arrived at 7:30 P.M.

Eric was glad to see me & he told me of his having a bicycle accident on Sunday & just getting out of the hospital on Tuesday so he's home from work for the entire week.

I'm leaving here Sunday morning—pushing on to Scotland to Edinbough & then looking for a crossing to Norway.

Today I was taken on a general tour by uncle "Eric" after a good nights sleep. Two letters were here from Carol which made me feel good.

I will write when possible but so far everything has come off without any trouble. I was very lucky to come as far as I did yesterday & come within 50 feet of Eric's home.

Must close for now, but try to have several letters waiting for me with news from home in Rosswangen for me.

Love,
Joe

Well hello there, Just the last few lines from Eric to say that everything is O.K. Joe and I are having a very good time and he's trying to get me to St. Louis. Bye for now—My love to you all.

Eric

Letter 3

(This letter was received, June 23, 1956)

June 19, 1956

Hello All—

Since I last wrote you—a great deal has happened. I guess I'm touched by a string of good luck, but here goes to bring you up to date on my travels.

In Preston, we journeyed to Southport on Friday & to Blackpool on Saturday, both places are large tourist attractions. We had an enjoyable time at both places & met many people. They are both about 20 miles from Preston.

Slept until 10 a.m. on Sunday & began hitchhiking north. My luck held out & I was picked up by 1st car driven by 3 people from London going to Glascow in Scotland. They took me 50 miles south of Glascow & I then headed north east to Edinburgh. I was picked up by Dick Fielding from St. Boswells, just north of Harwick. I told him I intended to lodge at a Hostel in Edinburgh. He invited me to spend the night as a guest in his home. Since he was going to Edinburgh the next day. We drove through the hilly country of Scotland—right through the valleys & arrived at his home at 7 P.M.

I was given a private room—well furnished & shown to the bathroom—all tiled, and quickly took a bath—my 1st in 5 days as Hammonds have no facilities whatsoever.

I dressed up for them & they had small cakes & breads prepared for me. We sat around fireplace sipping tea & then went to Dryburgh Abbey, a famous old place built in 1140.

Returned home around 10 P.M. for dinner—it still was daylight out, and we sat & talked to 1 a.m. The bed was the best I've had—very soft & good sleeping. I was awakened at 10:30 and given an American breakfast of Shredded Wheat—eggs, bacon and bread & jelly—with a glass of milk. I was treated like a King—Dick is a building contractor foreman & took off on Monday to show me around Edinburgh—34 miles to the north. Try to follow my trip on a map if you can. I'm recording my travels daily & keeping an exact diary.

Now I set about trying to get passage to Bergen, Norway, but no passengers ships go from port. I went to Norwegian Lines & they directed me to talk to the Capt. of the freighter "Royal" Here I sat with the Captain & he said he could take me on board as an Assistant Deck Mate—the only trouble was she was sailing on Saturday June 23 & then going to Copenhagen instead of Norway. I told him I'd be back to go with him if I couldn't find something else. Stopped truck & asked if he was going to Newcastle & he in turn hailed truck that was going there—loaded with 10 ton of fish. It was now 6 P.M. & I was on my way to Newcastle—120 miles due south along the coast.

Arrived here at 9:45 & went to Y M C A where Hostel was—but it had been discontinued & so a Mr. Stevenson directed me to a private home- called a "Dig" where I got lodging for night and breakfast of cornflakes—eggs, bacon, breads & jelly & tea all for 12–6 (12 shillings & 6 pence) about $1.75.

Why yesterday I only spent 40¢ all day & day before I traveled from Preston to the Fielding home, not spending one penny. The people from London who picked me up bought my lunch & afternoon tea.

This morning I booked passage to Bergen, Norway—my ship sails at 4 P.M. tomorrow. Please pay film bill when Eckman gives it to you & I'll pay you back when I can.

Love,
Joe

Letter 4

(This letter was received June 29, 1956.)

June 23, 1956

Dear Family—

Here I am in the center of Western Norway, experiencing beautiful sights that are beyond all comprehension. I've stayed in 2 Hostels—one in Voss for 28¢ and the other in Baldstrand for $1.02 which included supper, bed and breakfast; then I paid them 28¢ to pack 4 sandwiches for me. Now I'm on an 8 hour bus ride to Olden where snow is on ground yearly. Bus is nearly the only way to get around. I've met many wonderful people in this land of the north. Last night I went to bed at 1 a.m. and it was very light out—I was able to read the maps by the light. Then at 2:30 the sunlight became brighter. I'm not *too* many miles from the Artic Circle & the weather has been wonderful—very warm.

    The crossing of the North Sea took 22 hours and I got sick for the 1st time. I'm fine now and I think of you, mother, each night I slip between the sleeping sack. The time flies fast. You know I'll have been gone 3 weeks this Monday.

    I won't be in Rosswangen to the 4th of July the way my trip is going. You can't make time in Norway, but don't care much—for the beauty is there to see.

I think I shall be in Stockholm in 4 days and then proceed on to Berlin after visiting a family in Denmark.

Haven't lost a thing as yet and only complaint is case weighs too much, but I carry it very little.

Hope you write as often as I do and that your health is all tops.

Oh yes, on the crossing of the North Sea I saw Mary Bauer and the grey haired man who wears a mustache. I don't know his name, but Mary played golf with Mother before.

Then 5 minutes later I met a girl hostelling who lives in Ladue who has been studying the past year in Edinburgh.

What a small world; you and Dad will have to plan a trip to this country, someday for you'll never forget the beauty. We passed over Mt. Pass and through cut in snow deeper than the bus. Ice was still on the lake which was like a crater on top of mountain.

I only hope I can bring my trip back to you in the form of the interesting slides.

Do write me and I'll be home soon—Miss you all & may God Richly bless our home.

Love,
Joe

Letter 5

(This letter was received July 2, 1956.)

June 29, 1956

Hello Again—

Since I last wrote you in Norway I have now seen some beautiful sights—the Mts. of Norway with snow so very deep was most impressive while the cold hearted Swedes has left a sour note of concern for them. I've stayed in 4 Hostels so far & enjoyed each one. Most important has been the wonderful people & connections I have met.

This morning I am on my way to Hamburg & then on to Berlin to visit east Berlin & the Russian Sector by bus. A 2 1/2 hour trip only costs 25¢.

Here in the Capitol of Denmark I am staying with a private family for 8 kroner a night and 2 1/2 kroner for Breakfast. Each kroner is equal to 14¢. The Hostel is on outside of town & this location is most convenient. Yesterday I had breakfast served to me in bed. I also visited the Tivoli—the famous amusement Park which is out of this world in beauty & spectacle at night—admission 11¢.

Last night I was invited for dinner by a Danish family as I inquired as such as I told you I would. They were most wonderful to me & we had excellent dinner with fresh strawberries & Danish Pastry.

Their son, Jerry, 24, is coming to Boston to study textile business in October. This family registers its name with the tourist information bureau & have guests to their home often.

My lodging is with a swell family who is in frozen custard business & have a nice apartment. When I first arrived I washed my clothes & took 1st bath since Newcastle—8 days ago—No Hostel had any showers.

I guess you'll want to know about this, as I was going to surprise you, but while hitchhiking in Norway a man from the local newspaper of Eastern Norway asked me to come to his office for an interview with editor. I was shown to his office & notes were taken on my various travels. A picture was taken of me studying the map & then one taken of me, trying to hitch a ride on the street.

This was to appear in the evening paper but I had to go on to Sweden & could not wait for the editor.

They took my address & said they would send a copy to you at home. I didn't want you to think an issue of the Sun Gazette was coming and have you throw it away.

Well, in one month I'll be sailing again & will be home soon. I'm really not homesick & I wish I could stay longer. Time has flown by quickly and seems to as long as I am busy.

Can hardly wait for some good home cooking & do hope a good steak or some fried chicken, mashed potatoes & milk gravy will be waiting for me at 10:33 on August 6th.

Must close for now & will next answer your letter from Rosswangen. Dad—everything is going fine & no difficulties have developed. I never knew travelling could be so interesting. Someday I'll again come back as I greatly enjoy these foreign countries & their hospitality.

HITCHHIKING THROUGH EUROPE DURING THE SUMMER OF 1956

It has been quite cold here as well as in Norway & I'm looking to a warmer Germany so I can wear the light shirts.

Bye for now—you have my love & I think of you always.

God bless you—
Joe

Letter 6

(This letter was received July 3, 1956.)

June 30, 1956

Hello Again:

Just arrived in Hamburg & bought through plane ticket to Berlin & Frankfurt for 115 marks or $28.00. I plan to spend 1 day in East Berlin & 1 day in West Berlin.

Left yesterday from Copenhagen & arrived in Flensburg where I was the guest of a Joe Klebe. I was hitching rides in Central Denmark, as I had gotten that far on 5 lifts when a bus stopped for me. I thought they were stopping to take me on as a paying passenger. Here the bus had 18 German people from Flensburg who had been 8 days in Copenhagen. They were singing & talking in German the whole trip—taking me across border. Also on the bus was the boy Joe who had also been picked up & he was on way to visit his aunt in Flensburg & asked me to stay with him after I inquired of him the whereabouts of the Hostel.

Had dinner of 5 potatoes & 2 herring & then we went to a school where he teaches the art of fencing. This was quite interesting & then we went to Gasthaus to drink good beer.

Had filling breakfast & bought knap-sack for 15 marks that listed for 25. I now carry the suitcase empty for the use of "U.S.A."

which greatly helps me get rides, and the knap-sack is not a burden at all as it fits nicely over shoulders. It has leather padded straps.

As to interesting experiences which happen daily, I was approached yesterday by 5 different Danish boys who asked for my name & address—as it is a hobby. Oh my—what next!

Carol, where I stayed last night, there is a girl of 14 who wants to write to an American & she asked if she could write you when I told her I had 2 sisters. She has your address & will write 1st, but you could also write her. She reminds me of you—as she is always on the go. Her address is Flensburg—Toosbuy Str. 3 I, but I now forgot her name.

I'm now outside the airport where spectators can watch the planes take off & just resting for a change. I have covered a great deal of ground & luck has been with me.

My lift to Hamburg was accomplished in one jump: I waited all of 5 minutes at edge of town and was taken directly to airport outside of the city of Hamburg. I'll have many things to tell you—some quite funny. Everything has been written down in the thick note book I took along and it is filled up with one hundred pages so far. I must buy a new one to continue my travels. I'm on 8th roll of film & should provide you with a fine evening of entertainment.

Going to eat dinner now—5 P.M. My plane leaves for Berlin at 9:40 & arrives at 10:50 P.M.

Bye.

Love,
Joe

Letter 7

(This letter was received Friday, July 13, 1956.)

July 7, 1956

Hello all!

Sorry I could not write from Berlin but now I have the chance. The flight from Hamburg was very good—55 minutes at 200 miles an hour. I arrived at 11 P.M. and had hotel 2 blocks away with washbasin, good bed, closet, table and large window for 6 marks ($1.44) I stayed there 4 nights and on Sunday took a 2 1/2 hour Army bus tour of East Berlin for 25¢. The east Sector of the Russians is a great deal of ruin and only Stalin Allee is a newly constructed street. The people do not dress with color and Russian soldiers are all over just waiting for an American to step out of line. The damage of ruins is a terrible mess—at one time Berlin was 80% destroyed and West Berlin is slowly recovering but by manual labor so unemployment is low.

I rented a bicycle and went touring on Monday & Tuesday; my plane left at 12:30 P.M. on Wed. and a rough flight was had to Frankfurt. From there went to Hahau & then Wurzburg & had hotel again for 6 marks. (Y.H. filled.) Then went to Rotenburg for a day & stayed in Y.H. 400 years old. Oh My—seeing is believing, but I had cot and 2 blankets for 50 pfg. (12¢). Walked the entire wall around town and met interesting people. From there I went by U.S. Army truck & many other lifts in a round about way to Dinkelsbuhle, Ulm, Tuebington & arrived in Rosswangen at 7:30 A.M.—today to receive 12 letters—3 from you, 2 from Grandma, 2 from Carol, one from Carol (Rice in Seattle) 1 from Carla in Calif, 1 from Dr. Hynek in Austria, 1 from Holland Am. Line on boat train information from Paris & my report card from College!

Johan is very sick & Julian is not too well off either. I walked from Endington & someone from town took my suitcase & knapsack to Rosswangen, Germany for me. Walk was only 3km an hr. At 7 a.m. I felt like walking.

Back in Berlin I visited all the main places of interest Potsdamer Platz, Brandburg Gate, Kanewe Dept. Store and many other places.

Had good time at U.S. Service Club for 6th Inf. Stationed there. My passport allowed me to enter & one night I saw American movie for 25¢ & next night drank 4 beer and 2 hamburger for 75¢. Saw "Bud" on sale for 25¢ but I drank German beer. There was a Trio to play music till 12 o'clock & I sat and talked English for a change; my German is getting better!

Attention Girls—I was picked up by a tennis player who was one of best 10 in Germany from 1936–1943 & he has two daughters, 13 & 15, the 13 year old writes to an American girl, but 15 year old wants to write to one of you- name and address follow:

Ines Koschel 13

Leistenstrasse 23

Wurzburg, Germany.

Please see that this girl & one in Flensburg are written some type of letter. Janet—this girl is best for you. If I do a few things for you (hint) you write these girls. You shall be surprised weekly with "little" surprises. I am in gut health; see that you are the same! The doll I won on ship I gave to Bernt who can walk. Rosswangen sends her Greetings your way.

Love,
Joe

Time flies fast. Be home in one month. My ship sails at 11 a.m. on July 29. We go to Southampton from Le Havre & then to N.Y. (for you Dad—plane to N.Y. on June 5th was very delightful. I slept most of way & got off for air in Washington D.C. & Louiville, Kentucky.

With my Knapsack—I do feel like the "Happy Wanderer."

Love,
Joe

Letter 8

(This letter was received Monday, July 16, 1956.)

July 11, 1956

Hello Again—

Just another one of my letters to bring you up to date on my travels. I have just totaled up expenses and from the time I left Saint Louis, June 5th, through July 10, I have spent $159.48 including passage to Bergen from England for $26.60 and plane fare from Hamburg to Berlin to Frankfurt for $27.60. This $159.48 does not include plane fare to N.Y. or ship passage, but includes all tips on boat—$10.25 and all living expenses! Quite a saving if I must say so. In fact, I'm quite proud of myself. Hope the gifts are arriving by now—I have paid for all of them and do believe I'm buying all sensible things, but will let you guess what they are until they come.

The weather here has been very warm & humid—about 80—I have worked in the fields, but easily become tired.

Two days ago I was in my room & little Anna, who knew I had gum & candy, came to knock on my door and ask for some. Then yesterday I went to the school during recess period and gave all MAC'S gum & some taffy to the children. They then posed with the teacher for a picture.

The time has surely gone fast; I can hardly believe I'm gone nearly 5 weeks.

Rosswangen has changed little, but the old house across the street is redone & Adler's House is all finished. They all want me to say hello to you from them & Big Anna said she is too busy to write. Today it is raining and I'm taking the time to write letters. I leave for Fussen in early morning via Kempton where a boy I met asked me to visit him. Dr. Hynek wrote me in Rosswangen and said I would be a welcome guest.

While hitchhiking the other day I was picked up by a couple (American man—Polish woman) and taken to their home in Ochsenfurt / Main and given the greatest American Dinner. His wife paints ties and they gave me one of the most beautiful I have seen. Only hope the weather holds out for the rest of trip for when it rains I become disheartened and it is hard to get a ride in the rain as I found out in Norway.

They have been feeding me well and I think I'm gaining pounds. I'm starting to get homesick now as sailing date slowly arrives. I've so many things to tell you, it is impossible in a letter.

My health is fine; now I've a small cold, but aside from that and getting stung by 3 bees, I'm in fine shape.

Alles ist sehr gut mit mich und es ist sehr schoen in Deutchland. Mine zimmer und mine Bett ist nich hart und ich schlaffe sehr gut. Ich essen and drinke der gut bier of Deutchland und in fuer woche ich comme nach St. Louis. Dis ist nich gut deutch, aber ist besser den last yahr.

Guten tag.

Love,
Joe

P.S. The boat trip to Bergen took 22 hours!

Letter 9

(This letter was received Thursday, July 20, 1956.)

July 14, 1956

Hello Again:

Well once more I have a pen with ink, and have loads to tell you from happenings of past 2 days. Spent 5 days in Rosswangen, leaving July 12 at 10 a.m., as Elsie, baby Berhardt, Anna & little Anna walked me to Endingen. Before that I was presented roses & other flowers. I also said goodbye to Johan in his bed & Julian for the last time. They had tears in their eyes as we pulled wagon with my suitcase & knapsack the 3 km. to Endingen. The night before we celebrated; 1st I went to Butz family for Wine & Conac, where the table was decorated nicely with strands of colored lights & "Auf Wiedersehn" was written on table in rose leaves. All were dressed up for me and then Elfriede and I went to kitchen of Josef where whole family was gathered for talking and drinking. My German is quite good & I was well understood. Surprising!

As we reached highway to Rottweil I was on wrong side of road and motioned for car to stop & he did—taking me to Schwenningen where in a few minutes I was taken to Donaueshingen. Here I was in center of city & waited until woman from Los Angeles in a very small car stopped and after a 10 minute rearrangement of her car I was finally crowded in. She took me to next town. She is very good friend of Mallincrodt's of St. Louis in Chemical Industry & asked me to visit them for her (16 Westmoreland) Next picked up by 4 people from New Jersey who took me to Konstanz on Boden See. I had to take bus to edge of City & surprisingly entered Switzerland. Picked up by old German officer of last war who took me to Arbon. He was prisoner of war 2 years in Texas. He gave me Ham sandwich. As I left him I also had 4 sandwiches. Elsie had packed for me. 6th ride of day came soon & I went to Ronschach; 7th took me to Breginz; 8th, a real hot rod—in sports car took me to Feldkirk, 9th took me to Bludenz. They were a family from Innsbruck, but were not going there that night. It was 6:10 and my 10th ride with 3 civil engineers from Innsbruck and I made same journey that we did by train. (Alsburg Express) last year only by car. We stopped at top of Mt. Pass for Cognac (39¢) and later stopped for dinner (2 beers 24¢. Soup 15¢ so I spent 78¢ that day. I was taken to "Gasthof Sailer" 2 blocks from Marie Thersia Street & had hotel room for 26 shillings $1.07. Had large room with twin beds and slept to 9 a.m.—Friday 13th. This day turned out to be luckiest of all for me. 1st I wanted to see how City looked after a year; went to Bank & then walked through old section as we did last year where bombed building was being torn down—new building still not finished. Thought I'd look for cars with white "W" on black license as that means Wien—Vienna. I asked several people with the "W" if they were going there & all said "No". It was 10:30 & I returned to hotel & checked out—heading for highway—#1 to Wien. As I was crossing center of City I saw car pulling away from curb with the "W" I hurried across street and asked them if I could go to Wien with them, only to be told them were Contracting business in Salzburg; next I asked if I could go there with them, but was given an evasive answer. I then told them I was lost in Innsbruck and asked if I could at least go to #1 on outside of city and was told to "get in." Car was driven by Dr.

Gatterer from Wien who was in tapestry business—who decorated the Opera House in Wien! He took me to edge of Innsbruck and then 153km. (92 miles) to Salzburg & dropped me off at Austrian-German border near Berchtesgarten & told border guard to try to get me a ride to Wien. In two min. I was in car with Lt. Gil Hall from Maine, stationed in Livorno, Italy. He & wife were on way to Linz, 118km (71 miles) from Salzburg. They were on way to adopt child & we stopped & he bought me beer as we sat in street café. He left me off outside Linz just as car from Virginia struck motorcycle from Austria—hurling driver through air. I got some shots of accident and stayed there an hour, before young girl took me 3km. to a busy intersection outside of Linz on by-pass to Wien. Here I waited to 6:50 when car passed me by and then made U turn to come back & pick me up. It was very small car and I sat in front with driver as 2 women held my case & sack on their laps. They took me 25km. (14 miles) and invited me to stay with them for the night. I elected to head for Wien—192 km. (115) miles to east. They pulled car to side of road and all 3 got out to stop cars with "W" on it for me but they nearly caused several accidents and I suggested it best I try alone. I bid them farewell and thanked them for their troubles. At 7:10 a car came by and stopped; there was a "White" "W" on license and sure enough he was going to Wien. He was salesman for trousers, Franz Diemat. He stopped for Espresso Coffee (Mein1) and bought me mine. We passed Schoenbrun and headed in to center of city. It was 10 P.M. and he took me to Café and called Dr. Hynek for me, paying for phone call, and then left for his home as Dr. Hynek came to pick me up. We had beer & coffee there and then drove to his house where I had my 1st bath in 10 days (since Berlin). and then dinner of fried ham & eggs. We talked to 2 a.m. about various things; they expected me a week ago. I leave here the 19th for Lausanne (5 days). They have 3 daughters, 9,13,15. Tomorrow we go to Mts. for senic trip. Tonight Traute is invited to their home & all 4 of us go to Dance. This a.m. called Thomas Mein1, but he is in France and his father spoke with me. Everything going great—Rosswangen to Wien in 1 1/2 days on $2.08. Now have spent $165.18 for 38 days ($4.34 average) & there was 29¢ mistake, overcharge, on last letter I sent you, but is correct to date. Thinking of you—Received your 2nd letter today. (From Halmar in Norway went to Aduarka (Spelling wrong)—then down west coast through Grotterni to Helsingborgh and ferry to Helsingborgh Denmark & to Copenhagen. (Didn't go to Stockholm.) (West coast of Sweden) Home in 25 days.

Love,
Joe

Letter 10

(This letter was received July 24, 1956.)

July 18, 1956

Hello All:

As you can plainly see, I am back in civilization again & I thought you might enjoy a letter you can read. The Hynek family has been very good to me. As you know, I arrived on Friday 13th and from my earlier letter you know my activities of Saturday. Sat. night Traute Zellinger came to the house at 7 P.M. and Mrs. Hynek had a delicious dinner of fried ham and a gut salad. The 4 of us then went to the "Musil" a nightclub in Grinzig for a few gin fizzes and dancing, but the dance floor was very crowded. We left at 11:30 and walked Traute to her bus by 12:00 so she could be home by 1 a.m. Sunday the Hynek family, his wife Elfriede, and their 3 children, Edda, 15; Eva, 13; & Erika, 9; all drove me to the Austian resort of Mariazell, 100 miles to the south-west. We drove through beautiful country and midway stopped for a picnic lunch Mrs. Hynek had prepared. We were going to Mariazell to take Edda there to stay with a friend for a week, as she had been invited there by her girlfriend who comes to Canada in Sept. to study. We drank much beer in café (2 bottles) and then Dr. accompanied me to mountain top via cable car similar to Innsbruck last year. From here we could see quite far. We returned to hotel for more beer and then drove to Wien. Arrived home at 10:00 P.M..

On Monday I had arranged to meet Traute in town and after hour walk seeing Rathouse, Opera House, St. Stephens Church, garden & the Volksopera, where we went last year, we went to aunts home for dinner (their big meal is at midday.) Her mother was there too, as Traute had taken off from work for the day. We all went to the Prater and I went on the Reisenrad, the big wheel which we did not get to go on last year. It is 100 meters high & has 30 cars which holds 25 persons each, but due to non use, only half the cars are on the wheel. We went in spook houses & on roller coaster & for a while I thought I was at home again. We stopped at outside café for another beer and then returned to aunts home for evening meal before I came home on Trolly, which must have been built before Civil War.

On Tuesday I had pleasure of meeting the Götzl Family, a very rich one that lives a 10 minute walk from Dr.'s home, and who is an old friend. They have 4 children, Christian 6, Tommy 12, Niki 15 and Peter 18, but he is away in Northern Austria. Also living with them is Pauline, a girl from Ireland, age 23 who has been more or less their 5th child for 3 years. Their home was built in 1860, but has just been completely remodeled & is quite the thing with glass gate for driveway which opens by electricity from inside of house after driver signals by pressing button & identifying himself. That night Dr. had invited 3 other Dr.'s to home for dinner and we had lovely meal. In afternoon, Mr. Götzl had served me Vermuth, at Hynek home we had plum brandy before dinner, beer with meal, and wine was served in living room as we sat & talked. Also, we were treated to ice cream! On Wednesday you might say we went shopping & then went to the Götzl home and drank wine as Ritz Crackers were served. That nigh both families went to a wine garden nearby where music was also played. We had brought along bread & cold cuts and ordered the wine which came directly from the barrel. In fact the winegardens are only a very short distance from the "wine garden" where we were served the wine in 1/4 liter glasses. The musicians came around and asked for requests and "It's a Long Way to Tipiary" and "The Stars & Stripes" were played. What a time we were having; as soon as we finished one glass of wine another was brought. I only had four glasses (1 liter) and then Pauline and I accompanied the Dr. & Mrs. to a café overlooking Wien on a nearby mountaintop. Here we could see the lights of the city below while dancing to good music. We returned home by 1 a.m. and I found myself sleeping right away. It is surprising what wine and a good wine it was, can do to you. Today we went to town to do more shopping. Today is the 19th. Nearly all the letter has been written today, as I only had time to write 1st paragraph yesterday. Now today is July 20th & I've just returned from a filling breakfast & shall pack as all my things have been washed & ironed by the maid. Last night I went to Götzl home for dinner of some Hungarian dishes & then we sat around drinking wine. We mapped my trip to Lausanne, going south from Wien to Lienz & across border to Bolzano in Italy to Merano, Mals Nanders, Chur, Briga, Sion and to Lausanne. I hope to be there Monday night & arrive in Paris on the night of July 28 so I can get my boat train the next morning. Returned home, it almost seems like that, and here was a woman & 3 children also from St. Louis visiting with the Hynek's. Even more remarkable is the fact that they live in Affton quite near our home & it took staying at the Hynek home to bring us together. Their address is 6505 Lansdowne Drive. Fl. 2-8693 one thing I do want to say, is that I have enjoyed all your letters, but Janet & Carol do have a buying sickness. I would think they could write about something, at times, other than of what to be sure to buy them. If I have time I shall try to do the things they ask, but they should know when to be satisfied.

 I am going to buy the Hynek household a plant for their home this afternoon, as they recently purchased this home after living here for 4 years. Their other home was completely destroyed in the war & all that remains is a bare lot. It seems my trip has gotten better day by day, always something happening that I would not have expected to happen the day before. Hope to be seeing you in 17 days. The time has certainly passed quickly and all has been most enjoyable. When I came to Götzl home the other day, little Christian asked me, "Joe, where is your horse?" He had seen a few Westerns and had come to believe all Americans rode horses. Another funny thing happened the other day—I was writing in my diary before going to bed and was bothered by the flies and as they would light I would find something to swing at them. After my 5th attempt a knock sounded at door and Mrs. Hynek came to see about the noises, thinking I was falling out of bed. While in Germany I bought the best pair of eye glassed, strong & good looking with new lens as I had my eyes tested by same person who sold me glasses. I can see better than with the old ones & had everything done in one day for $15.60 I went to a reliable place & got quite a buy and have had them since July 10, all working nicely with no complaints. Well, must close—Love to all

Joe—The traveler.

Letter 11

(This letter was received July 30, 1956.)

July 24, 1956

Hello All:

Here's Joe at it again to bring you up to date on all the latest. Since my last letter I bought the Hynek family a beautiful plant that stands 40" high. Had such food as fried chicken & pork, not to mention the many glasses of wine I've guzzled. Sat, July 21, Dr. took me to highway going south to Klagenfurt. In 10 min. was picked up by Bleyuert Omer & wife from Wien who took me to Wiener Neustadt directly south of Wien. I had to wait all of 2 minutes before Dr. August Wipoel, a lawyer from Wien picked me up. He said he could only take me 15 km. when he stopped, but I replied that was better than none. We had gone 10 km when he said he had a friend who was driving to Italy for a vacation & he would ask him if he had room for me. The two were going to drive down together to the island of Grado, just off the coast of Trieste and not far from Venice. August put me off at town of Neunkirchen and told me to wait till he & friend came for me. It was now 12:20; Dr. Hynek had left me at 11:05 a.m. I waited in triangle of grass & ate lunch Mr. Hynek had given me. Police officer on foot wanted to know what I was doing (Austria has officers stationed along road on foot since cars cost too much) Explained to him in good German why I was there, but had to wait to 1:30 for car with travelers to come back for me. Other man was Anton Urban, 31 year old man whose father ran a nut & bolt factory. I had made plans to go with them & forgot about the other plans I had made. Trip went to Klangenfurt & Villach & on to Udine. They took me to small town on road to Venice (Cervignano.) Arrived there 11:55 p.m. Anton inquired at hotel for room & found one for 70¢. There was fight being televised & crowds gathered in public places making much noise.

I've just come back to finish this & one of the kids must have gotten to my masterpiece. Please excuse this. The noise carried on well into the night under my window, one being a bed with an end piece too short for me, and the other a mattress on springs on the floor. I slept on the latter, or tried to sleep, for I was awakened at 3:30 by a group of people singing and playing music under my window. It was getting light & I watched the festivities until they boarded a bus at 3:45 a.m. Arose for good at 7:30, dressed and walked to edge of town to try to get a ride from traffic from Trieste. Reached this point at 8:10 & at 8:30 a small van similar to our stationwagon, but without windows on side, & driven by Italian & his wife who could not speak English, stopped for me.

They took me in their van, as I was forced to sit in back with high-chair & dust mops etc. There was no air back in this prison, & I was greatly relieved when they stopped for me. Here was a man with a Swiss license plate who had come from east of Trieste that a.m. & was headed for Switz. I had planned to go near Venice, but it was not too hard to change mind when I had a long ride ahead. Hope you can follow my trip from here on a map, but we went to Tremiso, just north of Venice & on to Vicenza & then to Verona where we stopped across from the old Roman Arena, 2000 years old where Christians were once placed with lions & gladiators performed. The man I was now riding with was Ernest Bass, a Jewish man from Basel, Switz.

He had spent 12 days in Yugoslavia & was now on way to lodge near Bellinzona. We also went to San Zeno Church, begun in 9th Cent. & then drove on to Brescia & took autobahn to Milano & then north to where he was to leave me off. He said he was in no hurry to reach lodge & drove me 100kkm. (60 miles) north to Domodossia. We had covered 550 km in day with him (330 miles). It was 6 p.m. & we found hotel which was very nice. He bought my dinner that evening for me & we got a good nights sleep. Next morning he had paid my hotel bill and then bought my breakfast. I forgot to tell you of the great Italian coffee. Day before he had stopped 4 times & believe me, the stuff is great! He dropped me at end of town, 12 km. from Switz. & went his way. I had been with him 23 hours. We were up at 6:30 & I was on road by 7:50. Here I waited & waited & waited. At 10:30 a car from Denmark stopped & said he would take me, but had no room. I pleaded to go with man & his daughter in their small car telling them I was in a terrible need of arriving in Switz. that evening. He took me over Simplon Pass & into Switz. to Brig. where we had wonderful view of Mts. not a cloud anywhere. We stopped for picnic lunch as they had everything with them, including a big bottle of wine. I rode with them to Suste, near Mt. of Leukerbad, arriving there at 3:50. Here I waited & waited until 5:30 when convertible driven by U.S. woman from Princeton stopped & took me to Sierre. It was now 6 & my hopes had faded of reaching the chalet. I decided to take train to Aigle & then to Ollon & this woman took me to R.R. where she bought me 1/2 liter of wine & left me to wait 30 min for the train coming at 6:30. Arrived Ollon at 8:18, which was 10 km (6 miles) from chalet. Began walking up Mts. please, not hills, & became quite tired. Heard drone of motor & stood in center of road and stopped car from Begium, which took me to chalet. It was now 9 P.M. & they were just eating so I was able to eat too.

 I was soon to be prepared for the shock of my life. This was no ordinary place of lodging; it was a place to come & worship the Lord.

You pay nothing but enjoy good Christian fellowship. Schaeffer family has 4 children. One is recovering from rheumatic fever; other is crippled with polio & has a brace as of 5 days. As we sat at table after dinner Dr. Schaeffer read from Bible & dwelt on subject of "Do I accept Christ as my Savior?" I too began to wonder & began to think. I thought I was a Christian, but now I wondered. Next Day, Tuesday, 6 of us climbed Mt. taking lunch with us. We didn't start to 1 p.m. as we had taken walk night before from 12 to 1 a.m. to lookout & viewed Rhone Valley & slept to 11 a.m. Sky was a deep blue all day & view was great. Could see Mont Blanco, highest Mt. in Europe. Took many photos & returned at 7p.m. to eat dinner & then attend Bible Class in Villars with guests as Dr. S. spoke message, but after each sentence it was translated into French & then German. The power of prayer of this family is remarkable. There is a long story behind their present work & I'll tell you when I come home. Yesterday I cut lawn & took trash to dump as part of odd jobs to do to help. You pay nothing, but give what you think you should when you leave. Food is all American & is it good! Lemon pie & chocolate cake; roast beef, chicken ala king; corned beef hash; & ice-cream. I think I'm home! Now last night I felt I must talk with Dr. & found time to before going to bed. I told him I thought I was a Christian, but now wanted to be sure, for I did want everlasting life & to be saved. He spoke with me, making me feel funny, & then put 4 questions to me; previous to this he read from John 3:36. When you find time to be alone, ask yourself—1. Do you believe God is really who He says he is? 2. Do you believe you are a sinner worthy of condemnation? 3. Do you believe that Christ actually died as in Bible? 4. Do you believe that Christ died for me personally?

If you believe these questions & can say yes, then you shall be saved & shall have everlasting life as John 3:36 says you will. It was a wonderful experience to know that Christ is my Savior. He shook my hand & asked me to pray aloud, after which he prayed for me as no one has ever prayed before. (Keep this letter personal) I'm here 5 days leaving July 28 on 8:52 p.m. train to Paris: arrive 6:05 a.m. Take boat train to Le Havre at 8 a.m. This is a wonderful way to end my travels... in a home where God seems to reside on a nearby Mt. top. Had 5 days of clear, warm weather. God is great; God is good; please worship Him as you should. My love to you all through Him, my Lord & now, Savior, Jesus Christ.

Joe

Letter 12

(This letter was received August 1, 1956.)

R.M.S. Ryndam
July 29, 1956
2 P.M.

Holland American Line

Hello All:

Thanks for your letter which I just received. My stay in the chalet was very good for me for I have come very close to God and His great works.

The weather has been exceptional; bright, sun, warm & clear.

Last evening, July 28, after an outdoor roast I was taken to Ollon by a GI who is staying there on leave. Train left at 8:44 and I arrived in Paris at 6:05 a.m. as I was on a through train from Aigle which is station I arrived at 8:52 p.m. Found empty compartment & pulled down shades & slept on one whole seat for a fairly decent night of rest.

A girl at chalet, who once lived in Paris for 6 months, gave me a Metro ticket to get from one station—where I arrived—to the other—where I departed from Le Havre. The boat train left at 8:33 a.m. and by 10:50 a.m. we were in Le Havre and I found myself in cabin by 11:00—cabin is small, but O.K. for 2 persons. My roommate is a German immigrant from Nuremberg, 18 years old—coming to U.S. to live.

Hope all works out with packages and will declare everything I have bought—and will you be surprised.

The channel is quite rough as we head to Southampton. I've just had 3 Sirloin steaks to eat & feel O.K. since I took a pill. Received letter from Jerry S. and Carol R. also. Hope Grandma & Aunt L. can come to airport with you—that's only 8 days and I'll be so happy to see you all—I love you & miss you so much.

Well, just had a little rest. The sea is very rough now, but we arrive in Southampton shortly.

It shall be nice to meet Adelaide & George at pier. We get in dock in morning, but I don't know what time.

Better close now—is better for me when I rest; God is with me so everything is going as He plans it.

I'm safe and on my way home—just wanted to let you know I did not miss the ship.

Love through Him—
Joe

About the Author

Joseph Hahn was born in St. Louis, Missouri and attended Westminster College, Fulton, Missouri, where Winston Churchill gave his famous "Iron Curtain" speech in 1946. He has written several short stories, but never pursued writing. He has worked in public relations with banks in savings and loans and was an examiner for the state. Joseph worked as a right of way negotiator for Missouri Department of Transportation (MODOT) for twenty-eight years and owned and operated five laundromats. On his hitchhiking experience in 1956, he recorded his daily travels into shorthand books faithfully before bedtime. Upon his return home, he typed up all the experiences, but never did anything with the finished product. He titled the book *Hitchhiking through Europe during the Summer of 1956*. He and his wife, Nubia, are retired. Joseph has been asked if he was going to have the account of his trip published. Thus, a simple diary written sixty years ago has reached book form.

CPSIA information can be obtained
at www.ICGtesting.com
Printed in the USA
LVOW01s2054021116
510793LV00007B/16/P

9 781683 483441